WHY WINNERS WIN

Why Winners WIN

Art Garner

PELICAN PUBLISHING COMPANY
GRETNA 1982

Copyright © 1981
By Art Garner
All rights reserved
First printing, April 1981
Second printing, November 1982

Library of Congress Cataloging in Publication Data

Garner, Art.
  Why winners win.

  Bibliography: p.
  1. Success.   I. Title.
BF637.S8G356   158'.1   81–382
ISBN 0-88289-267-3   AACR1

Manufactured in the United States of America

Published by Pelican Publishing Company, Inc.
1101 Monroe Street, Gretna, Louisiana 70053

This book is affectionately dedicated to:

My late father, Tom B. Garner, who taught me by example the importance of effective human relations skills.

My mother, Eleanor Garner, who had tremendous faith and convinced us that we could achieve our goals in life.

My sister, Annie Ruth Parker, who has a caring and sensitive heart and who has supported me with encouragement.

My brother, Thomas L. Garner, who always challenged me to do my best and showed concern and interest in my achievements.

Contents

Acknowledgments

It is very difficult, if not virtually impossible, for a writer to identify all the people who have influenced his or her personal and professional life.

Teachers, coaches, supervisors, administrators, colleagues, ministers, friends, relatives, and my family have taught me so many valuable lessons. Their patience and humanistic concern stimulated me to continue my efforts toward a self-actualizing life. They saw and encouraged the development of things in me that I was unable to perceive. My life has been richer and more exciting because of their faith in my potential.

The author wishes to express his gratitude to Barbara Fitzpatrick for her assistance in typing and editing this book, and to my favorite college student, Dr. Estelle Helm, who has carefully edited the final copy of this book and provided me with many hours of inspiration and assistance. Dr. Helm taught me more as a student in my classes than I taught her.

Special thanks goes to my wife, Ann, for the years of encouragement and devotion she has given me. Her words of praise were available and given when I needed them the most. I am also indebted to our children, Alan and Kim, for the years of enjoyment and love they have provided. Their interest in "Dad's work" always filled me with pride.

Above all, I am grateful to the Lord for the strength to begin and complete this task. His grace and strength have given me the mental, physical, and spiritual energy necessary for this challenge.

I hope you will enjoy reading this book as much as I have enjoyed writing it. I trust that it will stimulate you to make any appropriate and necessary changes to enrich your life. Your success depends on what *you* can get out of *you!* The time you spend reading this book will have been well invested if an illustration, quotation, principle, concept, or anecdote helps you actualize more of the potential God has given you.

May your path be filled with many opportunities to help others!

WHY WINNERS WIN

CHAPTER 1

Your Most
Important Quality

*"Every adversity carries with it the seed of an
equivalent or greater benefit."*

NAPOLEON HILL

Several years ago a young boy saw a "Help
Wanted" sign in the window of the drugstore in
his home town. He went in and asked to see the
owner. "I'd like to check on the job you have
advertised in the window," he said.

"Fine," said the druggist. "We need someone to
help us in our business." He told the boy they
needed someone to make deliveries to customers
who telephoned their orders to the drugstore.

The young boy said, "I have six questions I
want to ask you."

The druggist replied, "Very well; ask them."

"First," the boy said, "I want to know how
much you pay. Then I want to know what kind of
health insurance program you provide. I want to
find out how many days of vacation time I'll get
each year. Then tell me how many holidays and
sick days you provide annually. And how much

time do I get off for lunch every day? And I have one more question."

"Fine," the druggist said. "I'm glad to answer all your questions."

"Well," the boy remarked, "I want to know if you have a bicycle I can ride to deliver the orders."

The druggist responded, "No, I'm sorry. We don't have a bicycle."

The boy quickly countered, "Well, you can forget it. I wouldn't have this job." And he walked out in a huff.

About two hours later another young boy walked by and saw the "Help Wanted" sign. He walked in with a big smile and asked to see the boss. A clerk pointed toward the druggist, and the boy went to the back of the store and waited patiently while the druggist filled a prescription for a customer. He then introduced himself and said he wanted the job. The druggist said, "Well, don't you want to know how much we pay?"

"No sir," the boy replied, "because you look like an honest man who will treat me fairly." The boy continued, "You see, sir, my mother is out of work, and we need the money, so I'm ready to start working right now."

The druggist said to the young boy, "I've just got to tell you about a boy who came in about two hours ago who also wanted this job. He had six questions which he asked me, and I answered each of them quite honestly for him. His last question was, 'Do you have a bicycle I can ride to deliver the orders?' I told him we didn't have one, and he walked out of the store after telling me he wouldn't have this job. I was very truthful with him. You see, we don't have a bicycle, but we do have a new station wagon you can use to make the deliveries."

What was the difference in the two boys? When we discover *that* difference, we have identified what it takes to be a WINNER. We have discovered the most important thing about every human being. It easily separates the WINNERS from those who wish they were.

One of my favorite stories is the one about the fellow who wanted to learn how to jump from an airplane and parachute safely to earth. During the instruction period the jumpmaster showed him how to strap the parachute on his back and how to make it open properly. The instructor told him, "When you hear the signal to jump, jump away from the plane and count to ten before you pull the rip cord. And if the chute doesn't open, pull the ring on the emergency cord. The parachute will open, and you'll float safely to earth, where a jeep will be waiting to take you back to the airport."

At eight o'clock the next morning the fellow was at the airport—ready for his first jump. He strapped the parachute on and climbed into the airplane. He stood in the door of the plane as the pilot flew over the jump site. The jumpmaster signaled for him to jump. The fellow took a deep breath and hit the air. He quickly counted: one

one-thousand, two one-thousand, three one-thousand, and up to ten one-thousand. Then he pulled the rip cord. Nothing happened. So he pulled the emergency cord—quickly. And nothing happened. He said, "Yeah, and I bet the jeep's not down there either."

This little story is meaningful because it places a unique emphasis on the importance of the winning concept in the story about the boy looking for a job at the drugstore. What do you think this important characteristic is? It's so important that I can hardly wait to share it with you. I've seen it enrich the lives of thousands of people. I have watched it transform the lives of those who have enrolled in classes I teach on motivation and personal achievement. This powerful attribute can turn your life around also. It happens every day in America. It can transform you into the kind of person you have always wanted to become. It really is the most important thing about you.

It thrills me that you are reading this book. It tells me that you want to enrich your personal and professional life. I love to see people change their lives and become more productive, because I know they will be much happier and will enjoy fulfilling lives.

A school administrator told me how a little first-grade boy fell down the steps of a school bus one morning and skinned his legs. During the morning recess the little fellow ran into another boy on the playground and knocked two teeth out. After lunch the little fellow was running outside on the pavement and fell and broke his arm. After the principal had taken him to the hospital where the boy's arm was placed in a cast, he decided to take the boy home before he was injured again. While driving him home, the principal noticed that the boy was holding something in his hand. He asked him what it was. The boy smiled and showed him a quarter he had in his tight little fist and said, "You know, Dr. Perritt, I've never found a quarter before. This is the luckiest day of my life!"

I'd say this little fellow is going to continue to be a WINNER in life because he is demonstrating that rare quality which is so necessary to be a WINNER. And *you* have this important quality also—at least to some degree. This book will help you develop this characteristic to a much greater extent. It will cause others to be drawn magnetically to you. I know you're on the right road. You're reading this book. The only people who read books like this one are those who want to "grow and glow." As a friend of mine says, "When you're green you grow, and when you're ripe you rot."

There's a beautiful story about a farmer who had lived on an old, broken-down farm all his life. The rain had washed gullies all through it, the trees were of little value for pulpwood, the farmhouse and barn looked like shacks, and the whole mess was located several miles from the main highway. So he decided to sell it all. He got in his old pick-up truck and drove to the newspaper office. He went in and told the secretary he wanted to run an ad in the paper to sell his place. She sent the farmer back to talk to the copywriter, who listened to him very carefully and then wrote the ad. It emphasized the beautiful rolling hills and the babbling brooks—not the gullies. It spoke of the variety of trees that enhanced the landscape and the possibilities of restoring the home according to one's own personal taste. And it talked about the secluded location where one could enjoy hearing the birds and smelling the lovely honey-suckles. The ad didn't mention the desolate location.

The copywriter read the ad to the farmer. He said, "Would you please read it to me again?" And he asked for still another reading. After hearing it a third time, the farmer walked over, picked up the piece of paper and said, "Now you look here, fellow, this farm ain't for sale. That's exactly the kind of place I've been wanting all my life!"

The farmer had lived for sixty years on that land. What caused him to have a different picture of the situation? It's all a matter of *attitude*, isn't it? And that's what this chapter is about. I fully agree with the adage, "Our attitude determines our altitude." Nothing is more important than our attitude. It separates the WINNERS from the losers.

The Stanford Research Institute conducted a study which concluded that twelve percent of our success depends on our knowledge and technical skills and eighty-eight percent on our ability to manage interpersonal relationships successfully. This implies a positive attitude, cooperation, enthusiasm, and commitment.

Talent is relatively inexpensive. You can buy it almost anywhere. Just think of the number of talented college football players who are never invited to try out for a professional team. Think, too, of the outstanding collegiate basketball players, baseball players, golfers, tennis players, and talented individuals in other sports who never make it to the "big leagues."

Look at the number of talented actresses, accountants, students who would like to enter medical school, teachers who want to teach, and a host of others who are refused admittance into their preferred fields. You see, talent is inexpensive.

Education is also relatively inexpensive. It is easier to become educated in America today than ever before. Any student who really wants to can get an education. Scholarships, loans, part-time jobs, and grants are available to needy and worthy students.

There's one thing, however, that you can't buy, even for a million dollars. And that is a positive attitude. It just isn't for sale. It comes from within.

Our society has witnessed tremendous and sometimes almost unbelievable scientific accomplishments. Space explorations continue to escalate. Medical researchers are probing into areas which they believe will provide answers to important health questions. Their answers will result in more comfortable living and longer lives.

Knowledge doubled for the first time in 1750, the second time in 1900, the third time in 1950, and the fourth time in 1960, and it presently doubles every five years. Research continues to probe deeper into areas little known to us only a few years ago. There have been more books published in the past twenty-five years than in the previous five hundred.

More than half of the jobs available to a young man today were not even in existence when his father was a boy. In fact, ninety percent of all scientists and technologists who have ever lived are alive now.

Monumental achievements have amazed us. But the greatest discovery of all concerns man himself. One of my favorite quotations is from the psychologist William James: "The greatest discovery of my generation is that human beings can alter their lives by altering their attitudes of mind."

WINNERS believe that something good can emerge from every situation, even though they cannot see it at the moment. That's where faith starts to work. I like the story of the rich father who wanted to ascertain the attitudes of his twin boys. He gave one of them a large pile of presents. The boy began complaining about the colors, the sizes, the shapes. To the other son the father gave a large pile of manure. This boy began singing, whistling, and shoveling the manure.

He looked up and said, "With a pile of manure this high, there's got to be a pony in here somewhere!"

This fellow is a WINNER. He'll make it in life. He has captured the spirit which Napoleon Hill suggested in the inspiring statement that "every adversity contains the seed of an equivalent or greater benefit." This success principle conveys the message that every cloud has a silver lining. We may not be able to see it, but it's there.

One evening on the way home from his office, Matthew Henry was robbed. Before going to bed, he wrote in his diary, "Let me be thankful, first, because I was never robbed before; second, because although they took my purse, they did not take my life; third, because although they took my all, it was not much; and fourth, because it was I who was robbed, not I who robbed."

A friend was telling me about an incident in the airport in Dallas. He saw this young boy in a wheelchair, smiling from ear to ear. He decided to visit with the boy, who was apparently waiting for his mother to return with some food. He asked the boy if he had been in a wheelchair all his life. The young fellow looked up at him with a refreshing warmth and said, "Not yet I ain't, Mister!" I don't know how long he had been crippled, but I do know he had a positive belief that some day he would be better. Don't you imagine that this attitude helped him smile a great deal each day?

One of the most rewarding experiences of my

life happened the day I met Ed Dohrman in Atlantic City. I was there to conduct a workshop for the annual meeting of the New Jersey Society of Radiologic Technologists. While I was checking into the hotel, Mary Vahey, the conference chairperson, walked over and invited me to have dinner with her and four others. After taking my luggage to the room, I met them in the lobby. Mary introduced me to Ed Dohrman and his seeing-eye dog, Yetta. I'll never forget that meeting and the next two days I spent with Ed.

There are many beautiful people in this world, and my traveling allows me to meet quite a few of them. While we were eating at Zaberer's Restaurant that night, I met another beautiful person—Janet, the efficient waitress who served our table. Noticing that Ed was blind, when she served his dinner, she whispered softly to him, "Your steak is at four o'clock, your peas at seven o'clock, and your potato at eleven o'clock." Her sensitivity to him prompted me to write a letter of appreciation to the manager of the restaurant complimenting her caring attitude.

The next morning I was waiting for the elevator on the fifth floor. When it stopped and the doors opened, I said, "Hello, Yetta."

Ed responded, "Good morning, Art. How are you? Isn't it a beautiful day?"

I replied, "Yes, Ed, it surely is. May I buy your breakfast?"

He replied, "I'd like that. But first I must meet

Yetta's needs." We walked slowly around the block while Yetta paused periodically.

After we ordered breakfast, I decided it was time to ask Ed how he was able to maintain such a beautiful attitude toward life. He told me his story. It moved me. Ed had been a radiologic technologist working in a large hospital. He had been in good health, enjoying his work. Diabetes caused him to lose his eyesight at the age of thirty-seven. Shortly after that his kidneys failed. Ed never gave up. He believed tomorrow would be better. His failing health necessitated a kidney transplant. Although the new kidney failed a few times, it did eventually function.

Ed was unable to learn to read braille because the diabetes had impaired his fingertip sensitivity. This stimulated him to spend his spare time listening to tapes. Ed had learned that "every adversity contains the seed of an equivalent or greater benefit."

While we were eating breakfast, Ed related the philosophy which helped him maintain a refreshing attitude toward life in the midst of difficult circumstances. He said, "Art, I decided when I lost my eyesight that I could be bitter, and no one would enjoy being around me. Or, I could be positive and try to encourage others. I'm glad I chose to be positive." I noticed during the convention that people were always standing around him. His smile warmed many hearts.

Three months later the phone rang one night

about ten o'clock at our home. When I answered it, it was Ed. "Hello, Art," he greeted me. "What's happening in your life these days that is exciting?" After we had chatted for a few minutes, I asked him what he had been doing lately. He replied, "Well, today I mowed the lawn."

I said, "Ed, you're blind. How in the world did you mow the lawn?"

He said, "I put a milk can at one end of the yard and another one at the other end. Then I tied a rope between them to give me some direction while I mowed."

I asked him what else he had been doing. He replied, "Well, last week I painted one side of the house in which we're now living.

I replied, "Ed, how many times does someone have to tell you that you're blind?"

He laughed and said, "If you keep painting over the same general section, you're bound to cover it all. When my wife, Barbara, came home she said I had more paint on me than I had on the house."

He then told me he had just completed building some shelves. He was a little disappointed that the shelves were one-eighth of an inch lower on one end. He had also been chopping wood for the fireplace.

A couple of months later, I telephoned Ed. I asked him what he was doing to enjoy life. He told me he had been riding his bicycle. I said, "Ed, what if you run off into a ditch?"

He replied, "Well, then I'll know I've gone too

far to the right." Oh, what a beautiful attitude, I thought.

Ed and I often corresponded over the following months. Barbara said he loved to walk to the mailbox and feel several letters in there. Every time I've used Ed's life as an illustration in one of my speeches, I've asked twenty-five listeners to write him notes of encouragement. One time Barbara told me that these letters helped keep him going. He couldn't wait for her to get home from work to read them to him.

One Sunday night I kept telephoning their home, but no one answered. Finally, about midnight, Barbara answered the phone. She told me that Ed had been taken in serious condition to the hospital in Albany, New York. Monday evening I called the hospital and talked to Ed. He said, "Art, it will be a while before I write you. This morning the surgeons had to amputate my right arm. But I'm going to learn to write with my left hand now." Tears filled my eyes as I thought of my lovely friend who was suffering greatly but still maintaining a refreshing attitude toward life.

Ed died the next morning. Along with a lot of other people, I'm a different and better person because of Ed Dohrman. He was a real WINNER.

Obstacles can be a WINNER'S steppingstones to greatness. For example, Demosthenes, the great orator, had a speech impediment which he conquered by placing pebbles in his mouth and shouting. Beethoven, one of the world's greatest composers, was deaf. Milton, the great poet, was blind. Abraham Lincoln was almost completely self-educated. The Wright brothers were bicycle mechanics by trade, not scientists. Winston Churchill overcame a speech impediment to become one of this century's greatest orators. Helen Keller, blind and deaf, became one of the great women of our nation and was admired throughout the world.

When I was in San Francisco recently, I boarded an elevator operated by Walter Henley, who was singing and whistling. A lady asked him why he was so happy. He smiled and said, "Because I have never lived this day before."

A negative thinker has the attitude of the old farmer who walked with his wife down to the train station to see their first train. When the farmer saw how large and heavy the engine was, he said, "They'll never get that thing to move." In a few minutes the engineer boarded, and the train started moving down the track. The old farmer looked at his wife and said, "Well, I'll tell you one thing. They'll never get it stopped." This old fellow had made up his mind to be negative—regardless.

Sometimes we may feel like my good friend, David Stone, who lives in Palm Springs, California. At the conclusion of a workshop I was conducting for the Loma Linda University Medical Center, David stopped by a clock shop to buy his wife, Nellie, a grandfather clock for her birthday. After paying for the large clock, he asked that it be delivered to his home that afternoon. The owner said it would be impossible because the shop was behind with its deliveries.

David said, "O.K., strap it on my back!"

The owner replied, "What? You're out of your mind! The clock is too heavy."

David said, "I paid for the clock. It's mine. Tie it on my back."

Reluctantly the shopkeeper strapped it on his back, and David started walking home. About three blocks down the street a drunk came out of a bar, ran into David, and knocked him down to the sidewalk. The clock lay broken in a hundred pieces all over the pavement. David stood up and said to the drunk, "Why don't you look where you are going?"

The drunk looked up at him and said, "Why don't you wear a wrist watch like normal people do?"

Someone said that all men are created equal, but it's what they do afterward that makes the difference. An individual's attitude determines to what extent he will develop his talents and in which direction he points his life. I've always been impressed by the philosophy of Oliver Wendell Holmes, who said, "The most important thing about a person is not where he stands, but in which direction he is moving."

Dad and Mother believed they could help make America a strong nation by rearing their children, attending church, supporting their city, and working hard at their jobs. During World War II both of them worked twelve hours a night, seven nights a week to provide for our family. After working all night on Friday, Mother would prepare breakfast, and Dad would take my brother and me fishing on Saturday mornings.

Mother always had a great deal of faith—in God, us, people, jobs, school, and the future. She truly believed that each of us could take the talents God had given us and become the kind of person each wanted to become. She believed that success depended on a positive and persistent attitude.

A WINNER closes the doors on past failures. By viewing our temporary setbacks as stepping-stones rather than stumbling blocks, we can build the kind of personal future that will be satisfying and rewarding. It's what we bring to life, not what life brings to us that counts.

Each morning brings us a fresh, new day. We can make of it what we will. The WINNER gets up each morning on the right side of the mind. He knows that the attitude he adopts early each morning determines the kind of day he will have. During the day he notices that attitude begets atmosphere.

Recently I was enjoying a cup of hot tea while reading the newspaper early one morning. Our daughter, Kim, came through the room, looked at me, and asked, "How do you feel this morning, Dad?"

"Wonderful, Kim," I said.

She responded, "Well, why don't you notify your face?"

Wow! Did I get the point! Now when I hear her getting out of bed and walking down the hall, I start smiling.

A WINNER knows that his attitude toward losing determines how long it will be until he wins. David Schwartz relates the story of a WINNER with a positive attitude. Benjamin Fairless, former chief executive of the U.S. Steel Corporation, suggests how we should think when things don't go our way. He said, "It depends on how you look at things. For example, I never had a teacher I hated. Naturally, I was disciplined just like every other pupil, but I always figured it was my own fault that the discipline was necessary. I have also liked every boss I ever had. I always tried to please him and do more than he expected if I possibly could, never less. I have had some disappointments, times when I greatly wanted a promotion and somebody else got it. But I never figured that I was the victim of office politics or bad judgment on the boss's part. Instead of sulking or quitting in a huff, I reasoned things out. Obviously the other fellow deserved the promotion more than I did. What could I do to make myself more deserving of the next opportunity? At the same time I never got angry with myself for losing and never wasted any time berating myself. I was determined to be persistent in the pursuit of my goals."

I'm very much inspired by the story of Steve Walle, a third-grade student at Cold Springs School in Missoula, Montana. The teacher asked the students to write something about Thanks-giving week for which they were really thankful. Steve's paper read: "Thanksgiving is special be-cause I get to go to my grandmother's house. She always has a meal waiting for us. She has some turkey and some mashed potatoes. My grand-father is nice and so is my grandmother. My grandfather is a mechanic. He works on tractors and drives college kids on the bus. They live three blocks from a candy store. They have a big house. I am thankful for being alive. I got run over about three years ago, and lost my sight. And I'm lucky to be here." His beautiful and heart-warming story was written in braille.

Millie Nye was in a personal enrichment class I taught recently. She shared some experiences which taught each of us a memorable lesson about thinking and acting positively. One of her days went something like this: When she got up one morning, she saw the toilet overflowing. Later she learned that her daughter had locked the keys inside the car. That evening she noticed the roof was leaking. The clothes dryer also broke that night. And another daughter accidentally broke a window in the house. All of this in one day!

Positive-thinking Millie took each of these thorny problems *one at a time* and did something constructive about them. At the end of that day she concluded, "I have no reason not to be positive."

What a fantastic attitude. She is a WINNER.

Millie had previously faced problems that few people confront in a lifetime. As a child, she lived in a series of foster homes and was eventually placed with Mr. and Mrs. Martin. She had three eye operations, as well as a constant struggle with asthma, but she turned into a smiling little girl because of the tender, loving care of the Martins.

She married a man whom she respected but did not love. That marriage failed after a daughter and son were born. She married a second time for love. Her husband, however, could not handle the responsibilities of marriage and parenthood. Left with three children to rear, she had difficulty with bad health and trouble finding work.

She now has a job she likes and feels that she will someday be an asset to the company. Don't you like her attitude? She wants not just a job, but an opportunity to be useful.

She feels life is too precious to take for granted. She appreciates her life now because of the obstacles she has overcome. She is thankful for her three normal, happy children. She feels a strong will and optimistic attitude will help her through future problems. She has truly made stepping-stones out of obstacles.

Which of the three in the following story would you want to hire to build you a new house? A reporter went out to a place where a construction company was erecting a large new building. She asked the first worker she saw what he was doing. He replied, "Laying brick." She came upon a second worker and asked him what he was doing. He responded, "Earning $7.50 an hour." And when she saw a third construction worker, she asked him the same question. His response was, "I'm building the world's greatest cathedral." I know which of these workers you would want—the same one I would. We'd want the fellow who takes pride in his work. He is the one who enjoys many self-actualizing experiences at work. He probably smiles, whistles, and sings at work, even if he sings to himself. His attitude and quality of work indicate that he is a WINNER.

You probably want to avoid being like the hypochondriac who died in Purdy, Tennessee. He left a note instructing the owner of a monument company to put this epitaph on his gravestone: "I told you people I was sick, and you wouldn't believe me."

WINNERS avoid criticizing, condemning, and complaining. They realize that when you're slinging mud you're losing ground. Losers spend a lot of time cutting others and themselves down. We have often heard that misery loves company. Some people criticize others in their attempt to bring them down to their own level.

There was a beginning teacher in Illinois who fell in love with teaching during her first year in the classroom. Because the school principal had not visited her classroom to evaluate her teaching skills, she assumed that she would not be employed the following year. At the end of the school year she took her materials to the office and prepared to say goodbye. The principal saw her and said, "We have enjoyed having you here this year and look forward to having you teach with us again next year."

She was quite surprised and replied, "Well, I haven't received a contract to teach next year, so I just assumed that you thought I had done a poor job and didn't want me back."

The principal said, "We really want you back. Your students have scored higher on their achievement tests than any of our other students in the last ten years. You've got to come back next year."

The teacher said, "It's easy to teach when you have such a great group of kids as I had. They were sharp, interested, motivated, and all of them had I.Q.'s of 150, 152, 153, and even higher." The principal asked how she knew that the students had such high I.Q. scores. She mentioned the materials he had given her at the beginning of the school year which contained a sheet of paper with the students' names and I.Q. scores on it. He smiled at her and said, "Those were their locker numbers."

Because she thought the students had high I.Q. scores, she had treated them all year as if they did. Her attitude was one of high expectations. She believed in the students. She *knew* they could accomplish the work. Her experience underscores the point that "attitudes are more important than facts."

My friend Helyn Yorke shared a beautiful

story with me. It was a letter written by a fourteen-year-old boy to an administrator at the Massachusetts Institute of Technology. It read:

> M.I.T. is my big aim. Besides receiving A's in algebra, I read everything I can lay my eyes on in all phases of the field of space and science, and go without shoes to save money. I need additional information about tuition, scholarships, and careers in space exploration and rocket engineering.
>
> "I am third in line of a family of five expensive, hungry children; and my father is a lobster fisherman. This adds up to the fact that what becomes of me will depend on me mostly.
>
> "Do you have any advice, so that every minute will count in the next three and a half years? I am coming to M.I.T. somehow, and you will be glad to see me.

I strongly suspect this young lad will continue to be a WINNER the rest of his life. He knows what he wants to do. He knows where he wants to go. He is searching for advice from the right sources to help him achieve his goals. His attitude is refreshing.

We can significantly enhance our relationships with others by imagining that each person we meet is wearing a sign around his or her neck which says, "Please make me feel important." And what does it take to make him feel important? Simply talk in terms of things which interest him, and he'll love being around you. Instead of asking questions which require a yes or no response, use the words *how, who, why, when, what*, and *where* to stimulate responses. For example, instead of asking, "Do you like your work?" ask, "What motivated you to go into this line of work?" In other words, you are talking the other person's language. Everybody loves to talk about himself. Being a good conversationalist makes you a WINNER.

You have noticed that WINNERS are good listeners. In our rapidly moving and highly advanced technological society, it is sometimes difficult to get someone to listen to you. Most people seem to be in a hurry. One can listen with interest by looking directly in the person's eyes while he is speaking or listening, really concentrating on what the person is saying and the meaning it connotes. It is also very helpful to watch the person's nonverbal body language and the messages conveyed.

I've also noticed that WINNERS are frog kissers. That's right—they kiss frogs! (I'll explain this later.) Have you ever felt like a frog? You know, it's when you have the "dropsies," and you wish you had the "upsies." It's when you want to feel energetic, but you feel fatigued; when you are lonesome but wish you had warm companionship; when you are being criticized but wish you were being praised; when you are selfish but wish very much that you were a giver; when you are not sensitive to the needs of others but wish you were a caring and concerned person; when you have procrastinated and are behind in your work but wish you were caught up; and when you are frightened but wish you had a strong faith.

My third-grade teacher, Mrs. Elsie Mae Dorsett, told us one time about a prince who was turned into a frog by a wicked old witch. The only way he could become a prince again was for some beautiful maiden to come by and kiss him. And, by and by, a miracle did happen in his life, just as it can in ours, and a lovely maiden came by and kissed the frog, and he turned back into a handsome prince. Obviously they lived together happily ever after.

Two college girls were at a park when a handsome frog came hopping up to them. He had such a friendly, pleading look that they took him back to the dormitory with them. There they fed and petted him. He responded with such gratitude that one of them leaned over and kissed him. He instantly changed into a handsome young man!

Do you believe that story? The dormitory matron didn't.

Words of praise have changed the lives of many frog-type people. Praise has the power to inspire others to reach just a little higher. You've probably noticed that a word or two of praise can bring joy that lasts for days.

The famous psychologist, William James, wrote, "The deepest principle of human nature is the craving to be appreciated." I suppose each person reading this book remembers a depressing time when he or she did something which he believed deserved recognition or reward, and didn't receive it. This indicates that praise is the greatest payment to receive for a job well done. It usually inspires us to reach a little higher in developing our skills. It also increases our morale, and we're more productive as a result. That's because a little bit of praising always does some spirit-raising.

WINNERS are careful to avoid deflating another person's ego. Lord Chesterfield gave his son some superb advice when his son asked, "How can I make people like me?"

"My son," Chesterfield explained, "make other people like themselves a little better, and I promise you this: they will like you very much."

We may as well admit it: we want people to like us. And the person who says he doesn't care if people like him will be less than truthful about other things also. To be liked is a psychological need each of us has.

We are contributing a great deal to a person's happiness and success when we express genuine appreciation. Such a gesture is particularly rewarding when we compliment an action or specific behavior the person has demonstrated. "Your tie really matches your suit well," or "That lemon icebox pie really satisfied my taste buds" are more meaningful than "You look great," or "That was a great meal."

Participants in the workshops I conduct on human resources development often ask me to suggest some guidelines to help them express appreciation to others. Over the past several years I have offered the following guidelines:

1. Search for things that are close at hand. Quite often we are looking in the distance to see something for which we should express appreciation. This habit causes us to overlook many lovely experiences and opportunities that are close to us.

2. Search for little things to praise. It doesn't have to be an earth-shaking experience or phenomenal discovery or invention to deserve praise. There aren't too many of these happening every day. You may wish to set a goal of finding two or three specific things each day to compliment.

3. Look for the right moment to express your appreciation. Usually the right moment is as soon as possible. The longer we wait to compliment the specific trait or action of the individual, the less powerful it will be. These comments will serve as positive reinforcement for the individual to replicate his or her performance.

In most cases it is usually quite meaningful to express your appreciation to the individual in front of others. This approach can multiply the effectiveness of your comments. However, in some cases it will be more useful to share your comments privately. For example, if your remarks would cause jealousy or friction, you'd want to approach the person when he or she is alone.

It is very effective to write someone a letter or

note expressing your sincere appreciation. I have found it very useful to keep several blank note cards and envelopes in my attaché cases in my desk at home and at the office, and in my car. Frequently I write notes while I'm at airports, visiting a doctor's office, or even attending faculty meetings. By having stationery with me, I don't have a good excuse for not writing. In fact, one Friday afternoon during a three-hour faculty meeting I wrote thirteen notes of appreciation. It was one of the most productive faculty meetings I ever attended.

Sometimes people we have never met can inspire us immensely. It happened to me one morning when I was in Atlanta to deliver a speech. As I was walking from my hotel room toward the elevator, I followed a well-dressed man down the hall. He stopped by a lady who was pushing a cleaning cart and said, "Good morning. I'm Bob Straw and I just want you to know how much I enjoyed sleeping in that clean room last night. The sheets were clean and I enjoyed the comfortable bed. And it was nice to take a shower in the clean bathroom. I hope you have a nice day."

I have a question for you. Do you think that lady cleaned all those rooms with more enthusiasm that day? Since that morning I have never passed anyone pushing a cleaning cart in a hotel or motel without saying something like that to her. If you have a second hand on your watch, you'll notice it takes only fifteen seconds to repeat what Bob Straw told the lady.

A few years ago someone suggested that "you can tell a great man by the way he treats little people." I've made an effort to observe the leadership styles of individuals at various levels in the management hierarchy. Invariably, those who treat others with respect and dignity motivate their employees to achieve higher goals, perform more efficiently, and have higher morale. Dr. Billy M. Jones, former president of Memphis State University, is an example of a leader who treats others the way he'd want to be treated. Every human being is important to him. He continually expresses appreciation to faculty members, administrators, the staff, and the community for their contributions to the university.

A real WINNER is someone who makes winners out of others. He is like the person described by George Bernard Shaw in *Pygmalion*. Eliza Doolittle says to Colonel Pickering: "You see, really and truly, apart from the things anyone can pick up, such as dressing and speaking, the difference between a lady and a flower girl is not how she behaves, but how she's treated. I shall always be a flower girl to Professor Higgins, because he always treats me as a flower girl and always will; but I know I can be a lady to you, because you always treat me as a lady and always will."

This little rhyme amplifies what Eliza was saying:

> *To sell Don Luther*
> *What Don Luther buys,*

You'd better see Don Luther
Through Don Luther's eyes.

This applies if we are selling cars, houses, insurance, services, ideas, or a marriage proposal. We'll be much more effective when we can see things from the other person's vantage point. Successful sales people know the value of projecting this kind of attitude.

It always excites me to read about people who develop and maintain a positive attitude toward circumstances and people. I love the story which reflects Abraham Lincoln's sensitive heart. It occurred in 1863, when he was busy trying to reunite a divided country. Each day his life was filled with decisions to be made which affected the lives of thousands of people. The easy decisions were made by his staff. He made the tough ones.

A soldier was sentenced to die because he had fallen asleep on guard duty one night. The boy's mother wrote to President Lincoln for help. Lincoln was extremely busy. He could have assigned the task to a subordinate, and no one would have blamed him for doing so. But he investigated the details surrounding the soldier's performance and learned that the boy had been on guard duty for forty-eight hours without any relief. He immediately issued a pardon for the soldier. Mr. Lincoln was a WINNER because of the way he treated "little people."

Jean Nabors, a graduate student in a university

class Dr. Leila Acklen and I taught, experienced the death of her twenty-six-year-old twin sister during the semester. At the beginning of the next class period she told us, "I learned that when you are gone, you are not remembered for things you have done for yourself but for things you have done for others." This advice, I hope, will motivate us toward a more "other-centered" philosophy. We've probably noticed many times that the happiest people are those who try to make WINNERS out of others. They realize that the greatest exercise in the world is reaching down and helping someone else up.

Perhaps you have heard of the group of researchers who set out to identify a common denominator among one hundred "self-made" millionaires. They wanted to share this profound research with the rest of the world. And what do you suppose they found in this group which varied in age from twenty-one to seventy, and whose educational backgrounds ranged from the third grade to Ph.D's? They found one common characteristic among the millionaires. They were all "goodfinders." They had the ability to find something good in every person and in every situation they encountered. The real WINNERS in life learned this attribute and developed the habit of practicing it. They weren't born with this trait. They practiced it, and practiced it, and practiced it until it became a habit, and their subconscious minds were programmed to look always for good things.

Why don't you get a sheet of paper and write down all the good things you can identify in some of the people you know? Then list some good things that have materialized because of some adverse experience you encountered. Practicing this simple technique will help you become a goodfinder—a WINNER.

In a motivation and personal growth class I was teaching one evening, a young school teacher told us how she had experienced beautiful serendipity as a result of a concern for an elderly lady. When she was in high school, her family lived across the street from an elderly lady who lived alone. Often she would take this lady out walking and sit with her in the park. Each week she would take her to the supermarket where the lady purchased her groceries.

Later, when the young lady was away attending college, she received a phone call to return home for the reading of the will of the elderly lady. Because the woman had lived primarily on social security, it was assumed that she had very little to bequeath. However, she had left her young friend property valued at $10,000.

My good friend from Texas, Herman Locke, taught me one of the most impressive lessons I've ever had. One day as we were stopping at a restaurant for dinner, we noticed a man staggering and falling against the building. Herman said, "That fellow must be drunk." We entered the restaurant and sat across from the man. After a few minutes Herman looked at me and said,

"Art, I owe someone an apology. That fellow over there isn't drunk. He's a double amputee and has to struggle just to get around." Although I'd always thought a great deal of Herman, since that day he has been a very special person to me. It takes a big person with a sensitive heart to apologize.

My favorite city to visit is San Francisco. My wife, Ann, and I love to ride the cable cars, visit Fisherman's Wharf, and eat at many of the city's famous restaurants. I am saddened at times to read of the people who have jumped off the Golden Gate Bridge to their deaths. Recently I read that over seven hundred people had jumped to their deaths. A couple of years ago one young man left this note in his apartment: "If, on the way to the Golden Gate Bridge, one person smiles at me, no one will ever find this suicide note." That morning this fellow needed a smile, and no one gave him one. Not one single person smiled at him! Question: "What if he had passed you?"

About seven one morning Eileen Burch telephoned and asked me, "Art, do you know what a smile is?"

I said, "No, what is a smile?"

She replied, "A smile is a gentle curve that straightens out many things."

Another friend sent me a description of a smile. I'm quoting it here, although I don't know its original source. It reads:

> A smile enriches those who receive, without making poorer those who give. It takes but a

moment, but the memory of it sometimes lasts forever. None is so rich or mighty that he can get along without it, none so poor but he can be made rich by it. A smile creates happiness in the home, fosters good will in business, and is the countersign of friendship. It brings rest to the weary, cheer to the discouraged, sunshine to the sad, and is nature's best antidote for trouble. Yet it cannot be borrowed or stolen, for it is something of no value to anyone unless it is given away. Some people are too tired to give you a smile. Give them one of yours, as none needs a smile so much as he who has no more to give.

There's a cute little story about a couple named Burton and Dorothy Jean Gooch that had been married for twenty-seven years and had never had an argument. That's right—twenty-seven years. Someone asked them how in the world they had managed to live together that long without having an argument. Dorothy Jean responded, "On our wedding night, we agree that Burton would always make the major decisions and I would make the minor ones. And to this day we have never had a major decision to make."

Although he may not always win, the WINNER knows that associating with other positive thinkers is good for him. It's like the farmer, Jack Roberts, from Knoxville, Tennessee, who entered his old horse in the Kentucky Derby. Jack said, "I know he doesn't stand much of a chance to win, but the association will be good for him."

WISDOM FROM WINNERS

WINNERS believe that a good attitude turns a chore into a cheer.

WINNERS know that how you think when you lose will determine how long it will be until you win.

WINNERS are convinced that you don't get a second chance to make a good first impression.

WINNERS believe that an optimist is a "happy-chondriac."

WINNERS believe that if you growl all day, you'll be dog-tired at night.

WINNERS know that a smile is so powerful it can even break ice.

WINNERS see a pessimist as one who feels bad when he feels good for fear he'll feel worse when he feels better.

ACTION SHEET
"The Most Important Thing About You"

Attitudes I Will Develop This Week

1.

2.

3.

4.

5.

ACTION SHEET
"The Most Important Thing About You"

Habits I Will Develop This Week

1.

2.

3.

4.

5.

ACTION SHEET
"The Most Important Thing About You"

Skills I Will Develop This Week

1.

2.

3.

4.

5.

ACTION SHEET
"The Most Important Thing About You"

The following list of people with a positive mental attitude are those with whom I will develop greater friendships this week:

1.

2.

3.

4.

5.

6.

7.

CHAPTER 2

The Secret Ingredient

*"Readiness for opportunity makes for success.
Opportunity often comes by accident; readiness
never does."*

SAM RAYBURN

One summer during my high school days I
worked on a towboat which pushed barges of
gasoline from Port Arthur, Texas, to Knoxville,
Tennessee, to Paducah, Kentucky, and to Cairo,
Illinois. This towboat, the *M.V. Codrington*,
often sat for hours waiting for other barges and
boats to go through the locks and dams on the
beautiful Tennessee River. Although my mother
and father never knew it, a friend and I would
dive off the barges and swim in the cool water on
those hot July days. If they had known this, I
probably would have had the opportunity to
work the rest of that summer at the service station
in the small town where we lived. But I was tired
of washing and greasing cars, repairing flats, and
cleaning windshields. I wanted to see something
other than what was under the hoods of cars and
trucks. And I was thrilled my parents gave me

permission to try something new and challenging.

Meanwhile, back to the barge where we were awaiting our turn to enter the lock . . . When the operator signaled for us to enter, our captain would blow the whistle for us to prepare the barges and towboat. The captain would maneuver the towboat and push the barges through the large steel doors that led into the lock. After we tied the barges, the operator would close the heavy doors and open the valves so the water could enter the lock and raise our barges. Sometimes it would take forty-five minutes for the water level to raise us to the dam. When we were level with this water, the other huge doors were opened, and we started up the Tennessee River again.

Sometimes our empty barges were hit with winds of eighty miles an hour. These winds kept our captain quite busy steering the towboat so that the cables holding the barges would not break and allow the barges to go where the river wanted them to go. Sometimes the water was so shallow that he slowed the engines so that our propellers would not hit the bottom and break. In other words, he adjusted the operating conditions to maximize our chances for a successful journey.

Sometimes the fog on the Mississippi was so dense that we had to tie the towboat and barges to the trees on the levee until the sun burned through the fog the next morning. But we never quit. We knew where we were going. Even when we had to dry-dock in New Orleans for repairs on the drive-shaft and propeller, we still didn't quit. We were on our way to a specific place.

Lock by lock we conquered the higher levels and mountains which stood between us and our destination. Armed with patience and persistence, our crew reached its destination. Our success in life can be favorably compared with our journey through the locks that raised us over the hills and dams. Too many people think that success in life is going to come in one big beautiful package.

Our big success is going to depend on our little successes as we sail through the channels of life. As the Chinese have told us for years, "A journey of a thousand miles begins with one step." And then, we might add, you must keep taking steps—one at a time.

Things seem to go smoothly at times in our lives. And then there are times when we have some rough sailing. Most of us don't go through life walking on mountain peaks. All of us must travel in the valley of frustration, anxiety, worry, stress, and despair. When you are experiencing these valleys, visualize those golden nuggets of self-fulfillment you enjoyed at the peaks of those previous mountain-top experiences. Remember that quite often it's down in the valley where the growth occurs. While you're in those valleys, ask yourself, "How can I use this experience creatively and constructively?" Your answer can help you be a WINNER. This world will be much better because you are a WINNER.

A WINNER is patient and realizes that behavioral and attitudinal changes often require time for successful implementation. The beautiful pecan trees my father planted did not produce pecans until long after he had planted them. With patience and care he nurtured them into large and productive trees. During the winter and spring he fertilized them, and he spent time watering them in the summer. Delicious pecans, years later, were the result of his efforts.

During the spring each year my father would use a horse or hire someone with a tractor to break the ground for our family garden. Then Dad would assign my brother, Tom, and me the task of breaking all the large chunks of dirt with a hoe. Because our hearts were at the basketball court, we'd work as fast as we could to finish the task. The next day Dad would take a hand plow and till the rows for planting. Then Tom and I would plant the seeds where he told us to. After watering them, we'd run to the basketball court again. We were motivated to play basketball, while Dad was motivated to raise vegetables for our family. He could visualize how those vegetables would look and taste in a few weeks.

Regardless of the preparation and work, I never saw us plant squash seeds, potatoes, corn, or other seeds one day and have those vegetables on our table the next day. Several weeks later, after we had watered the plants and hoed the grass away, my sister, Annie Ruth, and Mother would pick the vegetables and cook them for dinner or can them to eat during the winter months. Those experiences taught us planning, patience, persistence, and cooperation.

My grandfather walked off and left my grandmother with five small children to raise. My father, who was in elementary school at the time, dropped out to take care of the cotton crop and provide food for the family. Although most people never knew it, my dad never returned to school to graduate. Perhaps a high school diploma wasn't as important or necessary in those days as it is today. Even though he didn't have a formal education, Dad could get along with anybody as well as handle his business matters appropriately. His human relations skills were so well developed that he could effectively interact with the mayor as well as the poorest citizen in town. People loved him throughout our small community. He was living proof of the saying that "when you don't have an education, you've got to use your brains."

In Las Vegas Floyd Johnston told me about a persistent lady who was determined to find a compatible husband. She married a rich oil man in Houston but divorced him after a year of marriage. Then she moved to Hollywood and married an actor who had starred in several movies. Six months later she divorced him. Then, of all things, she met a preacher in Kentucky and married him. She lived with him for three years before they were divorced. She moved to Florida and married an undertaker. Someone asked her why she had married all those fellows. She replied, "One for the money, two for the show, three to make ready, and four to go." That lady was really optimistic! Perhaps she was somewhat like the eighty-four-year-old fellow from Arkansas who married a twenty-two-year-old girl and bought a five-bedroom house next to an elementary school.

My wife and I spent a lovely week in Honolulu one summer when I was conducting a motivation and communication workshop. One afternoon we went out to swim and enjoy the sun and sand on beautiful Waikiki Beach. After we swam for a while, we sat on the beach visiting with some people we had met from Ohio. I noticed that a lady had come down to the beach with her two small children. She sat there while the children began walking toward the sea. They walked into the water just as a large wave came in. The wave knocked both boys off their feet. One of the little fellows jumped up laughing. The other boy was crying as he ran to his mother. The second reaction is the kind some people have when an adverse situation knocks them down. WINNERS believe that adverse situations in life make them better. Losers, on the other hand, become bitter.

One of the most rewarding experiences of my life happened one year when I directed a motivational and personal achievement program for a high school football team. I'll never forget one of the players named Rusty McClure. He was a hard-hitting, powerful fullback on offense, and he loved to play linebacker on defense. He didn't mind hitting or getting hit. He loved competition and winning. Early in the season Rusty's jaw was broken. A surgeon wired his jaw together and told him he was through playing football for the rest of the season. But the surgeon didn't know Rusty very well.

The next Friday evening I walked into the dressing room and saw Rusty dressed out and ready to play. I asked him what he was doing. He mumbled something and indicated that he was ready and eager to play football. Because his teeth were wired together, the only food he had had all week was liquid. He drank a lot of milk shakes during the month he was in this condition.

That night the coach allowed him to run with the ball on offense. As I recall, he gained about eighty yards in that game. When he came to the sidelines to rest for a few minutes, I felt sorry for him but was inspired as I watched him desperately trying to catch a breath of air with his teeth wired together. I can still see the agony on his face as he stood by me in that hot football uniform with the temperature hovering around ninety degrees. You can imagine how he inspired the other players with his desire and dedication.

The next Friday evening Rusty was dressed out and ready to play again. I could tell he had lost some weight. It had been fourteen days since he had eaten any solid food. Rusty played every play on offense that night. It was still hot and the humidity was high, but not as high as his desire to play and win. My heart ached as I watched him gasp for fresh air in the clouds of dust.

In the third week the coach allowed Rusty to play both offense and defense. This meant playing the entire game, and that's what Rusty wanted. He was still losing weight. For twenty-one days he had consumed liquids through a straw. He was still drinking those milk shakes. I sometimes wonder if he still likes milk shakes. But he made it that night on the field. It was thrilling to watch him cross the goal line with the football for a touchdown.

Rusty was really glad to see the next Friday evening. It was the last game he'd have to play with his wired jaw. He played well again that night as he gained more than one hundred yards running the football. Wouldn't a T-bone steak have looked good on his plate the next week?

At the end of the season a head football coach of a university called and asked me to write a letter of recommendation concerning Rusty and his potential. I wrote the coach that I had never seen a football player with the desire Rusty had.

WINNERS can take a *minus* and make a *plus* out of it. Their eyes are always open to creative opportunities for growth that negative situations can provide.

Failures provide WINNERS with opportunities to learn ways that do not work. As Charles Kettering said: "Every great improvement has come after repeated failures. Virtually nothing comes out right the first time. Failures, repeated failures, are fingerposts on the road to achievement.''

Sometimes the WINNER realizes that he has to try another way in order to succeed. Jack Robertson, a paraplegic because of an automobile accident when he was nineteen years old, has been sitting in a wheelchair teaching students at an elementary school in Scottsdale, Arizona. At one time he had been an excellent swimmer. He decided that he wanted to be the first paraplegic to swim the English Channel. Jack spent two years developing, perfecting, and practicing a new free style windmill stroke.

Jack swam for eighteen hours in the English Channel before the tides forced him to be pulled from the water when he was within a few hundred yards from the shore. Back at the hotel in Folkestone, England, he declared, ''I think I made my point. I have proved that such people as me can get off their backsides and do what we want to do.''

WINNERS just don't give up easily. They have the tenacity to hang in tough. Like our son, Alan, who was the pitcher on a little league baseball team in Texas. Someone asked him what the score was. He replied, ''It's 27-0.''

''Well,'' said the adult, ''I guess you all are really discouraged.''

Alan looked at him and said, ''No sir. Why should we be discouraged? We haven't gone to bat yet.''

I love this exciting attitude. I'd want him on

my team if I were coaching another little league team again. He has a WINNER'S attitude.

WINNERS are inspired by the words of James J. Corbett:

> Fight one more round. When your feet are so tired that you have to shuffle back to the center of the ring, fight one more round. When your arms are so tired that you can hardly lift your hands to come on guard, fight one more round. When your nose is bleeding and your eyes are black and you are so tired that you wish your opponent would crack you on the jaw and put you to sleep, fight one more round—remembering that the man who always fights one more round is never whipped.

Theodore Roosevelt once observed, "Far better it is to dare mighty things, to win glorious triumphs, even though checkered by failure, than to take rank with those poor spirits who neither enjoy much nor suffer much, because they live in the gray twilight that knows not victory nor defeat." Roosevelt reminds us of the persistent attitude of that great inventor Thomas Edison. He said, "I never allow myself to become discouraged under any circumstances. The three great essentials to achieve anything worthwhile are: hard work, stick-to-itiveness, and common sense."

A real WINNER has the persistent attitude of one young lad who lived near Boston. Because he really needed a job, he began looking in the newspaper want ads every day. When he saw a job opening in Boston, he sat down and wrote the best letter he could and mailed it to P.O. Box 1935 in Boston. He carefully described his qualifications, interest in the job, and his willingness to work hard and learn. He waited nearly two weeks, but there was no response to his letter. He sat down and wrote a second letter and mailed it to P.O. Box 1935. Two more weeks passed and still there was no response.

This young man was not a quitter. He wrote a third letter describing his desire and determination to work for the company. He was disappointed when two more weeks passed and no word had come from the company. Probably ninety-five percent of our population would have felt they had gone the second mile and could justify quitting. But not this WINNER. He wanted that job badly enough to go a step further.

He boarded the train to Boston. He walked from the train station to the main post office. Upon entering the building, he inquired of the postmaster as to ownership of P.O. Box 1935. The postmaster informed him that it was against policy to release such information. Surely it was time to give up and look for some other job. No one would blame him now. But not this WINNER.

He walked around the post office for a while and came up with a beautiful idea. He located the box and stood over to the side, waiting. He waited for two hours, but no one came to get the mail from that box. Another two hours passed, and still no one came. Finally, toward the end of the day, a man arrived and collected the mail from the box. He followed the man for several blocks and into a large office building. When the man entered the elevator, he followed. The elevator stopped at the eleventh floor, and the man got off and walked into the office of a brokerage firm.

The young boy entered the office and asked the secretary if he might see the manager. The secretary was so impressed with the boy's pleasant attitude that she ushered him in. The boy introduced himself and told the manager that he had written three letters applying for the job the company had advertised, and that no one had responded to his letters. He told the manager he wanted to work so badly for the company that he had boarded a train to Boston, waited all day for someone to pick up the mail from P.O. Box 1935, and followed the man to this office. He then said, "And I'd like to have the job with your company. You'll be glad you hired me."

The manager was so impressed with the young man's attitude and persistence that he hired him. The young man started working as hard as he could to learn about the company and the details of his work. His attitude, persistence, and dedication resulted in a very successful career as a financial analyst. This WINNER'S name? Roger Babson.

Could you drive a car if you had no hands or arms? Would you be capable of typing without fingers? And could you tie a child's shoe strings if you were armless? Could you catch a fly in the air with your feet? It would take a very special person to accomplish these things, wouldn't it! Bonnie Consolo can do it! I've seen her engaged in these activities. It's almost one of those experiences which you have to see to believe.

Bonnie Consolo was born without arms. She was reared by two loving and caring parents on a small farm in Kentucky. She was one of five children and was the only one "handicapped." As a small girl she was given the responsibility of taking care of her baby brother while the rest of the family worked in the fields. That experience captured her heart and developed in her a burning desire to achieve a goal in life—to marry and have a family. She never lost sight of this goal and her burning desire moved her toward it.

In high school Bonnie learned how to type by using her toes. And she could type twenty-five words a minute! She also enjoyed her class in shorthand—or, as she called it, "shortfoot." Also, she took a class in driver education. She passed the driving test the first time she took it—and the car was a stick shift! When the girls played basketball, she usually kept the score. But guess who was chosen first when they played soccer?

After graduating from high school, Bonnie went to a rehabilitation center in Staunton, West Virginia because someone thought she needed to be rehabilitated. A few months later the occupational therapist called her into his office and asked, "Are you ready?"

She replied, "For what?"

He responded, "Your prosthesis."

She asked what that was and he told her it was artificial arms. She tried to refuse but he insisted that she learn how to use them. After a lot of training she finally mastered a few basic skills. But she could do all those things without those heavy, awkward, cumbersome arms! Why should she burden herself with them?

Bonnie left that center and moved to Florida where she worked as a PBX operator. While living there she found the best place for those "awkward arms" was in the closet! A newspaper reporter wrote a story about Bonnie's life and published it nationally. A gentleman named Frank Consolo, living in Redding, California read it and began writing her. After months of corresponding, she moved to California. Later they were married and are now the proud parents of two attractive sons, Mark and Matt.

This outstanding lady attributes so much of her success in life to her mother. When she was a small girl, her mother would require her to learn all the fundamental skills necessary to take care of one's self. When it took other children only a few seconds to button a button, sometimes it would take Bonnie several minutes. But her mother "made her do it." The same was true relative to dressing herself or tying shoes. Bonnie always knew her mother was available and would help her if she really needed it. Her mother laid the beautiful foundation for her to become the self-reliant person she is today.

Bonnie told me one day that a turning point came in her life when she was thirteen years old. She began to wonder why she had to be so different from the other girls in her school. She became depressed as she compared herself to others. Then one night things came together. She decided that God had put her on this earth for a particular mission. And that mission was to develop her talents and show others what one could do with a "limited" body. She could prove to the world that the most important thing is not what we have lost, but what we do with what we have left that really counts!

Believing that others would be inspired by her life, Bonnie portrayed her attitude and talents in a provocative and amazing film entitled, "A Day in the Life of Bonnie Consolo." If you haven't seen this film, you have missed a great one. The film has won numerous national awards. I've shown it to many audiences where I have given a motivational speech or conducted a workshop. Without exception, every group has been inspired by it. Also, Bonnie travels around the country speaking to various groups. I hope you have an opportunity to hear her personally.

Today, Bonnie and her family live in Westerville, Ohio. She enjoys cooking for and taking care of her family. That hits her hot button!

WINNERS *make* things happen. They don't

sit around waiting for something to happen to them. They are aggressive individuals who put energy into their desires and positive thoughts. They know that good things will happen in their lives as a result of the seeds they plant and the territory they cultivate.

The philosopher Kierkegaard often related the story about a flock of geese that headed south to avoid the cold winter snows. After a few days of flying, they landed on a farm and ate a great deal of corn. When the flock started to fly off the next morning, one goose decided to stay a little longer and enjoy the delicious free corn. He planned to leave the next morning, but the corn still looked good. He gave the same reason for staying the next several days. He fully intended to fly south soon.

His procrastination helped create a habit pattern. Then cold weather hit the area. The goose either had to fly south or freeze to death. He started running across the field to build up enough speed to fly, but he had one problem: he was too fat to fly. Procrastination cost him his life.

Winston Churchill's positive attitude and indomitable spirit during the dark days of World War II were reflected in the encouragement he gave the British people. He said, "Tomorrow will be better. The day will come when we will win. The final victory will be ours." After the war, Churchill was invited to speak to the boys enrolled in the school he had attended. The headmaster told the boys to bring notebooks and copy down everything their guest said, because they were to hear the greatest living Englishman. Churchill walked to the platform and looked at the faces of all those boys. He realized that life would hold many opportunities as well as challenges for them. His complete speech was simple: "Never give in, never give in, never give in, never, never, never, never!" He then sat down. These words are just as powerful and meaningful today as they were then.

One of the speeches I deliver throughout America contains three tremendously important points relative to personal and professional achievement. Here they are:

1. PERSISTENCE
2. PERSISTENCE
3. PERSISTENCE

A retired executive once stated that the secret of every successful businessman he had known lay in three little words: "and then some." The man who got ahead was the one who would do what he was assigned to do, and then some. He was the man who worked the hours required by his contract, and then some. He would treat the men under him fairly, and then some. This businessman was simply applying the Biblical principle of going "the second mile." This persistent attitude is a noticeable characteristic in all WINNERS.

Persistence is often the determining attitude that separates the WINNER from the loser. The

WINNER doesn't give in, doesn't give out, doesn't give over, and doesn't give up. He's somewhat like my friend Joe Villemez. Joe's nephew went to him for some important counseling. It seems that the boy had fallen in love and wanted to marry this beautiful girl, but he didn't have any money and couldn't find a job. Joe, the wise counselor, told the boy he had a solution to the problem. He had located a job for the boy in a city about fifteen hundred miles away. The boy responded, "But I can't go. She'll forget all about me while I'm over there for a year working to save money so that we can get married."

Joe said, "David, that's no problem. Just write her a long love letter every day, and she'll always be thinking about you." In desperation the boy decided to try it. And sure enough this concept of spaced repetition and persistence worked. When David returned home in a year, he found that his loved one had married the postman.

In my judgment, Calvin Coolidge gave us a most provocative insight into the concept of persistence. He said,

> Nothing in the world can take the place of persistence. Talent will not; nothing is more common than unsuccessful men with talent. Genius will not; unrewarded genius is almost a proverb. Education will not; the world is full of educated derelicts. Persistence and determination alone are omnipotent. The slogan 'Press on' has solved and always will solve the problems of the human race.

The Duke of Wellington said that the British soldiers at the Battle of Waterloo were not any braver than Napoleon's soldiers, but they were braver for five minutes longer.

The WINNER develops persistence in all his pursuits. He reflects the attitude toward life of the man who built a successful business on the philosophy that "it's always too soon to quit."

A WINNER doesn't sell himself short. He continues striving, pushing, and tugging to achieve his objectives. You've probably read or seen copies of the famous children's books written by Dr. Seuss (actually Theodore Geisel). The first book he wrote was rejected by twenty-seven publishers. They critiqued his manuscript and concluded that it contained too much fantasy and verse. Theodore Geisel believed in the book. He believed in his writing ability. He was persistent. And because of his persistence the *twenty-eighth* publisher liked the unusual approach Geisel had taken in his writing. The company bought it. Millions of books by this writer have since been sold. The next time you try something and don't succeed, ask yourself, "Have I tried twenty-eight times?" WINNERS sometimes have to.

WISDOM FROM WINNERS

WINNERS believe that failure is the path of least persistence.

WINNERS don't make tomorrow's meal with yesterday's garbage.

WINNERS say, "Patience is keeping your motor in neutral when you feel like stripping the gears."

WINNERS get ahead because they do more than is expected . . . and keep on doing it.

WINNERS know there is no such thing as failure—only new beginnings.

WINNERS believe that success is that point in life where preparation and opportunity meet; but a great number of people don't recognize it because it comes disguised as hard work.

WINNERS are aware that procrastination is the grave in which opportunity is buried.

ACTION SHEET
"The Secret Ingredient"

This week I will be persistent in the following pursuits:

1.

2.

3.

4.

5.

CHAPTER 3

Keeping Your
Hot Button Hot

*"Nothing worthwhile was ever accomplished
without the will to start, the enthusiasm to
continue, and the persistence to complete."*

WAITE PHILLIPS

Someone has said that there are four kinds of
people in America. *First*, there are those who
make things happen. These individuals have a
positive attitude about themselves, others, their
jobs, families, and America. They are the builders
who believe that life is worth living. When they
fall down, they get up and get on with the
business of living. They realize that how you
think when you lose will determine how long it
will be until you win again. They know that a
good attitude turns a chore into a cheer.

These people who make things happen agree
with the words of wisdom from W. Clement
Stone, founder of the Combined Insurance Company: "One's attitude is the only thing over
which he has absolute, complete control." These
WINNERS are the ones who turn stumbling

blocks into steppingstones. They see things and situations from creative, constructive viewpoints.

Second, there are those people who *watch* things happen. They are in the group that is neither for nor against apathy. They don't oppose those who are involved in creative and productive activities. For reasons of their own they choose not to become involved in the exciting adventure of attempting new experiences. In far too many cases this feeling is projected because the person fears failure. This fear of failure is probably, of all obstacles, the greatest deterrent to growth and achievement in a person's life. He fears that if he tries something and it fails, people will look with disfavor or pity on him, and that a parent, spouse, or friend will say, "I told you that wouldn't work!" And then he'll feel guilty as a result.

Where would America be today if scientists and technologists had refused to dream, attempt, or experiment because they might have failed? We wouldn't be reading by electric light bulbs, listening to the radio, riding in airplanes, driving cars, and seeing the significant reduction in diseases such as polio. WINNERS win because they believe that victory is possible any time they're active in improving themselves and trying to improve this world for others.

Third, there are those who simply *wonder* what has happened. Periodically, they wake up to see the results of something that has happened and wonder, "What in the world has happened?"

They are probably not happy with themselves and wonder "how others always get the lucky breaks."

A WINNER worries, but not very much. He knows that worry is a counter-productive emotion. He is aware that worrying is holding onto a mental picture of what he doesn't want to happen. It's like the fellow who was sentenced to die in the electric chair. His lawyer kept telling him not to worry; everything was going to be okay. One day the prison officials came to get the condemned man. As they were walking to the electric chair, he asked the guards if he could make one last telephone call. The guards agreed. He telephoned his lawyer and complained, "I thought you told me not to worry. I'm on my way to the electric chair. What advice do you have to give me?"

The lawyer replied, "My best advice is: don't sit down."

Fourth, there are those who usually *criticize* what has happened. These folks are born in the objective case and stay in the kickative mood. Their eyes are always open for opportunities—opportunities to criticize others. They refuse to participate in constructive activities. They belong to the group which follows this adage: "Why be disagreeable when, with a little effort, you can be a real stinker!" And you'll notice that most people avoid spending much time with members of this negative club.

There isn't a single person in this world who

can make us think negatively, unless we allow him to. We control our thinking. If someone else influences us to think negatively, it only shows that we have given him permission to make us think that way. Our bosses, parents, children, spouses, friends, enemies, co-workers, and anyone else can program us to think negatively only if we allow them to.

Recently, when I was fulfilling a speaking engagement, I had the privilege of sharing the platform in Moline, Illinois with the writer, Sidney Harris. In visiting with him prior to the time we were to speak, I asked him about a lovely editorial he had written some years before. The editorial had been about his walking with a friend to a newsstand where his friend purchased a newspaper every day. When they arrived at the newsstand, Sidney's friend warmly greeted the owner and politely asked for a newspaper. The owner rudely shoved the paper at him, complained that the man didn't have the correct change, and directed more verbal abuse at him. On the way home Sidney asked him if he purchased a newspaper there every day.

"Yes, I do," he replied.

"And does he always treat you that way?" Sidney asked.

"Well, I must tell you that he does," his friend replied.

Sidney then said, "Why don't you buy a newspaper somewhere else?"

His friend then offered this fantastic response:

"I refuse to let him dictate how I am going to act."

What beautiful advice! WINNERS are positive and enthusiastic regardless of the way others around them act.

Dr. John O'Brien, research professor of theology at the University of Notre Dame, says the word "enthusiasm" comes from two Greek words, *theos* and *entae,* which mean "God within you." Isn't this a beautiful concept? God wants you to be a WINNER. As Ethel Waters said, "God doesn't sponsor any flops." God feeds the birds, but they have to go and get the seeds.

An exciting Texan I know, Larry McKenzie, defines enthusiasm as "inner excitement." That is the best definition I've heard. It suggests that enthusiasm isn't necessarily shown by loud talking, backslapping, or other external behavior. In fact, genuine enthusiasm must fit one's personality to be effective. For example, Dr. Jonas Salk was filled with enthusiasm, or inner excitement, as he quietly worked in his research laboratory discovering the polio vaccine.

The Bible says that with faith we can move mountains. I believe it. God didn't say the mountains would be moved immediately. But they will be moved! Think of yourself as a co-worker with God. Each day you're praying for His will to be done in your life. You and God are a majority. That's why I love to repeat each morning those exciting words from Psalms 118:24: "This is the day the Lord has made; we will rejoice and be glad in it."

While I was a post-doctoral fellow at the University of Southern California School of Medicine, I was impressed by a plaque I saw in a building on the main campus. It contained the words of Waite Phillips: "Nothing worthwhile was ever accomplished without the will to start, the enthusiasm to continue, and the persistence to complete."

The epitaph for too many people could read: "Died at 43. Buried at 67." It's obvious that these people reduced their efforts for growth and excitement when they were forty-three years old. These are the ones who need to be reminded of all those people who achieved their goals in life after the age of forty.

Recently I was delivering a speech in the lovely MacDonald Hotel in Edmonton, Alberta. After the presentation some members of the planning committee invited me to lunch. One of the fellows knew that I collected ideas for my speeches. After lunch he gave me a copy of a book entitled *How to Succeed Without Working*. Now, that title sounds fascinating. In bold print on the first page was the word IMPOSSIBLE. The rest of the "book" contained blank pages on which to take notes.

You've noticed that WINNERS have a sense of humor. They can laugh at themselves and also laugh *with* others and not at them. They're like the fellow named Hal Walker, who applied for a job as a vice-president of a large company in Marked Tree, Arkansas. The owner decided to ask him some questions to test his ability to make important decisions. He said, "Hal, if you were standing down by the train station and saw two trains coming toward each other on the same track at forty miles an hour, what would you do?

After thinking for a moment, Hal responded, "I'd go home and get my brother."

"What?" the owner asked. "You'd go get your brother? Why in the world would you do that?"

"Because he ain't never seen a train wreck before," Hal responded.

WINNERS are not spectators in the game of life. They are active participants in this exciting adventure. They refuse to sit on the sidelines and watch things happen. They want to make things happen. They're not like those timid souls who are afraid to participate because they might be rejected by someone, or they might get hurt, or they might fail. Mother used to tell us that old Uncle Hank was always going to do something, and he finally did. He died.

The WINNER knows that life is a real game in which every day is the Super Bowl. But he knows that it's much more important than that professional football contest. For example, there are no "time outs" during which the clock of life is stopped. It keeps moving—all the time. Also, there are no substitutions in the game of life. You have to play your own position. No one can substitute for you—no one. Your success depends on what you can get out of *you*. Not what any coach, boss, spouse, or parent can get out of you, but what you can.

Life is not a scrimmage either. It's the real thing.

When I played football, the coach had us run a particular play. Then he would stop, critique the play, and we'd run it again. And sometimes we'd run it again, and again, and again. Life doesn't provide us these options. None of us can relive any single day, regardless of its successes or failures. After twenty-four hours, that day is gone forever. That's why it's such a fantastic idea to awaken each morning and get up with enthusiasm on the right side of the mind.

Arnold Toynbee once stated, "Apathy can only be overcome by enthusiasm, and enthusiasm can only be aroused by two things: first, an ideal that takes the imagination by storm; second, a definite intelligible plan for carrying that ideal into practice." This idea indicates that we need to set a goal that we simply must reach, then build the fire of a burning desire under it. Enthusiasm is an attribute which can be developed by thinking about a worthwhile goal until it obsesses you. Enthusiasm will propel you to achieve those goals. George Matthew Adams once suggested, "Enthusiasm is a kind of faith that has been set fire."

Enthusiasm is as contagious as measles and as powerful as dynamite. It can move mountains of apathy and increase production to undreamed of heights. Enthusiasm is to the WINNER what rocket fuel is in the cylinders that launch our astronauts into space. It creates motion. It causes things to happen.

Last summer a boy from New York City was hiking at night in the Rocky Mountain National

Park. He asked Alan Hewitt, the guide, "Is it true that a grizzly bear won't attack you if you're carrying a flashlight?"

"That depends," the guide answered, "on how fast you're carrying it."

Some folks are turned on to activities which really excite them. They remind us of the question: "Does success come before enthusiasm, or does enthusiasm come before success? In my judgment, enthusiasm comes before success. It's the driving force that helps a WINNER achieve his goals.

Positive desire and negative fear are the two strongest psychological forces within the human being. Desire is not something that can be measured by a standardized achievement test. In my judgment, it is the strongest force, and it can move people to achieve seemingly unattainable goals. WINNERS have a strong desire to achieve. They think, plan, talk, and act with an "I can" attitude. They pay the price to win.

Someone asked Frederick Williamson, a former president of the New York Central Railway, his definition of success. He offered this:

> The longer I live, the more certain I am that enthusiasm is the little recognized secret of success. The difference in actual skill and ability and intelligence, between those who succeed and those who fail, is usually neither wide nor striking. But if two workers are nearly equally matched, the one who is enthusiastic will find the scales tipped in his or her favor. And the one of second-rate ability with enthusiasm will often

outstrip one of first-rate ability without enthusiasm.

Don't you just love to be around optimistic people? There was an old man in Ohio named Tharon Lee who was in his last days. The family was called to the hospital for the final hours. The family doctor was called to examine the old gentleman and give his prognosis. No member of the family was willing to tell the old fellow how much his condition had deteriorated; so the doctor leaned over to tell the old gentleman he had only a short while left and to ask if there were a final request. In a whisper the old fellow answered, "Yes, get me another doctor."

Harry Truman once said, "I have studied the lives of great men and women; and I found that the men and women who got to the top were those who did the jobs they had in hand, with everything they had of energy and enthusiasm and hard work."

Ask yourself: How would an enthusiastic person perform the work I am doing? Perhaps you'd like to write some things down and then review them each week for a month. As you implement these "energizers," you'll soon discover that it's more fun to go to work each day.

The WINNER isn't always the individual who has the most, but he is always the one who gives the most. He knows that it's when we've given more than we're asked that we have given our best. George Bernard Shaw said, "I don't believe in circumstances. The people who get on in this world are the people who get up and look for circumstances they want, and, if they can't find them, make them." The individual with enthusiasm will sometimes experience temporary defeat; but this doesn't stop him, because his enthusiasm lifts him up and keeps him going.

Sometimes even WINNERS find it a challenge to please everyone. Perhaps you've felt at times like the cab driver who was working in Los Angeles for a company that had acquired a reputation for being late in responding to telephone calls. The president of the company admonished the drivers to resolve the problems by responding more rapidly to the calls.

The next day Tony, one of the drivers, was cruising down the street when a lady called for a taxi. The radio dispatcher relayed the message immediately to all the cab drivers. Tony realized that he was directly in front of the lady's house. He quickly stopped his cab, walked briskly to the door, and rang the doorbell just moments after the lady had completed the call. She came to the door and he announced, "Lady, you called for a cab. I'm your driver, Tony."

The surprised lady looked at him and said, "Young man, I'm not going to ride with anyone who drives as fast as you."

WISDOM FROM WINNERS

WINNERS believe that it isn't the load that weighs us down; it's the way we carry it.

WINNERS believe that most folks don't really fail; they just quit trying.

WINNERS know that failure will never overtake them if they have a burning desire to succeed.

WINNERS are convinced that the best place to look for a helping hand is at the end of their arm.

WINNERS believe it is not how much we have, but how much we enjoy that brings happiness.

WINNERS look for the best in others because doing so brings out the best in themselves.

ACTION SHEET
"Keeping Your Hot Button Hot"

In order to experience a more productive and rewarding week, I am enthusiastically going to give more than is expected of me in the following ways:

1. Employment

2. Family

3. Religion

4. Community

ACTION SHEET
"Keeping Your Hot Button Hot"

This week I will conquer the thief of enthusiasm —procrastination—by taking action on:

1.

2.

3.

4.

5.

ACTION SHEET
"Keeping Your Hot Button Hot"

I will also conquer the second thief of enthu-siasm—indecision—by making decisions on the following matters:

1.

2.

3.

4.

5.

ACTION SHEET
"Keeping Your Hot Button Hot"

To conquer the third thief of enthusiasm—an unorganized day—I am going to accomplish these six things tomorrow in the order of their importance:

1.

2.

3.

4.

5.

6.

CHAPTER 4

Mirror, Mirror
On the Wall

*"It is when we've given more than we're asked
that we have given our best."*

A wise old man lived in a cave a few miles from
a village. People from the village often went to
the old man for advice and counseling. They
found that his answers were always correct. Two
boys decided one day that they were going to trick
the old man. Their plan included catching a bird
and having one of them hold the bird in his hand.
They planned to approach the old man and ask,
"Is the bird I hold in my hand alive, or is it
dead?" If the old man answered "Alive," the boy
was to quickly squeeze the little bird in his hand
and kill it. He would then open his hand and
prove the old man wrong. If, however, the old
man said, "The bird is dead," the boy would open
his hand and show him that the bird was alive.

The boys walked out to the old man's cave. One
of the boys said, "Old man, is the bird I hold in
my hand alive, or is it dead?" The old man

thought for a few moments and responded, "That depends on you. Its life is in your hands."

The WINNER realizes that *his* life is primarily in his hands. He can choose to use it or abuse it; mend it or break it; be somebody or nobody, an asset or a liability.

You can select your own epitaph today. WINNERS know their epitaphs. They live every day to epitomize them. I told my wife I want this epitaph on my tombstone: "He died learning."

Every day I try to do something to improve my mind. I may read a book, listen to a cassette tape, hear some motivational speaker, do research in a library, watch some informative or inspirational program on television, or visit with someone to discuss something. Just as I exercise and watch my diet to care for my body, I feel it is important to do something to improve my mind. I believe *you* think the same way. That's why you are reading this book.

After visiting the Alps someone related the story of the monument he had seen to a famous mountain climber who had died while trying to climb a dangerous pass. The epitaph on his tombstone read: "He died climbing." What a powerful thought. Like most of us, you're probably not terribly excited about being rushed to the cemetery in a casket. WINNERS know, however, that they're writing chapters each day in their lives, and they want the chapters to be productive.

A farmer in Kankakee, Illinois advertised for someone to work on his farm. After running the ad in the paper for three weeks, he finally received a phone call about the job. He invited the eighteen-year-old boy out for an interview. After showing him around the farm, he asked the young fellow, "Can you drive a tractor?"

"No sir," the boy replied.

"Well, can you operate a milking machine?" the farmer asked.

The boy responded, "No sir. I've never done that either."

The farmer asked several more questions and received negative answers to each one.

The farmer was growing short in patience and asked, "Well, what *can* you do?"

The young fellow said, "I can sleep when the wind blows."

The farmer didn't understand what he meant, but he needed help so badly that he gave the boy the job. A few days later a storm came up in the middle of the night. The wind was blowing about fifty miles an hour, accompanied by thunder, lightning, and rain. The farmer awoke and ran to the barn to check on the animals and the equipment.

He went to the room where the boy was sleeping soundly. Rather than trying to awaken the youth, the farmer ran out to check on the animals and equipment. He found the barn doors securely fastened. The animals were in their shelters and secured. Then he remembered a hay pile that was surely blowing away, but he found it covered well with canvas. On the way back to the house the farmer remembered what the boy had said: "I can sleep when the wind blows." And he understood.

This story reflects an attitude of pride. Pride in oneself and in one's work. It also speaks to the important work ethic that was much stronger in the past than it appears to be in our country today. A better world really does begin with *me*. The WINNER knows that he can change his world. He makes things happen by taking positive action.

The WINNER believes that the greatest freedom in the world is the freedom to become the best he is capable of becoming. He accepts the profound truth expressed by Ralph Waldo Emerson, "What lies behind us and what lies before us are tiny matters compared to what lies within us." Indeed, your success depends on what you can get out of *you*.

A friend recently told me about a tramp who was sitting on a park bench. As he watched a fellow walk by in a three-piece suit—obviously a successful person, the man said, "There, except for me, go I." This provocative statement characterizes the lives of many people. It seems that a lot of folks these days are itching for things they're not willing to scratch for.

Have you noticed how many people quit looking for work as soon as they find a job? Last December I went into a shoe store to buy a pair of shoes. The manager was standing by the door and I asked him, "How many people work here?"

He replied, "About half."

Some ten minutes later a salesman came to assist me. I asked him, "How long have you been working here?"

He said, "Ever since they threatened to fire me."

We have two chances of making good without working: slim and none.

A friend once told me about a young boy who went into a grocery store and asked permission to use the telephone. He called and asked to speak to Dr. Walter Murphy. He asked, "Do you need someone to mow your yard and clean the flower beds?" Dr. Murphy told him that he didn't because he already had a boy working for him. The boy asked if the worker did a good job and was dependable. Dr. Murphy assured him that the boy did excellent work. He thanked the doctor and hung up the receiver.

As the boy was leaving the grocery store, the manager, who was impressed with the boy's attitude, told him that he had a job opening and could use him. The boy responded, "Thank you, sir, but I already have a job. I'm Dr. Murphy's boy. I was just checking up on myself."

In my judgment, it's a good policy to watch the person in front of the one behind you.

As the popular motivational speaker Zig Ziglar says in his bestselling book *See You at the Top*, "Get rid of that stinking-thinking," and what we need is a "check-up from the neck-up." Zig places the responsibility for personal growth and achievement directly on our own shoulders. And that's where it should be.

Is there a common denominator among the personal traits of WINNERS? Yes. It is the capacity to make yourself do what needs to be done, whenever it needs to be done, whether you like it or not.

A few years ago a young man graduated from Arlington Heights High School in Fort Worth, Texas. He completed his freshman year of college at Texas Tech and went back to the Fort Worth area to find summer employment. Since he had enjoyed singing so much, he auditioned for a job at the amusement park, "Six Flags Over Texas." At the conclusion of the audition, he was told that he wasn't good enough to be a singer. Although disappointed, he did not give up. He spent the summer working as an operator helping people on and off rides at "Six Flags." This positive attitude and persistence paid off very well for John Denver. He believed in himself. He reflected the beautiful truth expressed by Eleanor Roosevelt, "Nobody can make you feel inferior without your permission."

WINNERS realize that it is impossible to please everyone. Tommy and Liz Lane were traveling in their car on their honeymoon. Before they arrived at the motel, the new bride said to her husband, "Please don't tell anyone that we're newlyweds because they'll laugh and make jokes about us."

When they entered the lobby to register, she stood back while he signed the directory. After spending the night there, they came back to the lobby area to pay for their lodging. She stood in the middle of the lobby while he paid the bill. As she stood there, other guests were frowning at her from her head to foot. She thought to herself, "I know he told them we are newlyweds. Just look at the expressions on their faces. I'll tell him off when we get in the car."

As they were driving off, Liz said, "Now tell me the truth. You told them we were just married, didn't you?"

He looked at her and said, "No, I didn't tell them we were newlyweds. I told them we were just good friends."

Sam Rayburn once said, "Readiness for opportunity makes for success. Opportunity often comes by accident. Readiness never does."

The measure of our success is not dependent on how much talent we have, but on how much we use it. Research tells us that nine-tenths of an iceberg is below water. Could it be that nine-tenths of your potential is out of sight—just waiting to be developed and used?

A WINNER is aware that his success begins with himself, and that no success principle will work unless *he* does.

WINNERS believe that with God's help they can do anything they really want to do. They believe in the passage recorded in Philippians 4:13, "I can do all things through Him who

strengthens me." God made each of us a WIN-
NER. God loves WINNERS. And we are WIN-
NERS when we are developing the talents God
has given us and contributing each day toward
making this world a more beautiful place in
which to live.

Frank Vander Maaten lived in Sioux County,
Iowa. The citizens were filled with pride because
of his unusual ability to play the violin. As a
matter of fact, they expected him to become
world famous. At the age of eighteen, he was
working one day in his father's blacksmith shop.
Accidentally, a red-hot iron fell on his left hand,
burning him badly. The burn was so severe that
only his thumb and four stubs remained on the
hand. This was the hand he used to touch the
violin strings.

Such an accident would seem to be a justifiable
reason to put the violin in the closet permanently.
And that's what everybody thought Frank would
do. But that thought wasn't on the mind of this
WINNER. This accident provided another opportunity for him—an opportunity to learn to
play the violin with his other hand. This stumbling block became a stepping-stone. Frank
learned to hold the bow in his crippled hand and
manipulate the strings with his good hand. It is to
his credit that he later became a noted violinist in
the Sioux City Symphony. WINNERS turn circumstances to their advantage—to help themselves and others.

A WINNER believes it is absolutely imperative

to have a healthy attitude about himself. If you don't like yourself, then who will? How we see ourselves is our ego. How other people see us is our personality. A healthy attitude toward ourselves suggests a confident pride in ourselves and our abilities. It's a belief and knowledge that we can achieve our goals. This does not suggest an ego trip in which one is all wrapped up in himself. Such a trip is of short duration. We don't want to be like the fellow who wrote a book entitled *The Four Most Beautiful People in the World, and How I Met the Other Three.*

Thomas Edison was asked by a young news reporter at a press conference, "Mr. Edison, how does it feel to have failed 10,000 times on this project?"

Edison looked at him for a moment, smiled, and said, "Young man, I did not fail 10,000 times. I simply found 10,000 ways that would not work."

This persistent attitude resulted in 1,093 inventions. Edison believed in himself. Although WINNERS don't always succeed at every task they attempt, they refuse to allow other people's opinions to kill their beliefs in themselves.

In her book *Think Mink*, Mary Crowley offers ten two-letter words to help make WINNERS out of those associated with her in the business she founded and has led to a sales volume of $100 million a year. Her advice: "If it is to be, it is up to me."

The measure of a WINNER is the size of the thing it takes to get him down. Show me a person who lets failure and defeat teach him wisdom, and I'll show you a WINNER. There is really no such thing as failure, only new beginnings. How we think when we lose will determine how long it will be until we win. As Dr. Alfred Adler has written, "One of the wonder-filled characteristics of human beings is their power to turn a minus into a plus."

Congratulations if you have failed and learned something helpful from your failure. Every inventor, musician, artist, athlete, scholar, scientist, and teacher has known failure. No one starts out a self-actualized person. Every person at some place and time failed to achieve his objectives or goals. Thomas Edison, Henry Ford, Jonas Salk, Franklin Roosevelt, and Michael DeBakey failed as they were learning, experimenting, and growing. I characterize these men as successful failures. They had deep beliefs in themselves. Their work has benefited millions of people. What if they had given up too soon?

WISDOM FROM WINNERS

WINNERS are those who can give without remembering and take without forgetting.

WINNERS firmly believe that the road to success is always under construction.

WINNERS grow happiness under their feet, while losers look for it in the distance.

WINNERS believe that the world owes them a living, but they have to work to collect it.

WINNERS find an opportunity in every difficulty. Losers find a difficulty in every opportunity.

WINNERS believe past experiences should be a guidepost—not a hitching post.

WINNERS view obstacles as opportunities to develop their achievement muscles.

ACTION SHEET
"Mirror, Mirror on the Wall"

The following list reflects my major strengths and assets: (Please include attitudes, skills, traits, emotional and physical characteristics, education, and personality traits.)

1.

2.

3.

4.

5.

6.

7.

8.

9.

10.

11.

12.

13.

14.

15.

ACTION SHEET
"Mirror, Mirror on the Wall'

The following written description portrays the mental picture I have of myself succeeding:

ACTION SHEET
"Mirror, Mirror on the Wall"

This week I learned these new things that improved my knowledge of my job:

1.

2.

3.

4.

5.

ACTION SHEET
"Mirror, Mirror on the Wall"

Each day this week I am going to look in a mirror and give myself the following pep talk:

CHAPTER 5

What You Set
Is What You Get

*Belief is the thermostat that regulates our
accomplishments.*

Recently I boarded a plane for a trip to San
Francisco, where I was scheduled to conduct a
three-day seminar. After we were seated, the pilot
spoke over the public address system: "Good
morning, ladies and gentlemen. This is Captain
Turner. Welcome aboard Flight 241, non-stop to
San Francisco. Our cruising altitude will be
thirty-four thousand feet. We plan to arrive on
schedule at 2:43 P.M. The weather is nice in San
Francisco, with sunny skies and a temperature of
seventy-five degrees. Please sit back and enjoy
your flight. If any of our crew can assist you,
please call on us."

Now, I like that kind of introduction to my
flights. The pilot knew where he was going, what
the departure and arrival times were, and what
some of the conditions would be along the way.

How do you think I would have felt if the pilot

had greeted us with these words: "Welcome aboard, ladies and gentlemen. We will depart sometime this morning on a trip to San Francisco. We'll leave Memphis International Airport and fly south for a while; we'll probably fly west for an hour or two, and then we'll probably turn north for a while. We haven't decided on the particular cruising altitude yet, but we'll try to keep the aircraft above the mountain peaks. We don't know the weather conditions in San Francisco. We're not sure what time we will arrive, but we can assure you we'll have a lot of fun on this flight."

How long would you stay on that plane?

This fabricated captain's speech reminds me of the cross-eyed javelin thrower. He didn't win many contests, but he surely kept the spectators alert and interested.

Our goals will have a great deal more power when we make them personal, state them specifically, write them down, have them compatible with our values, state them positively, and make them challenging enough to motivate us to attain them.

Goals are the key to success. If a person doesn't have any goals, he won't know when he scores. I am reminded of two basketball teams lining up for the tip-off. Before the referee blows the whistle to begin the game, two men bring out a ladder and remove both goals. The referee then says, "Let's play ball!" How can the fellows play basketball if there are no goals? Who will know when someone scores? Who would enjoy this kind of a game? This is analogous to a person's not having specific goals for his life.

There is a powerful proverb which states, "Before you can score, you must have a goal." Exactly how much money do you want to earn next year? How many books do you plan to read this month? What kind of house do you want to own? How much time do you want to invest in service to your community? What kind of person do you want to be spiritually? How much do you want to weigh in six months? What particular skills do you plan to develop or improve in the next twelve months?

It is imperative that we define the target for which we are shooting, or we will never know how close we come to hitting it. We must define the height we want to reach, or we'll have no way of knowing when or if we've reached it. Without goals there is no way we can measure our success and achievement.

Goals help us build self-confidence. Because self-confidence is built upon successful experiences, setting and reaching goals enhances this attribute. In the goal-setting workshops I conduct, I often suggest that participants may want to begin by writing simple, achievable goals. For example: to read one specific book this week, or bake a cake for someone, or sign up for some exercise program, or write two letters in the morning, or call on three new prospective clients.

Several years ago there was a popular play on

Broadway. It ended with this powerful benediction, "May your dreams be your only boundaries." This is a phenomenal prescription to take every day. Before you retire at night, when you awaken each morning, and during the day, "dream your impossible dream." Each of us is limited only by the boundaries of our imagination. It is important to raise our sights above those things around us and catch a higher vision of the things we want to do with our lives. We'll find this advice in the Bible: "Look up! Set your mind on things that are above, not on things that are on the earth."

If we spend an inordinate amount of time on things around us, we may become quite discouraged. This dissipates our ability to dream and reach out toward important goals.

My favorite sport in high school was basketball. For three years my brother and I played on the varsity team. Because I played the guard position, it was my responsibility to bring the ball up the court. I developed the habit of looking down as I dribbled the basketball. It was impossible for me to see where the other players were positioned on the court when I had my head down. During practice sessions Coach Calvin Hastings would yell, "Art, look up!" With his encouragement and instruction, I broke that habit. When our son, Alan, played basketball, I noticed that he dribbled with his head up so that he had a clearer view of where he was going and where his teammates were.

You probably remember the lesson Jesus taught

Peter about walking on the water. Jesus told Peter to walk toward him on the water. Peter was progressing well on top of the water as long as he kept his eyes on Jesus. When Peter looked down at his feet, he saw the waves, became frightened, and began to sink.

One of the greatest lessons I have learned in life is that of the self-fulfilling prophecy. This concept clearly suggests that we become what we imagine; that we become what we *expect* to become. While we vividly picture ourselves achieving our goals, we will move toward their achievement. As Napoleon Hill stated, "What the mind can conceive and believe, it can achieve."

Psychologists tell us that we move in the direction of our present dominant thoughts. This is why it is essential to fill our minds with goal-oriented thoughts. This process nourishes one's subconscious mind with the proper mental food. The subconscious mind operates much like an automatic guidance system of a modern missile. It receives a set of planned instructions, monitors the course of the flight, and makes appropriate corrections to remain on course.

Without goals our minds wander aimlessly. Probably ninety-five percent of the adults who inhabit spaceship earth have no specific goals for their lives. This means they function like ships without rudders.

One summer while I was working on a towboat, we were pushing several barges of gasoline up the Mississippi River. The boat hit some heavy object under the water and the rudder was broken. We were adrift—unable to control our direction. The towboat and barges turned wildly as we helplessly floated downstream. Our captain finally made radio contact with another towboat, and it came to our rescue.

You can decide today—right now—that you are not going to drift aimlessly any longer. You are going to join the elite five percent who set goals and, as a result, achieve much more in life than do those without goals. One of the exciting things about living is that it is never too late to set specific goals for our lives.

All human progress was first visualized in someone's mind. This is true in business, education, medicine, engineering—in all endeavors. Christopher Columbus cherished a vision of a water route to the Indies, but discovered, instead, a "new world." Henry Ford dreamed of mass production of automobiles. Thomas Edison dreamed of inventing a technique to illuminate homes and offices in America. Dr. Jonas Salk cherished a vision of developing a vaccine against the dreaded polio. They all proved this point: to actualize, you must visualize.

A burning desire is often more important than knowledge. A study of the life of Thomas Edison reveals that he had little formal training in chemistry, mathematics, physics, or electronics— subjects ordinarily considered essential for an inventor. This great inventor, who obtained 1,093 patents, had a burning desire which could not be extinguished by discouragement or lack of adequate resources. He was willing to pay any price to achieve his goals.

Guidelines for Setting Goals

Decide specifically what you want to achieve in life.

WINNERS know what they want in order to achieve it. As Will Rogers said, "In order to succeed, you must know what you are doing, like what you are doing, and believe in what you are doing." The things you achieve by reaching your goals are not nearly as important as what you become by reaching them.

I suspect that when most of us look back over our lives, we'll be somewhat like the fellow, Amakel. One afternoon he was riding his camel in a caravan with a group of merchants who were traveling to a distant city to sell their merchandise. A voice out of the sky spoke to Amakel and said, "Get on your camel and ride by yourself to an oasis ten miles west of here. When the stars come out tonight, pick up all the pebbles you see by the oasis and put them in your pockets. And in the morning you will be both glad and sad."

Amakel did as he was instructed. After he had picked up several pebbles, he became tired and went to sleep. He awoke several times during the night wondering what the voice meant about feeling glad and sad. When the sun warmed his face, he rubbed his eyes and stood up to stretch. He reached into his pockets and pulled out the pebbles he had placed there. When he looked in his hand, he knew then what the voice meant. The pebbles had turned into jewels. He was glad he had picked up many of them but sad he had not picked up more.

You have the power TODAY to decide on the number and quality of "pebbles" you want to pick up. It's a very important decision for you to make. I want you to make the decision to do with your life what you really want to do. I wrote this book to help you become a greater WINNER. God wants you to be a WINNER. He created you and has given you talents to develop. Your love for God will be shown by what you do with those talents. Also, I hope you're making a great deal of money, because I believe the more money you're making, the more people you are serving.

Here are some examples of specific goals you might set: "Within two years I intend to be a district sales manager, or earn $50,000 a year, or complete my college degree in accounting, or save $10,000 within three years for a down payment on a house." This procedure removes us from vague generalities and establishes specific targets toward which we can direct our energies.

It is imperative that you write your goals down. This helps crystallize your thinking and aids in making them concrete and specific. Otherwise, the goals remain vague and abstract.

In the space below take approximately fifteen

minutes and write your lifetime goals. You'll want to interpret these goals from your present perspective. As you write these lifetime goals, consider at least these important areas: personal, physical, financial, social, intellectual, spiritual, family, career, and community.

LIFETIME GOALS

1.

2.

3.

4.

5.

6.

7.

8.

Because most people have not been involved in any type of goal-setting workshop, they write most of their goals in very general terms. For example, they include such things as wanting to make more money, enjoying more happiness, becoming a better salesman, or achieving more success.

Next, I'd like for you to take fifteen minutes and write in the space below the specific goals you plan to achieve in the next three years.

THREE-YEAR GOALS

1.

2.

3.

4.

5.

6.

7.

8.

It's time now to write the specific goals you are going to achieve during the next six months. As you write your goals, avoid using the words "more" or "better." When either of these terms is used, the goal is probably not nearly as specific as it should be. In the space provided below, write your goals for the next six months.

SIX-MONTH GOALS

1.

2.

3.

4.

5.

6.

7.

8.

Each of your goals carries a different value. Some are more important than others. Because this is true, you'll want to go back over your Lifetime, Three-Year, and Six-Month goals and rank them by priority. From each list place the number "1" beside the most important goal on that list, the number "2" beside the next most important goal, and continue until you have placed a number beside each goal on your different lists. This procedure is very necessary because it helps you identify those goals which are the most important and on which you should spend more time. It also breaks each goal down into achievable activities.

But how are goals achieved? Goals are achieved through activities. These activities are simply steps you'll be taking along the way toward achieving your goals. For example, one of your goals may have been to insure financial security. Your activities to achieve that goal might be to purchase one hundred dollars worth of stock each month, place one hundred dollars in the bank each month, or invest a certain amount in real estate.

In the space below, write your top three Lifetime Goals. Under each goal write as many activities as you can that will help you achieve each goal.

LIFETIME GOALS and ACTIVITIES

Lifetime Goal #1

Activities:

A.

B.

C.

D.

E.

Lifetime Goal #2

Activities

A.

B.

   C.

   D.

   E.

Lifetime Goal #3

   Activities
   A.

   B.

   C.

   D.

   E.

THREE-YEAR GOALS and ACTIVITIES

Goal #1

   Activities:
   A.

B.

C.

D.

E.

Goal #2

Activities

A.

B.

C.

D.

E.

Goal #3

Activities

A.

B.

C.

D.

E.

F.

G.

H.

SIX-MONTH GOALS and ACTIVITIES

Goal #1

  Activities

  A.

  B.

  C.

  D.

  E.

Goal #2

  Activities

  A.

  B.

C.

D.

E.

Goal #3

Activities

A.

B.

C.

D.

E.

You can always go back and revise your goals or activities according to your needs and desires. You have written these on paper, not in concrete. Our goals change as our values change. You'll also find it necessary sometimes to modify your activities to achieve your goals. Such modification usually indicates growth on your part.

Periodically I find it helpful to ask during the day, "What am I doing with my time right now?" You will find it beneficial to write this question on a three-by-five index card and leave it on your desk, put it in your pocket, tape it to the refrigerator door, or place it in some prominent location where you can see it as a reminder. It can help you reflect on the activities on which you need to spend your time to accomplish your goals.

All your waking minutes should not be spent in activities to achieve your top few priority goals. You need time to do things which relax, inform, or entertain you. You need time to be you. The amount of "free" time varies with each of us. If your schedule seems to stay full most of the time, you will probably need to schedule some time for recreational activities. Your feelings of accomplishment will be greater as you develop a well-rounded schedule which meets your personal needs.

Perhaps there are some additional strengths which you need to develop that will help you achieve your goals. Do you need to become more enthusiastic, develop a more positive attitude, organize your time better, reduce your food consumption, quit smoking, or become more flexible? Please continue your efforts toward a more rewarding and productive life by completing the following exercise.

STRENGTHS I NEED TO DEVELOP

1. Attitudes I Need to Develop:

   A.

   B.

   C.

   D.

   E.

2. Skills I Need to Develop:

   A.

B.

C.

D.

E.

3. Habits I Need to Develop:

A.

B.

C.

D.

E.

It's a fair question for you to ask: "Does this goal-setting process work?" Thousands of people who have used it say that it does! It has worked effectively in my life. This process has helped me achieve more things in my life than I ever dreamed of achieving. For more than twenty years I have researched the lives of successful people. They were goal-oriented individuals. They knew where they wanted to go, what they wanted to achieve, and when they wanted to arrive. They were achievement-oriented people. They could visualize exactly what they wanted. And they asked this important question: "What am I willing to give up in order to achieve my goals?" They also asked, "Is the gain worth the pain?" As a graduate student in one of my classes, Debbie Gallimore, used to say, "Dr. Garner, those questions are *heavy!*"

Let me share with you a few examples which, I believe, validate this goal-setting process. One fellow in my class named Bob Carter set a goal to earn $25,000 a year within a three-year period. He wrote down the activities he was going to use to make his goals a reality. One of his activities, incidentally, was to get another job. Within three years he was earning over $50,000 a year, and this year he will probably earn over $100,000. As they say in Texas, "That ain't all bad!" Bob decided that the "gain was worth the pain." His goals were very clear, and the daily visualization of these goals motivated him to achieve them. Bob made a move to improve, and it paid off. America is a country in which this can be done. God bless America!

A lady in another goal-setting workshop set a goal to earn a college degree in early childhood education within a five-year period. This middle-aged lady had never entered college, and she planned to go part time so that she could meet the needs of her family. This lady, Joe McKenzie, will receive her degree this year from a major university.

Another lady, Joan Lee, used goal-setting to achieve an important objective in her life. She specified the goal to become a director within a certain time in Transart Industries. She listed the activities she needed to engage in, ranked them by priority, and took action. Today she is a director in this fine business.

It's extremely important to keep our eyes on our goals. Let it be our magnificent obsession. We think about it constantly. We have to achieve it. We really want it. It hits our hot button! In the goal-setting workshops I conduct, participants have found it very helpful to get a piece of poster board and glue on it some pictures or symbols which remind them of their goals. You, too, should get a detailed picture of the kind of house you plan to own, or of the clothes you plan to purchase, or of the car you are going to buy, or the college from which you plan to graduate, or the kind of career you plan to pursue. You'll want to divide this poster into three sections, which include Lifetime Goals, Three-Year Goals, and Six-Month Goals.

Several times each day you will be motivated toward achieving your goals as you look at pictures of things you plan to achieve. My mother used to say, "Out of sight, out of mind."

Have you ever heard the name "Gerry Dorsey"? Probably not very many people have. He was a singer who wanted to have a successful career entertaining audiences. He spent several years singing in small night clubs, then decided to make some changes. He found a new manager. The manager was unable to book him anywhere because his name was associated with failure. The manager decided to change Gerry's name. Within four years he became a superstar—and a millionaire. He had changed his name to "Engelbert Humperdinck."

Sometimes we have to try another way to reach our goals. Although one road may have an insurmountable obstacle, there are other roads which can lead us to our goals. God never closes one door without opening two more. Faith can move mountains. Winning requires persistent faith.

It is important to picture your goals as though they had already been achieved. Picture yourself *being, doing, or having something*—a *fait accompli*. Avoid picturing the individual steps you think should be taken to achieve what you desire. Because your conscious mind is limited by your five physical senses, it cannot know the best direction to take. Your subconscious mind operates twenty-four hours every day on all levels and in all directions. It does not have the limitations that are characteristic of the conscious mind.

In his book, *One More Step*, James Dillet Freeman has included a challenge to all of us:

> A hill is not too hard to climb
> Taken one step at a time.
> One step is not too much to take;
> One try is not too much to make.
> One step, one try, one song, one smile
> Will shortly stretch into a mile.
> And everything worthwhile was done
> By small steps taken one by one.
> To reach the goal you started for,
> Take one step more . . . take one step more.

WISDOM FROM WINNERS

WINNERS can take a negative environment and make it a training camp for personal growth.

WINNERS see something positive in everything that happens.

WINNERS develop the ability to see difference where others see only likeness, and likeness where others see only difference.

WINNERS believe the best angle from which to approach any problem is the try-angle.

WINNERS hold a picture of what they want to happen, while losers hold a picture of what they don't want to happen.

WINNERS believe that a specific goal is a dream being acted upon.

WINNERS ask, "What am I willing to give, or give up, to achieve my goals?"

WINNERS believe that obstacles are the things you see when you take your eyes off your goals.

we turned away from the lake and walked along the edge of a field dense with glossy broad-leaved plants, which Nina told me were sugar beets. Finally, we scrambled up a steep bank at the back of the field, and I found myself gazing down into a wide channel of slow-flowing water, bordered by lush grass and bright yellow flowers on either side, glinting invitingly under the high sun.

"*This* is the drain?" I said.

Nina grinned. "Yep. Milner's Drain. It takes all the rainfall from the fields all the way along — it's glorious fresh water, not swampy like the lake."

Jonas was already stripping off to his swimming trunks, and I half turned away, heat flaring in my cheeks.

"Where does the water go to?" I asked, gazing as far up the channel as I could see.

"To the sea, of course," Nina said.

Jonas sounded mildly annoyed. "Don't say *of course*. How's she supposed to know?" He gave me a serious look. "It's all re-claimed land, the Fens — it used to be mostly under the sea. The water's drawn out by big pumps now, and the coastal walls stop it flooding back in again."

"Oh my God," Nina said. "I've just re-membered why I hated school."

"Oh, very funny." Jonas turned away, preparing to dive into the water. I watched his muscles tense. "You hated school because you can't stand being told what to do."

He dived in cleanly, creating the smallest of splashes. I held my breath as I watched him glide under the silvery green surface.

"We're eight feet below sea level here, did you know?" Nina said brightly. "If those sea walls gave way . . ."

She didn't wait for me to respond, but stepped to the edge of the bank and dived in too. My heart rattled, and I scanned the horizon. How fast would the water come rushing inland? How quickly could we run back to Raven Hall? Did the family keep a store of food upstairs, in case of this eventuality?

"Beth!" Nina called from the water. "Come in — it's wonderful!"

I checked that Jonas was still swimming away from us, not watching us, and I took a flying leap and plunged in feetfirst. My head went right under, and the shock of the cold took my breath away, even once I'd surfaced. Nina swam closer.

"You okay?"

I gasped in great lungfuls of air, and then I laughed.

56

"Yeah, you were right. It's freezing. But I love it."

The three of us swam for a while, and then we floated, chatting lazily, as the sun blazed down on us. Nina showed me a newt peeking out from the long grass on the bank, and the newt and I stared at each other for several seconds before it pottered away. It was the first one I'd ever seen. Jonas pointed out a buzzard circling overhead, silhouetted against the blue dome of a sky, and I heard its *kee-yah* call. I learned that the cheerful chirruping coming from somewhere nearby was a reed warbler.

Eventually, we hauled ourselves out of the water and sat drying on the bank with dragonflies flitting around us. I was much paler than the other two, and I draped my T-shirt across my shoulders, not wanting my sunburn to get any worse. If I wasn't allowed to cycle into the village to buy sun cream, how would I get hold of any? Would Leonora let me add it to her shopping list? I'd ask Nina later, I decided, when we were alone.

"There's a party tonight," Jonas said casually, after a spell of companionable silence. I assumed he was directing this at Nina rather than me, although he kept his gaze fixed on the blade of grass in his hand. "A load of kids in the village. You could come, if you wanted to sneak out?"

Nina rolled her neck, considering. "We can't. Not tonight. My parents are kind of twitchy at the moment. I think they'd be on the lookout."

Her use of the word *we* — her assumption he was inviting both of us — gave me a glow of reassurance. I didn't miss the implication that she'd snuck out on previous occasions.

"Okay." Jonas tossed his blade of grass aside and looked directly at me. "Maybe next time."

My pulse jumped, and I looked away, turning to Nina.

"Why are your parents twitchy?" I said. "Not because of me, I hope."

When she didn't immediately reply, Jonas gave her a speculative look.

"Did you know," he said, "that Markus's dad is flying over from the States? He's booked himself a room at our place at the weekend. Is he coming to see you?"

"Markus's dad?" I said. "As in" — I looked at Nina expectantly — "your grandad?"

Nina's voice was surprisingly harsh. "Yeah, great, he's finally decided to visit, after all these years. He left the country when I was a tiny baby, never even sends me a birthday card — I mean, it's nothing to do with wanting presents, but — he's never acted like a grandad at all, even though he's the only grandparent I've got." She made a noise of disgust. "And suddenly he wants to come and meet me."

Jonas and I exchanged a look. He seemed just as unsettled by this outburst as I was.

"That's weird," I said. "Do he and your dad not get on? Did they have an argument or something, and now he wants to patch things up?"

"I don't *know*, Beth." Nina jumped to her feet. "And I don't want to talk about it. I'm going back to the house. Are you coming with me, or not?"

I glanced again at Jonas, who showed no sign of moving. I kept my expression light and got to my feet.

"Of course I'll come with you," I said.

Jonas said nothing further, and Nina and I left him lying there in the long grass, his golden arm shielding his face from the sun. We headed back along the edge of the field, talking of other things, and gradually her good mood returned. But I was careful not to mention Markus's father again, and, privately, I added him to my growing list of prickly subjects where Nina was concerned.

We retraced our route all the way to Raven Hall, and the cool air of the entrance hall felt like a welcome-home caress on my skin.

SADIE

January 2019

The silver Mercedes S-Class arrives precisely on time, gliding between the hatchbacks parked along Sadie's narrow street like a swan parting a flock of scruffy mallards. Sadie isn't quite ready. She dashes to the bathroom to touch up her lipstick, then makes a last-minute change back into her own shoes — hers are more comfortable than the pair the company sent. The rejected ones she slips back inside the suitcase. Then she makes one final check of her reflection in the hall mirror. The ivory silk dress is perfect; she's never worn anything so glamorous.

The doorbell rings, and she flashes herself a quick grin in the mirror before hurrying to open the door. The chauffeur helps her with her luxurious coat, and he carries her case as he escorts her out to the car. *I could get used to this,* Sadie thinks.

The night is bitterly cold, and once they've left the main roads, there's nothing to see through the windows but the occasional lit-up farm buildings in the darkness. They could be heading anywhere in the black night. Sadie forces herself to relax against the leather seat; this isn't an audition — she already has the part. No need to feel jittery. Drinks, dinner, and a game. It's going to be fun.

She runs through her character details in her head automatically: Miss Lamb, newly arrived in the area, seeking employment at Raven Hall . . . She locks eyes with her reflection in the blank window by her side, and she gives a wry grimace. Here in the real world, Miss Sadie Langton is twenty-eight. She can barely pay her own rent, and she's never had a relationship or a job that's lasted longer than twelve months. She summons her mother's voice in her head: *"You don't need money or a man to make you happy, Sadie. But you do need to think before you act. You're too impetuous."*

Her mother was fond of dishing out advice like that — statements that always seemed carefully rehearsed; her mother wasn't one for spontaneous heart-to-hearts. Growing up, Sadie learned that excessive displays of emotion on her part sent her mother into retreat, as if feelings were things that should be kept private and not shared, even between daughter and mother. When Sadie, aged eleven, came home from school in tears because she'd been given a detention for something that wasn't her fault, her mother ate nothing that evening and drifted upstairs to bed before it had even grown dark. When Sadie's first boyfriend rang her at home to tell her he was dumping her, her mother remembered an urgent appointment and went out for the rest of the day, leaving Sadie to sob on her bed all alone.

The car slows as they approach the sparse lights of another village, and Sadie lets her reflection blur for a moment, focusing instead on the little she can see of the houses they pass. She never doubted her mother loved her when she was growing up; she just wished they could have been more open with each other.

Around the time Sadie left home, when she was eighteen, her relationship with her mother grew spikier, no doubt fueled by what her mother described as Sadie's *"irresponsible attitude to employment."* Sadie was drawn toward acting, thrilled to be signed by Wendy at the drama agency, starry-eyed at the prospect of earning a living by pretending to be something she wasn't . . . but it quickly became clear that she needed a backup income. So she lurched from one part-time job to another, keen to keep some of her time free in case, one day, Wendy was to ring with a truly exciting opportunity . . .

"You're too optimistic," her mother had told her, only a few months ago.

Sadie had laughed, but the comment had stung. "Why does that have to be a bad thing, Mum?"

"You need to stick with one job for a while. Your CV must look terrible. How many times have you been sacked now?"

"It doesn't —"

"Four, isn't it?" Her mother knew full well it was four.

"In ten *years*, Mum. And it was never —"

"And how many other jobs have you just walked out on?" Her mother's sigh filled the stuffy sitting room with her disappointment. "Please, just *try* to think things through a bit more calmly, will you? Before making snap decisions."

"You mean, *Grow up, Sadie*," Sadie had replied. "Don't you? You can just say it. I know that's what you're thinking."

Her mum had sounded weary. "I just want you to be happy . . ."

The car hits a bump in the road, and

Sadie's focus is jolted back to her reflection in the glass. She asks her mirror image, silently, *Are you happy?* Scraping money together from one month to the next, auditioning for sometimes quite dubious jobs, eating beans on toast every night . . . Her reflection's serious expression softens into a smile. *Happy enough* is the soundless reply. *And this job tonight will make me a whole lot happier, when I get paid.*

A brightly lit B and B sign marks the end of the village, and they're quickly plunged back into the darkness of yet another country lane.

"We've made good time, miss," the chauffeur says from the front — the first time he's spoken since they set off. "We're almost there now."

A minute or two later, they swing off the road, and Sadie spots the grand house lit up in the distance, familiar from the images she's seen online. It reminds her of an ocean liner, all lights blazing in a sea of black. She peers around the chauffeur's hat, her pulse quickening. The tower is still there, she sees. But the ivy has been cleared away — that's promising.

They pull up by a flight of steps, and the chauffeur leaps out and strides around to open her door. She takes his gloved hand

and steps lightly onto the gravel, one high heel after the other. A stunningly beautiful woman in a long emerald green evening dress comes down the steps toward her, all black hair and dark eyes and heavy mascara, her arms opened wide in greeting.

"Welcome to Raven Hall," the woman says grandly. "I'm Lady Nightingale, your hostess. And you must be Miss Lamb. Please — do come in, out of the cold."

She waits, watching, hidden behind the scratchy leaves in the garden border.

Eventually, there's movement by the back door. The fluffy dog lifts its head. A hand appears, gripping the doorframe. Someone is stepping out cautiously onto the veranda, taking their time about it.

Is this the new owner of Raven Hall?

It's a woman in her forties. A loose summer dress billows over her bloated frame, and her pale hair is scraped back into a ponytail, creating the impression that her head is too small for her body. She shuffles across the veranda and collapses onto a swing seat with a groan that rolls out across the lawn. The fluffy dog springs up beside her and nestles into the folds of her dress, and she rests one puffy hand on its little head.

Almost immediately, a second woman, much younger, appears in the doorway. In stark contrast to the figure on the swing seat, this one is dressed to show off her slim frame: bright orange crop top, tight-fitting denim shorts, enormous hoop earrings. She hovers briefly on the veranda without saying anything, then swivels and disappears back inside the house with a swish of her waist-length hair. The swing seat rocks and creaks, and the older woman tips her head back and closes her eyes.

So, these are the new owners of Raven Hall. A slow-moving woman and her spoiled brat of a daughter.

She watches the woman on the swing seat for a while longer, but her resentment is an ache inside her rib cage, and her powerlessness makes her restless. She creeps back around the border of the garden and escapes over the curved branch, into the farmer's field. Insects buzz all around her, and she stands perfectly still for a minute, thinking, weighing up her options. She needs to get back to the village; she's got a long journey ahead of her, to return to her lodgings. But before that, she has a decision to make.

She lifts her chin and retraces her steps around the boundary wall, until she reaches the point where she'll have to veer out into the open — where she might be seen. Before she leaves, she places her palms against the warm stone wall again, and she tells Raven Hall, "Don't forget me. I'll come back."

BETH

July 1988

Each evening of my first week at Raven Hall, when Markus arrived home after work he asked me how my day had been and how I was settling in. By Thursday, I was able to give him a genuinely unforced answer.

"It's been a brilliant day, thanks. I really love it here."

He beamed, before hurrying away as usual, to check on his other projects. There was always a ditch that needed clearing out, or a broken piece of guttering that needed mending, or on this occasion some old gazebos that needed to be retrieved from the stable block before Leonora followed through with her threat to hire a grand new one for their upcoming party.

Leonora grew more tense as the week wore on. She carried around guest lists and food lists, and I heard her several times chasing up the caterers on the phone. Nina and I spent our days outside, exploring routes around the lake, swimming with Jonas, or rowing halfway across to the island, shelving the oars and stretching out in the sunshine with a good book each and a picnic for when our stomachs began to rumble. But that Thursday evening, after Markus had gone off to look for the gazebos, Leonora told Nina to go and tidy her bedroom, and then she asked me whether I'd mind doing her a favor.

"Of course," I said. "What is it?"

"There's a dress in your wardrobe. I wondered if you'd try it on for me. I want to see if it fits you."

I hesitated. The dress had looked rather restrictive and uncomfortable, and I was perfectly content in my shorts and T-shirt; I didn't enjoy dressing up. On the other hand, Leonora had been nothing but kind to me, and my new life at Raven Hall had so far been one carefree day after another. I didn't want to seem ungrateful.

"Okay," I said.

"Come down and show me when you've got it on."

I hurried upstairs and lifted the blue checked dress down from its hanging rail. My prediction was right — when I pulled it on, it felt tight and scratchy, and I no longer

71

felt like Beth Soames at all. There was a big cheval mirror in the corner of the room, and I examined my reflection morosely. It wouldn't be easy to scramble into and out of the rowing boat wearing something like this; I felt sorry for the olden-day girls who had to wear such things all the time. But I did as Leonora had requested, and I went down to the drawing room to show her.

"Ah, Beth." She set aside her party list as if she'd forgotten she was waiting for me, but I wasn't fooled — her bright eyes scrutinized me intensely, and there was a twitchiness in her movements. She walked in a circle around me, tweaking at the fabric, and then she lifted a lock of my hair, which was tangled from swimming in the lake that afternoon.

"Here," she said. "Come and sit down. Let me brush your hair."

Warily, I sank onto a chair in front of the black marble fireplace. A fine mist coated my cheek as she sprayed something over my head. But as soon as she began to pull the brush through the tangles, I felt my muscles relaxing, and the smoother the brush's strokes became, the more soothed I felt. I closed my eyes and inhaled her rose-scented perfume, and the pleasant chemical fragrance of the spray, and the background

72

lavender-and-polish smell of Raven Hall.

The sensation on my scalp took me back to a time when my mother used to brush my hair each morning before school. Sometimes she'd braid it into two long pigtails, and I'd skip all the way to my primary school, enjoying their thump-thump on my shoulders as I bounced. My brother, Ricky, used to walk tall in his high school uniform beside me, and he'd laugh at my enthusiasm and call me Skippy. I could have sat there and let Leonora brush my hair forever; I didn't want her to stop.

"Now," Leonora said finally. "Let's see. Shall we plait it?" I nodded, my eyes suddenly stinging.

Deftly, she divided my hair into two sides and wove a pair of plaits, producing blue ribbons from her pocket to tie at the ends. When she was finished, she stepped back, and it was only then that I noticed Markus hovering in the doorway. Leonora's voice was rather sharp.

"What do you think?"

She was looking at him, not at me. I kept quiet as Markus took a couple of steps into the room.

"Yes," he said. "That'll do."

Then he spun on his heel and was gone.

Leonora turned away from me and picked

up her party list. "That's fine, Beth. You can change back into your own clothes now."

I felt I'd missed something. I was strangely bereft, as if a spotlight of maternal attention had been trained on me for the last ten minutes, then abruptly turned off. I watched her for a couple of seconds, but she didn't lift her gaze from her list.

"Okay, then." I hurried back upstairs, dragged the stiff dress over my head, and slid back into my own comfortable clothes before I glanced in the mirror again. The plaits looked all wrong. My reflection gave me a shiver of unease. I tugged off the ribbons and unraveled Leonora's careful weaving until I had restored my loose blond mane. I flung the dress into the bottom of the wardrobe and went off to find Nina.

There was no mention of the dress the next morning, but when I returned to my bedroom after swimming in the afternoon, something made me want another look at it. I creaked the wardrobe doors open and saw that the dress was no longer in a crumpled heap at the bottom: it was back on the hanger in the same place it had been when I first saw it. I banged the doors shut and held my hands against them for a moment. Then I rubbed the goose bumps from my skin, and I went off to look for Nina.

Up in Nina's turret bedroom, we peered at the activity on the back lawn. A team of men in white tunics was assembling a huge gazebo — Leonora had got her own way, after all. Others were arranging garden furniture into companionable circles on the lawn. Leonora and Markus strolled hand in hand, observing the workers, and I studied the dress Leonora wore — a pretty, knee-length pale green summer dress. Nothing like the thing she'd made me try on last night. She looked elegant and relaxed.

I sighed and turned away from the window. "Do you have parties here a lot?"

"Nah." Nina was restless, and I sensed she wouldn't be happy to stay up here for much longer. She, too, turned her back on the window. "My grandparents used to throw parties here all the time, but my parents only do it once every couple of years, when Dad thinks he needs to butter up his clients. He says it brings the work in."

"Oh." I chewed my lip. I wanted to ask more, but I didn't know which grandparents she meant, and since her grandfather seemed to be a touchy subject, it struck me as best not to mention any of them.

"They sent out invites for this one ages

ago," Nina continued, "but I think Mum regretted it afterward."

"She does seem a bit stressed." I frowned. "Wait. Are we supposed to dress up for this?" I was thinking of Leonora's intense gaze as she tweaked at the sleeves of the blue checked dress and straightened my plaits. Maybe she didn't approve of the clothes I'd brought with me, or perhaps it was my wild hair she didn't like — it was months since I'd last had a haircut or been bought anything new to wear. I glanced at Nina. Her T-shirt was an expensive brand, her shorts less faded than mine, but the differences weren't *that* great, surely? I opened my mouth to ask her why her mum had wanted me to try on the blue dress, but again I hesitated.

"Nah, don't worry about it," Nina said. "We're not invited — we'll have to stay out of the way." She picked up a book, then put it down. "God, I'm so bored, and there's no time to swim again and get dry before dinner. Let's go downstairs."

We clattered down the spiral staircase and then down the next flight to the wood-paneled hall. From there, we could see into the kitchen, and through the open French doors to the workers on the lawn. Leonora and Markus were now sitting at one of the garden tables, pouring themselves drinks.

"I know," Nina said. "I'll show you my dad's study. He's got some amazing collections."

She pushed open a door I hadn't yet seen behind and took me into a large square room, screened from the bright sunlight outside by a slatted blind. A green-topped desk, as long as a bed, stood over by the window. It held a neat stack of paperwork, a pot of pencils, and one large spread-out diagram of a garden.

"Why doesn't your mum work in here?" I asked, thinking of the cluttered laundry room that Leonora used.

Nina shrugged. "She's never liked this room."

"Are you sure we're allowed in?"

"Of course." But she spoke softly, and she pushed the door gently closed behind us.

The wall opposite the door was made up entirely of bookshelves, from floor to ceiling. But only half the shelves held books; the rest were stuffed with all sorts of treasures: enormous glossy shells and bulbous pieces of pottery; a stuffed bird on a branch, and a brightly painted globe; a wooden bowl on three legs and a log carved into the shape of a drum. Two of the other walls were lined with mismatched cupboards and cabinets, and these, too, boasted collections of objects. The room felt more like a museum than an office.

"Here," Nina said, "I'll show you . . ." She strolled in a loop around the room. "These are shells from the Philippines. And coral Dad collected when he was diving. These are pearls."

"They're amazing."

"There's a cello in there." She patted a black instrument case leaning against one of the cabinets. "And these are fossils — that's an ammonite, and a trilobite, I think. What do you like best?"

I was tempted to say the cello, but I forced my gaze to move on around the room.

"Those orange spiky shells," I said. "They remind me of hedgehogs."

Nina's grin was delighted. "They're my favorite too." With great care, she picked one up. It filled her cupped palms, and she showed me how its top and bottom halves were hinged at the back.

I moved my head to examine it from different angles, keeping my hands clasped behind my back. "I love it."

A sudden noise outside the door made us both jump — footsteps were passing, accompanied by the chinking of glasses.

Nina hurried to set the shell back down.

"The caterers are here." And just like that, the tour of the room was over. "Come on. Let's see if there're any goodies in the fridge. We can sample them to make sure they're okay for the party tomorrow."

SADIE

January 2019

Raven Hall's entrance hall is warm and welcoming after the icy wind outside, and Sadie gazes in awe at the portraits and the huge bronze vases of hothouse flowers and the gorgeous foliage weaving up the banisters of the central staircase. She barely registers the chauffeur setting her suitcase down and leaving.

"What a beautiful house," she says.

"Bloody hell." Lady Nightingale lunges toward the floor, trying to catch the cards and papers she's just dropped.

"Oops," Sadie says. "Here, let me help."

Together, they gather it all up. The cards are for the game, Sadie sees; they're numbered, and they're now in the wrong order. There are little envelopes, too, all with animal names on them, and sheets of paper similarly mixed up.

Lady Nightingale gives her a rueful smile.

"I'm Nazleen," she says, dropping the cut-glass accent. "You're one of the other actors, aren't you? I'm so glad I didn't do that in front of a real guest. I've got so many things to remember; I can't —" She glances around at the multiple doors leading off the hall. "Do you think there might be a desk or something, down here, where I can sort these out?"

A young man in black tie hovers by Sadie's suitcase. "Shall I show you up to your room, miss?"

"Do you know if there's a desk we can use somewhere . . . ?" Sadie asks him, but the young man merely looks anxious.

"We're not allowed in the other rooms."

"Right, okay." Sadie indicates her suitcase. "Well, if you don't mind taking my case up now, I'll go up and find it in a minute." She turns back to Nazleen. "Come on, I'll give you a hand."

The two doors that stand already open reveal beautifully furnished interiors — one a drawing room with bright flames crackling in a black marble fireplace, the other a grand dining room with silver cutlery and crystal glasses sparkling on a snow-white tablecloth. They ignore these rooms and work their way down the hall. The first door they try is locked; the next opens into a dimly lit cloakroom filled with racks of coats. Then Sadie finds a door with the key still in it, and she unlocks it.

"In here," she says. "It looks like it used to be someone's study."

Nazleen darts in after her and closes the door behind them.

"The next guests could be here any moment," Nazleen says, "but it won't take long."

She takes the paperwork over to a dusty green-topped desk and spreads it out. Sadie stands in the center of the room and turns in a slow circle, gazing at the many curious objects lining the walls. Shells and corals, mysterious bits of pottery, a heavy-looking cello case. Cobwebs trail from every surface, and Sadie could believe no one's been in here for thirty years.

"Okay," Nazleen says. "I'm done. I'd better get back out there." She consults one of her sheets of paper as they return to the brightly lit hall. "So, Miss Lamb's room . . . ah. Top of the stairs, turn left. You're in the second room on the left. You're supposed to be taken up there to freshen up, and then come back down for drinks at seven."

"Got it." Sadie watches Nazleen draw herself up in an effort to regain her former composure. "You sure you're okay?"

"Yeah, I'm fine." Nazleen's smile holds a trace of embarrassment. "I just really want this job, you know? I'm hoping it'll turn into a long-term contract. So I can't afford to mess it up."

Sadie hasn't considered that the hostess job might not be a one-off, and she wonders fleetingly whether she should try for it herself. Nazleen is a few years older than her and might have more relevant experience, but Sadie rather likes the idea of taking on the hostess role. She peers up the broad staircase. Perhaps she'll see how this weekend goes first, and then she'll ask Wendy to make some enquiries.

When she reaches the landing, she looks right, toward the room that appeared to show soot around its window in the photo she saw online. The whole corridor appears to have been recently wallpapered, and its skirting and coving freshly painted — she can still catch a trace of the paint smell in the air. There's no evidence of any fire damage. She turns left and makes for her allocated bedroom, and her heart lifts when she opens the door. The room is warm and beautifully furnished, with a high bed, a solid-oak wardrobe and drawers, and soft Turkish rugs laid over the carpet. A cheval mirror of darker wood stands in one corner, and a vase of pink roses sits on the bedside table. Her case has been laid out on a trunk near the window.

She strolls to the window and slides her hands down the thick embroidered curtains before parting them to peer out into the night. A pair of headlights is approaching from the direction of the road, and she glances at her watch — it's almost six thirty. As the car draws closer, she catches a reflection from water to the side of the driveway, and she remembers the lake from the photo, now swallowed by darkness. Another set of headlights appears in the distance, and she wonders how many guests have been invited to play this game.

It doesn't take her long to freshen up. She's eager to get the evening started, and she listens impatiently to the other arrivals being shown to their rooms. She almost sticks her head out the door to say hello and size them up, but she's mindful that she's being paid rather a lot for this, and she probably ought to behave as instructed. At ten to seven, she can wait no longer. She checks her appearance in the cheval mirror, straightens her pearls, and descends to the drawing room.

Nazleen rises gracefully from a sofa near

the fire as Sadie enters. The young man who earlier took Sadie's case to her bedroom now offers her a glass of champagne from a silver tray. Sadie tries not to grin as she takes it; she must remember her part — newly arrived, looking for employment . . . She joins Nazleen by the black marble fireplace, and they perch side by side on the sofa and sip their drinks simultaneously.

"Thanks for helping me out earlier," Nazleen murmurs.

"No problem."

Sadie's gaze roams around the room. Crystal wall lights and table lamps lend the air a shimmering quality, and there are more vibrant flowers in here, and abstract sculptures on the polished wooden side tables. She runs her free hand over the velvet of the sofa. So much in here looks brand-new. Such a contrast to that dusty study.

"How many guests are coming?" she asks.

"Seven." Nazleen touches her necklace, as if checking it's still there. "Well, six of you, plus me. I know I'm the hostess, but I don't know the answer to the mystery either. It's my husband who gets murdered."

Sadie flinches, then feels silly. "In the game," she says. "Of course."

"Yes." Nazleen laughs softly, her gaze on the door. Male voices are drifting closer; it sounds as though at least two guests are making their way down the stairs. "In the game, I'm the lady of the house, and my husband has — well, I'm not supposed to tell you that yet. But you have to work out who's responsible and how it happened."

"Excellent." Sadie, too, turns an expectant face to the door. "It's going to be fun."

Nazleen rises just as gracefully as she did before, and her upper-class accent has returned in full force.

"Welcome, gentlemen," she says as she crosses the room on her narrow heels.

Sadie sips her champagne like a new-to-the-area young lady hoping to land a job, and she thanks her lucky stars for whatever made the company pick her for this outrageously civilized role.

Then she, too, rises to greet the new arrivals.

BETH

July 1988

On the Saturday — the day of Leonora and Markus's party — Nina sent me upstairs after lunch to grab some blankets and cushions from her bedroom.

"Why?" I said.

"It's a surprise. I've got to persuade Mum first." Nina grinned at me. "But I always get my own way in the end."

By the time I returned with an armful of blankets, Nina was cheerfully packing a selection of party food into a big wicker basket, and she added bottles of Coke and a torch, and a game of Scrabble.

"Where are we *taking* all this?" I asked, but she merely laughed.

"It's a surprise; I told you. Just wait and see."

Leonora hurried across the kitchen from her office. "I'm going to get changed now." She hesitated at the door, looking back at us. "Nina, I'm really not sure about this. You'll get cold and bored, and you know you can't come down halfway through . . ."

"It'll be *fine,* Mum," Nina said, rolling her eyes, and she grabbed the basket and headed out into the garden. "Come on," she called back to me, her dark eyes sparkling. "Trust me, Beth. You're gonna love it."

I followed her across the lawn, straight to the back of the garden, but I hesitated as she deliberately stepped into the flower bed and squeezed her way between two dense bushes farther back in the border. It was only when I spotted the ladder, partially hidden in the foliage, that I realized what she'd brought me to.

"Oh, you've got a tree house!" I peered up at the wooden planks among the branches. "This is so cool. It reminds me of" — I'd been about to say the Famous Five, but I tried to think of something more grown up — "*Swiss Family Robinson.*" I felt a twinge of embarrassment at the random comparison, but one of the great things about Nina was that she never tried to make me feel small.

"I know. It's amazing, isn't it?" She set the basket down and scrambled up the ladder. "You'll have to pass everything up to me. Careful. Don't shake the Coke."

We arranged our blankets and cushions with care, and then we sprawled out in our little hideaway and peered through the gaps between the planks and surveyed the garden.

"It's brilliant," I said. "We'll be able to see everything from up here. This is a genius idea."

"I know." Nina grinned. "I can't believe Mum thinks we'll get bored — there'll be way too much interesting stuff to watch. I can't wait to see them all arrive, and the ladies' dresses, and their shoes, and their hair, and their jewelry . . ."

"Do you think anyone'll see us up here?"

"Nah, they'll all be drinking too much, won't they? And they'll be too busy gossiping and eyeing one another up to notice us."

I liked this way of joining in the party — as a hidden observer. It felt thrilling, almost illicit, even though Markus and Leonora knew we were up here. *Perhaps this is what it's like to be a spy,* I thought, and I scanned the garden, assessing the current situation. I wondered how much longer we had 'til the first guests arrived.

Tables and chairs sat in clusters on the lawn and under the giant white gazebo. Strings of white light bulbs hung in romantic loops from tree branches and all along the veranda railings, already glowing softly even though we still had hours of daylight left. At one end of the veranda, a bar had been set up, and a red-cheeked man in a white shirt and black bow tie was bustling around it. Nina and I had examined it surreptitiously on our way past: bottles in every different color; glasses in every size and shape imaginable; dishes of lemon and lime segments; mint leaves; glacé cherries; cubes of pineapple speared onto cocktail sticks . . .

"I wish I could try one of those cocktails," I said. I'd only ever tasted cider and an occasional sip of my parents' wine on special occasions. The thought of alcohol made me wonder what Jonas had drunk the other night, at the party in the village. I blurted out my question to Nina before I could think better of it.

"Why won't your mum let you mix with other people? Is she afraid of germs or something?"

"Yeah," Nina said without meeting my eye. "Something like that. It's just one of those things."

"Were you ill when you were little?"

She shrugged. "I don't remember."

"Have you ever been in hospital?"

"Yeah, once, when I got an ear infection."

"Huh." I shifted on my blanket and thought about the hundreds of hospital appointments I'd attended over the years with my brother. Sometimes Mum would find someone to babysit me, but mostly I'd had to trail along too, and they were *so* boring. "I guess you're lucky, then," I said. And then, more quietly, "I guess we both are."

A dramatic *pop* made us peer out again. The first guests were emerging from the French doors onto the veranda, and they gathered by the bar, chatting and laughing, while the red-cheeked man poured champagne into tall, elegant glasses. As we watched, Leonora and Markus joined the group, bringing a couple more people with them from the house. Leonora wore a shimmering green dress that went right down to her shoes, and her hair was pinned up; she had a string of pearls around her neck. Markus wore a suit so dark green, it looked almost black, and underneath that was a white shirt, open at the collar, with no tie. I turned back to Nina.

"When's your —" I hesitated, but my curiosity overrode my instincts. "When's Markus's dad coming to see you, then?"

"Tomorrow afternoon." Her voice was low.

"How long for? Has he got other grandchildren? What are you going to say to him?"

"Oh, Beth, give it a rest." She rolled away on her blanket and crossed her arms over her face. "Can we just drop the subject of *me*? Please."

Chastened, I asked no more questions, watching in silence as the lawn filled with people. Music started up, and the chatter of the guests grew louder. Eventually, Nina suggested we eat our picnic, and then we wrapped our blankets tightly around ourselves and continued to watch the party as darkness gradually fell. Leonora had been right all along: we grew cold and bored. In the end, we both dozed off.

We were woken by Markus, poking his head above the top of the ladder and laughing at us in the beam of light from his torch. The garden was completely dark, and we blinked at him, disorientated.

"Come on, sleepyheads," he said cheerfully. "Party's over. Everyone's gone home. Mum's making you hot chocolate indoors to warm you up. Come back inside."

The following morning, Nina was sick.

"I should never have let you stay up in the tree house for so long." Leonora fussed around Nina's bed, feeling her forehead and straightening her blankets.

Nina's face was a ghastly color against her

pillow, almost green. She waved at me feebly, indicating I should step back.

"No point you catching it too." She gave me a pained smile, then clutched at her stomach.

I hurried back to my own bedroom and curled up on my bed, guilt gnawing at me. I shouldn't have asked Nina all those questions about germs and illness last night — what if this was my fault? What if I'd somehow — despite my protestation to Nina that I didn't believe in such things — what if my questions had somehow tempted fate?

I closed my eyes, unable to push away memories of the worst night of my life. I'd asked a lot of questions that day too: Why did Ricky always have to fall ill just before we went on holiday? Would we still go, even if his cough got worse? Why couldn't he stay behind, with Mrs. Jackson from next door?

I'd bought new sunglasses that morning from C&A — thick black frames, glamorous reflective lenses. I knew they'd transform me from a round-faced twelve-year-old into a cool teenager as soon as we arrived at the beach. But while I was still lying awake in bed that evening, Ricky's cough *did* get worse, and I heard other worrying noises too. Mum yelling that they didn't have time to wait for an ambulance. Dad running next door to get Mrs. Jackson to babysit me. The squeal of tires as the car roared away. Mum, Dad, Ricky . . . I never saw them again.

I wore my sunglasses to the funeral, and I barely took them off for the rest of that summer. I wore them while Caroline explained why I could stay with her in her apartment for just a few nights. I wore them while the staff at the children's home went off to find me a music stand for my alien new bedroom. Those sunglasses masked my emotions; they made me feel less vulnerable, less naked. And by the time they eventually broke, I didn't need them anymore — I'd learned to present a calm face to the world, no matter what I was feeling inside.

I sat up on my bed and frowned at my reflection in the cheval mirror across the room. Of course, Nina's illness wasn't my fault, just like my family's accident wasn't my fault. Nina had caught a bug; that was all. With all those strangers passing through the house before the party — caterers and waiters and gazebo people — it was hardly surprising.

A soft tap at the door made me jump. I smoothed away my frown as the door was pushed open. Leonora poked her head in, as if not sure what she might find.

"Ah, there you are." She hesitated. "Are you okay?"

I nodded quickly. "I'm fine."

"Good." She came in and closed the door gently behind her. "I need to ask you a favor, Beth."

My heart lifted a little. Leonora and Markus had been so kind to me. I'd happily do anything to show them how grateful I was.

"Of course," I said. "What is it?"

She walked across to my wardrobe, pulled open the doors, and gazed at the blue checked dress for a long moment. If she thought it strange that I hadn't hung any of my own clothes in there yet, she didn't comment. She gave herself a little shake and lifted the dress down from the rail.

"The thing is," she said, turning to face me, "we're in a bit of a pickle. Markus's father is coming to see us today. He moved to the States after Nina was born, and he always said he'd never come back, because this place holds a lot of . . ." Her gaze drifted up to the ceiling. "Bad memories. His wife died here . . ." When she dropped her gaze again, her expression was clouded, and she looked at me as though not really seeing me. "But for some reason . . ."

"He's changed his mind."

She blinked and gave me a tight smile. "Exactly. And the thing is . . ." She came toward me with the dress clutched against her chest, and she perched on the bed as if about to confide a great secret. "Obviously, Nina's in no fit state to meet him this afternoon. So we're very much hoping you'll help us, Beth." She gave me an earnest, pleading look. "We'd like you to put this dress on, and plait your hair, and pretend to be Nina, just for a little while."

I stared at her. "But — he'll know I'm not Nina."

"He won't. He's never met her. He never asked for photos, and we never sent them."

Sympathy for Nina blossomed in my chest — her only living grandparent, and he'd never even asked for a photo of her.

"Can't you just explain to him she's ill?" I asked.

"The thing about Markus's father is" — Leonora closed her eyes and grimaced, as if remembering some previous, traumatic encounter with him — "he likes to get his own way. He's flown thousands of miles to meet his granddaughter today, and —" She opened her eyes again and looked sorrowfully at the dress in her hands. Then she thrust it toward me. "Just — trust me. All our lives will be much easier if we give him what he wants."

I wasn't convinced, but I took the dress from her anyway. Leonora and Markus had done so much for me; of course I'd do what they asked, even though it sounded bizarre.

"Okay," I said. "I'll try my best."

"You're an angel." Leonora placed her hand over mine. "Thank you. And don't look so worried. Just think of it as — a little game."

Sadie

January 2019
And so the game begins.

Nazleen leads the two men across the drawing room toward Sadie. *They look like father and son,* Sadie thinks; they share a similar wiry, angular frame. The elder must be over seventy, but his gaze is sharp, his expression suggesting a lively enjoyment of the situation they find themselves in. The younger man looks to be in his late thirties, and he has softer facial features and collar-length dark hair.

"Professor Owl," Nazleen says to the older man, "allow me to introduce Miss Lamb."

Before Sadie can shake Professor Owl's hand, he grabs hold of hers and bows over it to kiss it. He doesn't mime either; the kiss is decidedly enthusiastic. Champagne whizzes through Sadie's arteries, and she feels fleetingly unsettled by their character names — lamb, nightingale, owl . . . As quickly as politeness allows, she withdraws her hand from the old man's talons, and then she laughs inwardly at her silliness.

"Enchanted, mademoiselle," Professor Owl says. "Please, call me Everett. Everyone else does."

She suspects they're not supposed to be using their real names, but she smiles anyway. "Sadie. It's nice to meet you."

He turns back to Nazleen. "My word, if all the guests are as pretty as you two, we're in for a marvelous evening."

Nazleen's professionalism doesn't falter, but Sadie's smile evaporates, and she turns away to greet the younger man as Everett and Nazleen fall into conversation. In contrast to Everett's dinner jacket and deep maroon waistcoat, this man is in black jeans and a casual shirt. He gives Sadie an apologetic smile.

"I'm Zach," he says. "Sorry about the old man."

"Sadie." She gestures at his clothes. "You didn't fancy dressing up, then?"

"Nah." He pulls a face. "I wasn't going to come at all, actually, but Dad talked me into it, last minute. He's been going on about how we should support local businesses and all that. I think he was just flattered they asked for his endorsement, really, you know."

"You live locally, then?" she says.

He drains his glass of champagne as if he's parched. "Yep. Born and bred just down the road."

The young waiter steps forward and refills Zach's glass. A photographer moves around the room at a discreet distance, taking pictures, and Sadie tries to ignore her. She declines a top-up of her own glass, and her gaze settles on an amateurish but rather charming painting of Raven Hall, hanging over a polished bureau in the corner.

"Well, it's a stunning house," she says. "Do you know the owner?"

"No." Zach peers around at the luxurious furnishings. "It's been empty as far back as I can remember. This is high-end stuff, though, isn't it? I hope the food matches up."

They both turn as the next guest enters the room: a dark-haired, high-cheekboned young woman in a striking crimson dress. She dips her head slightly as Nazleen leads her across the drawing room toward the others. She must be in her early twenties, Sadie thinks. Everett can't take his eyes off her.

"Everyone," Nazleen says, her accent slipping slightly, "this is Miss Mouse."

Miss Mouse nods a meek hello around the group, and she sidles over to stand next to Sadie.

"So, er— have you come far?" Sadie asks her, for lack of a more inspired question.

But before Miss Mouse can answer, Everett butts in.

"Owl and Mouse — we'd fit rather well together, wouldn't you say?" He looms closer to the young woman, and she blinks back at him, a flash of stunned repulsion in her eyes. Sadie gives Everett a steely look.

"Step back a bit, would you?" Sadie says to him firmly. "It's too warm in here to huddle together."

Thankfully, Everett's attention is diverted by the arrival of another new guest — a man in his forties, who hovers in the doorway.

"Colonel Otter," Nazleen says loudly. "Welcome. Do come in."

By Sadie's side, Zach makes a pleased sound. "Ah. I didn't know Joe was coming."

Colonel Otter — Joe — is a good-looking man, a few years older than Zach and more athletically built. But he hesitates in the doorway for a moment longer, as if he thinks he's in the wrong place. The reddish tint in his brown hair clashes rather unfortunately with the bright yellow waistcoat he's wearing. *Someone had a field day choosing all these outfits,* Sadie thinks. She smiles at the idea that, according to her alibi card, she and this reluctant-looking man supposedly took a stroll around the garden together earlier.

"Well, well." Everett strides toward the man, barging ahead of Nazleen. "Joe, old chap, how've you been?"

Joe's gaze jumps around the room as he shakes Everett's hand.

"I'm fine, thanks," he says. "I didn't know you two would be here."

Zach goes to join them. "Good to see you, mate."

Joe must be another local, Sadie guesses, drafted in alongside the hired actors for this trial event. As the men talk, Sadie turns to the young woman next to her and sees that she's ducking away from the photographer's camera.

"Are you okay?" Sadie asks her quietly, feeling an unexpected surge of protectiveness toward her. "I'm Sadie, by the way."

"Genevieve." The young woman widens her eyes. "Yeah, I only got offered this job a couple of days ago. I just — I didn't realize everyone would be so . . ."

"What?" Sadie says. "Old?" She laughs. "They're taking photos for their website.

They've got to appeal to the right demographic — people who can afford a murder mystery weekend . . ."

The young woman pulls a face. "I'd hoped they might be *nicer.*"

"Ah." Sadie shoots a dark look at Everett. "Well, some of us are nice, honestly." She gives Genevieve what she hopes is a reassuring smile. "Shall we stick together?"

But Genevieve merely looks at her sideways, as if trying to puzzle her out.

Zach rejoins them by the fire, and Sadie sighs with relief; he seems the easiest person here to chat to.

"So, what's the history of this house, then?" Sadie asks him. "Why did the previous owners abandon it? Do you know?"

Zach's expression is vague. "Oh, someone died, I think. I was just a kid; I don't really know what happened. It's always been empty, as far back as I can remember. Dad said the owner went off to live abroad."

"It seems criminal," Genevieve says, "to leave a beautiful house like this empty for so long. The owner should be ashamed of himself."

Zach wags a finger at her. "Or herself. How do you know the owner isn't a woman?"

Genevieve smiles graciously. "Fair point."

Sadie glances at the door; she's waiting for the final guest to join them. There are six of them so far — three men and three women — and she wonders who the seventh will be. Will it have to be another woman, to balance out Nazleen's — or rather, Lady Nightingale's — mysteriously missing husband in the game?

Again, the waiter comes to refill their glasses, and this time, Sadie accepts a top-up. Zach must be on his third glass, at least. The photographer has disappeared, and Sadie's stomach gives a low rumble. If the last guest doesn't make an appearance soon, their dinner will be late.

Finally, there's movement by the door, and a formidable-looking silver-haired woman in a rich blue evening gown glides into the room.

"Mrs. Shrew," Nazleen cries. "How kind of you to join us."

Mrs. Shrew's gaze sweeps over them all, and her expression slides from distaste to something more like horror. Sadie hopes she's another actor, merely playing her part — because if not, the poor woman looks like she'd rather be anywhere but here.

She decides to take the long route back to the village: around the lake, across Milner's Drain, and up through the fields to the main road. She wants to distract herself from that scene on the veranda — those two women, the new owners of Raven Hall, the interlopers who stole her house. Also, she has a decision to make before she reaches the village. So yes, she'll take the long route back, and she'll hand the rest of her day over to fate.

Walking around Avermere has always soothed her, even in the terrible days after her mother died, when Daddy locked himself away in his study and Raven Hall itself seemed to creak with misery. Today, she can feel her spirits lifting already. She passes the old tree stump and slows her pace, rolling up her sleeves in the gentle sunshine.

Flag irises nod at her from among the long grass as if recognizing her as an old friend.

Memories drift through her mind as she strolls along.

Here is the tiny stone beach, only a dozen feet wide, where her mother taught her to swim, and where they brought their picnics every summer. It reminds her of her first experience with the pain of sunburn, and her mother taking her out to the kitchen garden and showing her how to turn strawberry leaves into a soothing lotion for her sun-scorched skin.

And here are more of her mother's much-loved medicine plants — cheerful button-headed tansy flowers, with their familiar camphorlike odor. As she dips her head to inhale the scent, a gray heron flaps up out of the vegetation by the lakeshore. It curves its flight path toward her, as if wanting to get a good look at her before it lifts away. She raises a hand in a silent greeting.

For a few golden minutes, she almost forgets that none of this is hers any longer — her beloved Raven Hall, her beautiful Avermere. But inevitably, her mind drifts on to the last days of her mother's illness. She remembers arranging daffodils in a jug by her mother's bedside, and seeing their vivid yellow reflected in the whites of her mother's eyes. She remembers her mother beckoning her forward . . .

"Promise me, lovely girl, you'll never leave Raven Hall. You'll bring up your own children and grandchildren here, and you'll teach them to love it as much as we do . . ."

Suddenly she's picturing those two dreadful women again, and resentment swoops back into her chest like a kestrel dropping onto its prey.

How can this have happened? The slow-moving woman on the swing seat, the long-haired daughter in her orange crop top . . . For a moment, she tries to imagine herself wearing such an outfit, and despite the lump in her throat, she almost smiles. Daddy would have been scandalized. He'd have said she was encouraging the boys. As if boys ever came within a mile of Raven Hall anyway. She sighs. Poor Daddy. He had no idea it wasn't the local boys he should have been worried about.

She thinks fleetingly of the young doctor. That's what Daddy always called him, as if it were his official name — the Young Doctor — even though she happened to know his name was Roy, and he was nearly thirty.

She hasn't seen the young doctor since the day Daddy died — not since they walked into Daddy's study together and found Daddy collapsed over the green-topped desk. For days afterward, she didn't think of anything or anyone much at all. But when the shock had begun to subside — when reality came creeping back in — she'd dared to hope that the young doctor might reappear. She'd even watched for him from the windows of Raven Hall, while the lawyers argued in low voices behind her.

But he didn't reappear. Not when the lawyers told her the estate was bankrupt and Raven Hall would have to be sold. Not when a distant relation of her mother's begrudgingly offered to take her in as a lodger, eighty miles away. Not when they dragged her, sobbing, down the stone steps and into a taxi on the final day . . .

She frowns and picks up her pace. She needs to decide — should she knock on the young doctor's door when she gets back to the village? He's the only person who ever showed an interest in her. And now, living at her distant relative's house, she has no one to talk to at all. But what might he say if she knocks on his door this afternoon? *"I've missed you,"* or *"I'm not interested"* — which is more likely? She's not an idiot — she knows he must have kissed other girls and told them they were special too, but . . . She plucks a daisy from the path and pinches its petals off as she marches along. *He loves me; he loves me not . . .*

"Hallo."

She almost dies of fright.

A very tall young man emerges from the low hedgerow — he must have been crouching down. Is he going to attack her? But he holds up his hands, and his smile is apologetic.

"I was just taking pictures of some toad-stools." He taps the camera hanging around his neck. "I didn't mean to startle you. Sorry."

"Who are you?" She's alert for any sudden movement, ready to run if he looks like he means her harm. But his expression is ear-nest, and he's careful not to come any closer.

"Sorry. I'm not trespassing, am I?" he says. "I'm just visiting for the weekend, for a house-warming party." He indicates the direction she's come from. "Raven Hall — do you know it?"

She's horrified to feel tears welling up, and she swallows hard. "Not really. A bit."

"Ah. Well." He looks away, toward the lake. "I thought this was all theirs, but — anyway, I should be getting back. My girlfriend will wonder where I've got to . . ."

His gaze slides back to her, and she feels it like an electric charge on her skin. *Of course,* she thinks. *The girl in the orange crop top. Of course, she's his girlfriend.*

She should say good-bye and walk on. But he hasn't moved to pass her yet. They stand there, holding each other's gaze, and she finds she can't walk on.

"Are you a photographer, then?" she says. "I mean, of wildlife, or something?"

His smile makes her heart skip. "Actually, I'm a student. In London. I'm studying horticulture. But I love it out here." He gestures at the stunted hedgerow on one side of them, the bank of nettles leading down to the lakeshore on the other. "I'd love to live somewhere like this when I graduate. How about you?"

"Oh, I'm —" She wipes her palms on her skirt. "I'm just visiting someone here too. In the village." She wrinkles her nose. "Or at least, I was thinking about it. I haven't decided yet."

"Oh, okay." He tilts his head. "Well, you've got a long walk ahead, but I guess you know that. Do you want to come back with me? I could drive you down there if you like . . ."

"No," she says. "I'm fine." She narrows her eyes. "I'm not lost, if that's what you're thinking. I used to live around here. I know the way."

"Oh, right. Great." He studies her with a puzzled smile. "Well, I'll probably be back this way some weekends, from now on. Maybe we'll bump into each other again."

She gives this suggestion some consideration. "Maybe."

110

"I'll try not to startle you so much, next time."

"You'd better not."

His laugh is gentle, like the breeze in the reeds. "It was nice to meet you, girl-who-isn't-lost."

She stares at him for a moment, drinking in his features, memorizing them to pore over later. Then she turns away and hurries on, without looking back.

BETH

I tugged at the neckline of the blue dress and frowned down at my salad. Leonora and Markus had barely eaten any of their own lunch either; they were too busy exchanging uncharacteristically snappy words across the dining table. I wished with all my might that Nina would skip down the stairs and interrupt the meal by announcing she was fully recovered and ready to meet her grandfather. But instead, I had to listen to her parents bicker while my skin itched and sweated under the uncomfortable fabric. I longed for the afternoon's visit to be over.

"We should sit outside, actually," Markus said. "Dad always liked the garden here . . ."

"We are — *sitting* — in the drawing room." Leonora enunciated each word with painstaking clarity. "And your father hated the garden, I remember you saying. And Beth

112

can't exactly play her violin outside, can she?"

"Can't she?" Markus sounded genuinely nonplussed. I jabbed my fork into a slice of cucumber and kept my gaze lowered.

"Of course she can't," Leonora said. "Stop trying to change everything at the last minute. We stick to the plan."

Markus's cutlery clattered onto his plate, and he held up his hands. "Okay, okay."

"Unless you're having second thoughts?" Leonora's tone was icy.

"Of course not." Markus's prompt reply seemed to mollify her slightly.

She turned her attention to me.

"So, *Nina,* let's run through it again, shall we? What do you like doing in your spare time?"

I straightened in my seat. "I like reading. Drawing. Anything to do with animals."

"And?"

"Oh, and playing my violin." I kept forgetting this part, since it wasn't true of the real Nina, but when I'd queried it with Leonora, she'd dismissed the question with a quick frown and a shake of her head.

Leonora scrutinized me now. "You will sound a bit more convincing when he's here, won't you?"

I met her gaze sheepishly. "Yes, I'll try."

113

They rose to clear the table then, and I peeked at my watch. Markus's father was due at three; I still had an hour and a half stuck in these silly plaits and this horrible dress, and all to trick a grumpy old man. I'd go along with it for Leonora and Markus's sake, but it seemed a daft sort of game to me.

The Rolls-Royce was late. Only by a few minutes, but Leonora and I had been peering through the drawing room window for a quarter of an hour by then, and her tension was contagious. It made me wonder exactly what she was afraid Markus's father would do if he found out his planned meeting with his granddaughter had been thwarted — by a sickness bug, of all things. He must be a desperately unreasonable person, I thought. I had no memories of my own grandparents, but in the photos of them taken with me as a baby, they looked to be kind, caring people. I hoped this so-called little game with Nina's grandfather wasn't going to turn into an ordeal.

All the more reason to play my part properly, I decided.

"Here he comes," Leonora said, and Markus sprang from the armchair he'd been pretending to relax in and marched out to the hall. A moment later, I heard the front door open. By the time the car came to a halt on the gravel, Markus was waiting on the bottom step. He held up a hand to the chauffeur and went forward to swing his father's door open himself.

I'd been expecting someone older, but Markus's father didn't look even sixty. He was just as tall as his son, and he had a thick thatch of white-blond hair that added at least another inch to his height. He unfolded himself from the car, and his expression when he turned to the house was severe. Leonora snatched me back from the window, out of sight.

"We'd better go and greet him," she whispered, and when I saw the way her trembling fingers fluttered to her throat, I felt a wave of sympathy for her. She was *frightened* of this man — it shocked me to discover an adult could feel this way. What on earth could he have done to her to make her fear him this much, and yet agree to let him visit?

In the hall, we came face-to-face with Markus and his father. The older man's gaze locked onto mine, and his stare was so piercing, I was convinced he could see right through my eyeballs and into my brain. Heat flared to my cheeks. Could he read what I was thinking? I hadn't said a word to him yet, but what if he already sensed I was an impostor? I glanced at Markus and then at Leonora, but neither of them met my eye.

The visitor's gaze left mine and jumped to Leonora, and I let out a shaky breath. *I'm Nina,* I reminded myself. *He's never met me before. Of course he'll believe it.*

"Ms. Averell." His voice was silky smooth but not friendly. "You look remarkably well."

Leonora stuttered something unintelligible, and I frowned, not understanding why his phrase had sounded like an insult rather than a compliment.

"And you —" Again, he stared right into me. "You are — ?"

I steeled myself. "I'm Nina, sir."

He raised his bushy eyebrows high, as if waiting for more, but then he turned to Markus and indicated the door to the drawing room. "Shall we?"

Leonora caught hold of my wrist as Markus and his father went into the room.

"We'll make some tea," she said, a little too loudly.

I followed her down the hall to the kitchen, my heart jumping uncomfortably. Had I done enough? Leonora pushed the kitchen door firmly shut behind us.

"You were perfect," she said. "We'll let

116

them talk for a while; then we'll take in the tea and cakes."

When we eventually joined the men in the drawing room, they broke off their conversation, and the visitor gestured for me to approach him. Markus flashed me an encouraging smile.

"So," the older man said, "tell me, Nina. Do you know who I am?"

I cleared my throat. "You're my grandfather."

"Hmm." He studied me. "I hear you're quite the musician. Is that right?"

This was a question I'd normally have been delighted to answer, but I felt a prickle of unease.

"Yes," I said, "I suppose so."

"Would you play for me now?" he asked.

Leonora was already carrying my violin case toward me.

"Okay," I said. "If you like."

I lifted out my violin and bow, and I took them across to the piano and struck an A, aware that all three adults were watching me intently. Usually, the act of tuning my instrument slid me into a calm, focused state, and I was desperate for that reassuring feeling now. I adjusted my bow slowly, waiting for the familiar scent of the resin to transport me back to my carefree childhood days, the way it normally did. But my heart continued to race, and I couldn't shake the sensation of Markus's father staring at me with those glittering eyes. I marched across to the black marble fireplace and positioned myself with my shoulder turned against him so that I didn't have to see his expression while I played.

I began too fast, and I hurried through the piece, feeling increasingly resentful as my bewilderment about the situation swelled. It wasn't a terrible performance, but it was nowhere near the best I could do, and by the time I reached the end, I was close to tears. I lowered my instrument and bow.

I don't know what I expected — polite applause, perhaps. A condescending comment from the man I was trying so hard to fool. But when I reluctantly turned to face him again, I was horrified to see he was crying. Fat tears slid down his pale cheeks, and he gestured for me to sit next to him on the sofa. I desperately wanted to run from the room.

But Leonora spoke sharply. "Nina."

It jolted me into action, and I forced myself to join him on the sofa. He placed one of his gnarly hands over mine and took a moment to compose himself.

"That was beautiful, my child." He gave me a surprisingly gentle smile. "You remind me so much of your grandmother, Anneliese. She played the cello every day of her life up until she —" His face contorted briefly. "Well, up until she grew too weak to hold it upright anymore. I'll tell you something else. She'd have been very proud of you."

I pictured the old cello case leaning in the corner of Markus's study, and I nodded mutely. But Nina's grandfather seemed to be waiting for a proper reply, and when I glanced at Leonora and Markus, they, too, were watching me with expectant expressions.

"Thank you," I managed to say.

At that, Markus's father tightened his grip on my hand. "Tell me, Nina. How would you like to come and live in America with me?"

Leonora made a choking sound, and Markus caught hold of her arm. His father's gaze was fixed on me, and either he didn't notice Leonora's reaction, or he chose to ignore it.

"There's an excellent music school in my city," he continued, "and lots of wonderful opportunities for a bright girl like you. You could live in a big, airy apartment, go out to fancy restaurants, see a different show every night of the week. How does that grab you?"

I stared at him, thinking of the real Nina, upstairs, ill, in her bed. *What would Nina say to this?* Nina, who swam in the lake and the water channels around here every single day in the summer; who could row across to the island faster than Jonas could swim to it; who loved her turret bedroom and her tree house and the acres of fenland she'd grown up in.

"Thank you," I said, "but I love living at Raven Hall too much. I think if I ever had to leave, I might die of a broken heart."

First, his white eyebrows shot up. Then they hunched down, and he pulled my hand closer to him, bringing his face right up to mine. I tried to wriggle away, but he wouldn't let me go.

"I see," he said, and his voice had become a growl. "I see exactly what's going on here. You've been brainwashed by your mother, haven't you? I should have guessed."

I scrambled to my feet, desperately trying to tug my hand free of his.

"Let go of me!"

"Dad," Markus said sharply.

Finally, his father dropped my hand with a look of disgust. He got to his feet in one smooth, furious motion, and he glared at Markus, his body quivering.

"I've seen enough," he snapped. "I'll think about what you said, but I'm very disappointed in you, Markus. You're my only son —" He cut himself off and stalked to the door. "I'll see myself out."

January 2019

Sadie deliberately hangs back as the guests set down their champagne glasses and leave the drawing room.

Nazleen leads the way, with an eager Everett hurrying to accompany her, for all the world as if he really is an owl, sizing up his prey. Mrs. Shrew has regained her composure, but her expression is now severe. When Joe offers her his arm, she grants him the briefest of smiles, and she allows him to guide her from the room. Zach and Genevieve follow, arguing mildly about some aspect of the architecture of the house. Sadie brings up the rear, wondering which of them she'll be seated next to at dinner.

The dining room is a striking mix of old grandeur and modern luxury. Dark wooden paneling gives way to a lustrous raspberry-colored wallpaper above; dozens of flickering candles set the crystal glasses twinkling and the silver cutlery gleaming. The table is set for eight, and as the guests seek out their place cards, they see the head of the table remains empty. An enormous portrait looms over it: a severe-looking gentleman with bushy eyebrows and a thatch of blond-white hair.

Nazleen, their hostess, hovers at the foot of the table while the others circle and find their places. Before they take their seats, she gestures theatrically at the portrait and glances around to make sure they're all paying attention.

"Ladies and gentlemen, this is my husband, Lord Nightingale."

On Sadie's right, Zach murmurs, "A bit old for her, isn't he?"

Sadie shushes him.

Nazleen continues. "I regret to inform you that this afternoon, Lord Nightingale was found murdered in his study. He was killed by a toxic powder that was delivered to him inside a sealed envelope. When Lord Nightingale opened the envelope, he inhaled the powder, and it killed him instantly." She looks at each of the guests in turn. "He died at three o'clock this afternoon, precisely."

Sadie thinks of her alibi card. She visited Lord Nightingale in his study between two and three . . . Her pulse quickens, questions already flitting through her mind.

"Now," Nazleen continues, "the envelope was addressed to my husband, and there was no stamp on it, so we know it didn't arrive in the post. Therefore, one of you must have delivered it to his study today. One of you, perhaps, slipped it under his study door, or left it discreetly on his desk, at some point this afternoon." She draws herself up. "As far as I'm concerned, one of you killed him." Her eyebrows lift meaningfully. "But you, of course, may suspect me."

Sadie glances at the other guests. They're all watching Nazleen with varying degrees of fascination — even sour-faced Mrs. Shrew.

Nazleen eases her shoulders down ever so slightly, and when she speaks again, her tone is calmer. *She's good,* Sadie thinks. *I can see why they hired her; she's really good.*

"Now," Nazleen says, switching effortlessly from wronged wife to dinner party hostess, "each of you should have read your preliminary alibi card, so you know certain things to be true about your own activities here today. You may refer to your cards as needed. Your task, ladies and gentlemen, is to question one another — and me, of course — on your movements leading up to three o'clock this afternoon."

Genevieve claps her hands. "How exciting!"

But Mrs. Shrew's voice injects a mood-destroying contrast. "Are you going to give us permission to sit down, Lady Nightingale?"

"Oh, er, yes, of course," Nazleen says. "Please, go ahead."

They all pull out their heavy high-backed chairs and settle into position before Nazleen resumes her instructions.

"Right, and, um, a new piece of information will be provided with each course — a new clue, if you like. Please remember, everyone, you must be truthful in your answers, but you don't have to share anything that you're not directly asked about." Nazleen holds a pose while the photographer points her camera at her, and then, finally, she reaches the end of her speech. "The last clue will be given at breakfast tomorrow morning, and then you will be asked to submit your theories and name your prime suspect."

Sadie beams at Nazleen, and Nazleen shoots her a grateful smile in response.

"Well," Everett booms. "This is all very jolly."

The young waiter appears in the doorway

with a loaded catering trolley, and the photographer helps him to wheel it in, while the guests shake out their pleasingly heavy napkins and gaze wide-eyed around the room. Sadie is seated directly opposite Joe, and she watches him watching the others for a few seconds, until suddenly their eyes meet. She finds it amusing and smiles, but he seems rather disconcerted, and he turns to Mrs. Shrew and murmurs to her, asking if she needs anything. Mrs. Shrew shakes her head. Sadie wants to start questioning everyone, but she can't decide which guest to start with, and she's distracted by the plate of food being set in front of her.

The first course is sea bass, served whole, with a light lemon-dressed salad. Sadie blinks down at the entire fish on her plate, and its blank pupil stares back up at her. Her appetite shrivels, and she glances enviously at Genevieve's vegetarian alternative. On her left, Everett is already devouring his fish, while the waiter moves around the table, pouring wine.

On the other side of her, Zach nudges her elbow. "Free food. Don't knock it."

"The chef has an impressive CV . . . ," Nazleen says, poking her fork into her own fish with an uncertain expression.

Everett strikes up a loud conversation

about local fishing sites with Joe, and Sadie is tempted to interrupt him and steer him back to the game they're supposed to be playing. But she's curious about the white-haired man in the portrait, so she takes the opportunity to ask a quiet question of Zach.

"Is he the real owner, do you think?" She lifts a tiny portion of sea bass to her mouth and is pleasantly surprised by how tasty it is. "Lord Nightingale, or whatever his name is."

"I'm sure the name's made up, and I've never heard of a lord around here," Zach says. "But yeah, I guess the portrait looks real enough. Dad'll probably know — ask him."

But Sadie's reluctant to interrupt Everett's rambling anecdote. She catches Genevieve's eye, and they exchange a brief raised-eyebrow grimace as Everett cracks a bad-taste joke. Sadie sips her wine, and before she can stop him, Zach grabs the bottle and tops her up again.

"Shouldn't we be asking each other questions?" she says to Zach. And then, "So, what were you doing, leading up to three o'clock today?"

He grins. "I was still in bed with a hang-over." But he takes pity on her and raises his voice. "Okay, I was in the library with

Miss Mouse all afternoon. I heard loud talking in Lord Nightingale's study at half past two."

The other guests rapidly switch their attention to Zach, except for Everett, who concentrates once more on clearing his plate.

"Is that right, Miss Mouse?" Sadie asks Genevieve.

Genevieve pats around her crimson lips with her napkin, and Sadie guesses she's buying time while she recalls the details on her alibi card.

"Yes," Genevieve says, "except I went to use the bathroom just after two. I was only gone five minutes, but . . ." She widens her eyes at Zach in mock horror. "It would have given you time to . . ."

Zach thumps the table enthusiastically. "I didn't deliver any envelope. I deny everything. I'm innocent, I tell you."

Sadie leans forward and tries to catch Joe's eye. "And where were you leading up to three o'clock, Colonel Otter?"

But Joe is already shoving back his chair, and he looks only at Nazleen, with an apologetic expression. "Please excuse me a moment. I need to use your phone."

The room sits silent in his wake, like a deflated balloon. Everett, the only one of them who seems oblivious, spears some-thing onto his fork and lifts it halfway to his lips before gazing around.

"Fish eyes," he says. "Very good for you. Omega-threes, you know." He pops the morsel into his mouth, and Sadie's not the only guest to turn her head away.

Sadie takes a large swallow of her wine, and once again Zach tops up her glass im-mediately; it's irritating. The only person who hasn't said a word since they took their seats is Mrs. Shrew, and Sadie studies her, still unsure whether she's playing a role or she's genuinely unhappy about being here.

"So, Mrs. Shrew," Sadie says brightly, "do you live locally too?"

The woman's lips pucker as if Sadie's insulted her, and for several seconds, Sadie thinks she's not going to answer. But even-tually she gives a sharp shake of her head.

"No, I traveled a long way for this." Her gaze rests on the pearls around Sadie's neck, and her expression tightens even further. "Believe me, I'm beginning to wish I hadn't bothered."

Zach snorts into his wineglass, and Sadie's mood dips. She feels out of place suddenly — the way Mrs. Shrew looks at her . . . Can the woman tell that Sadie's never been inside such a huge mansion before, never eaten such a lavish meal or worn such beautiful clothes and jewelry? But as soon as she recognizes her reaction as embarrassment, she shakes it off. Sadie's just as good as anyone here, and she won't let them make her feel inferior.

The waiter clears their plates deftly, and as he leaves the room, Joe comes back in.

"The phone line's dead." Joe's voice is tight with annoyance.

"Oh, I'm so sorry," Nazleen says. "They were supposed to reconnect it last week. I'll chase it up on Monday morning."

"But" — Genevieve half stands in alarm — "I haven't got a mobile signal either."

"That's something you have to expect," Everett says complacently, "out here in the Fens." He grins wolfishly at Genevieve as she sinks back onto her seat. "Don't worry, my dear. I'll look after you."

Sadie smooths the tablecloth in front of her. She's tempted to blurt out, *Did you cut the telephone wire, Colonel Otter?* but she senses the feeble joke would worsen Joe's mood, and she's keen to get the game back on track so they can all start enjoying themselves. The waiter returns with the freshly restocked trolley, and Sadie excuses herself from the table and walks to the window. She parts the thick curtains and peers out at the faintly lit gravel. The chauffeur-driven cars have all gone, unsurprisingly, but two ordinary-looking cars sit over in the shadows by the stable block.

We can drive to the village for help if we need to, she thinks, and then she smiles at herself for letting Joe's discovery unsettle her. Of course, they won't need to go for help — she's being ridiculous. It must be the fish eyes that have made her jumpy. She lets the curtains fall back and returns to the table.

Their second course looks more appetizing: panfried partridge breasts with celeriac chips. Nazleen makes a show of pulling out the next game card, and again, she pauses for the photographer to take some pictures. Then she lifts her chin and waits for her six dinner party guests to give her their full attention.

"Ladies and gentlemen," Nazleen says, "I, myself, heard footsteps approaching and leaving my husband's study on two separate occasions this afternoon. Either one of them might have been the person who delivered the envelope to Lord Nightingale."

"*If* we're to believe you," Zach says, but he's smiling, waiting for Nazleen to tell them more.

"One set of footsteps belonged to a

woman," Nazleen continues. "Clearly high heels. The other must have been a man's — they were heavy, like boots . . ."

Genevieve rolls her eyes as if she's struggling not to protest at the wording. Sadie shoots Nazleen an encouraging smile. Yes, the company could do with a more politically correct writer, but it's good to gain new clues, and Sadie would dearly love to be the guest who solves this mystery — why shouldn't she be the winner? And besides, what if Nazleen is secretly assessing Sadie's and Genevieve's performances tonight? Sadie doesn't want to damage her chances of being reemployed by this company, and she certainly doesn't want to put tomorrow's paycheck in jeopardy.

"What else can you tell us?" Sadie asks.

Nazleen gestures around the table. "It's up to all of you, now. You need to ask one another more questions . . ."

Sadie turns immediately to Zach. "Were you wearing men's shoes when you left the library?"

Too late, she realizes this wasn't the right question, and she flinches as a ripple of laughter passes through the other guests. Even Mrs. Shrew's lips twitch, and Nazleen gives Sadie a surprisingly grateful look. For the first time, there's a real feeling of

132

camaraderie in the room, and Sadie feels mildly astonished that she was the one to create it.

"I'm afraid not," Zach says. "I was wearing pink stilettos."

"I was so surprised when I saw him," Joe says, "I almost dropped the envelope I was carrying." They all laugh again. "Joke!" Joe adds. "Joke. It wasn't me who poisoned him . . ."

"Do you call it poison," Zach says, "if you inhale it? Because I thought . . ."

But he's interrupted by a shout of annoyance from Everett, who scrapes his chair back noisily as he lurches to his feet.

"What's the matter?" Joe says.

"Damn lead shot in the partridge." Everett leans forward and spits out a tiny metal pellet, which pings onto his plate surprisingly loudly. "Nearly broke my bloody tooth on it."

"I'm afraid" — Genevieve's tone drips with gleeful malice — "that's something you have to expect, out here in the Fens."

Everett coughs and glares at her, and Sadie turns her face the other way to hide her own smile. Mrs. Shrew positively beams down the table at Genevieve, and even Zach is grinning. Nazleen tries to smooth things over. She calls back the waiter and asks him to let the chef know about the shot, and she apologizes to Everett until even he has to concede it's no one's fault.

"Please," Nazleen says to the rest of them, "do carry on."

Sadie's not sure whether Nazleen wants them to carry on eating, or to continue questioning one another, but she sets her cutlery down neatly on her plate and resolves to do neither until her head has cleared a little.

BETH

July 1988

We sat in silence in the drawing room after Markus's father stormed out. First came the slam of the front door, then his angry footsteps across the gravel, then the double slam as he and the chauffeur got back in the car. The engine started. The sound of it faded. Finally, just when I thought my tears were going to spill over, Leonora rose and came to me, and she wrapped her arms around me.

"You were wonderful, Beth."

I inhaled her rose scent and felt myself relaxing.

"Yes, very well done," Markus said. "You played it beautifully."

But they both spoke cautiously, as if they weren't sure themselves exactly what had just happened. And it was soon clear they no longer required my company.

"Don't wake Nina, will you?" Leonora

said to me as she and Markus headed out to the terrace with a bottle of wine. "Leave her to rest, okay?"

But I was too unsettled to know what else to do with myself, so I crept up the spiral staircase and tapped cautiously on Nina's door.

"Come in."

She still looked pale, but her eyes were brighter than earlier. She patted the bed next to her, and I decided I'd rather have her company and risk catching her bug than sit in my own room alone with my churning thoughts.

"What on earth are you wearing?" she asked, and she reached out and tweaked the end of one of my plaits. "And your hair. You look funny."

"Your grandfather came," I said.

"Oh." She glanced at her alarm clock. "I forgot. Is he still here?"

"He —" I didn't know where to start.

"Beth? What's the matter?"

I wondered, suddenly, whether Nina already knew about the game. I wasn't sure if that would make it better or worse. Perhaps this was the sort of thing her parents did all the time. Maybe she'd laugh. Maybe I was worrying about nothing.

"He — I — They made me dress up, and

I had to pretend to be you, Nina. Your grandfather believed I was you." I gazed earnestly at her. "Your mum said if I didn't, he'd be angry you were ill, and he —" I didn't know what he'd have done, but I knew it must have been something truly awful.

But Nina was shaking her head. "You're making this up, right? This is a joke."

"No. I swear. That's why I'm wearing this dress. And your mum plaited my hair, and —"

"You're saying you took my place?"

I stared at her, hesitating. "Yeah. They asked me to."

"You mean you actually called yourself Nina? And pretended my parents were your mum and dad?"

I nodded miserably. "I was only trying to help."

She sank back into her pillows, staring at me, and then she turned her face sharply away, and neither of us spoke for a minute. Then —

"Can you go, please?" she said. "I'd like to be alone now."

For the next couple of weeks, Nina wore her resentment like an outer layer of clothing. She was sulky around her parents and short-tempered with me. I tried to talk to her about it, but she refused to discuss it, glaring at me fiercely when I made further stuttering attempts to apologize.

"This is *my* home" was all she'd say. "And *my* family. Just remember that."

How could I possibly forget it? I was acutely aware of my position as a guest at Raven Hall. I had no family of my own to return to, and my once-happy childhood home was now inhabited by oblivious strangers. I was entirely dependent on the goodwill of Nina and her parents.

I spent hours alone, keeping out of Nina's way, mostly playing my violin — it was the only way I knew to numb my fears and soothe my loneliness. One evening, a few days after Markus's father's visit, I was approaching the top of the stairs when I heard Markus answer the phone in the hall and say, *"Ah, thanks for ringing me back, Caroline."* I retreated to my bedroom and shut myself in, my heart pounding. He might have a client called Caroline, I told myself — but deep down, I was convinced Markus and Leonora had decided I was no longer a suitable companion for Nina, and they were demanding my aunt come and collect me. And she would take me straight back to the children's home; I was sure of it.

I cried myself to sleep that night. After everything I'd been through in the last couple of years — losing my parents and brother; being treated as a nuisance by my aunt — Raven Hall had felt like a haven, a second chance at having a happy life, of feeling safe. I couldn't bear the thought of being sent away.

For days after that, I felt as though I were holding my breath, even though Caroline never did turn up to collect me. Leonora and Markus continued to behave quite normally toward me, but I knew the real decision lay with Nina, and she remained distant and uncommunicative.

In the end, it was Jonas who mended our friendship.

It was a particularly warm morning in early August, and Nina and I were finishing our breakfasts — without conversation — in the dining room, when we glimpsed a blur of movement through the window: Jonas arriving on his bike.

"I'm desperate for a swim," he said when we went out to meet him on the gravel. "Are you two friends again, now?" He'd joined us swimming a couple of days earlier, but Nina's constant sniping at me had driven him to go home early.

I dropped my gaze and waited to hear

Nina's answer.

"I expect Beth would rather stay in the house," Nina said. She gave me a pointed look. "In *my* house, that is." She turned back to Jonas. "But I'll come."

I stepped back, ready to leave them to it, my mind already drifting to my violin and the music I would play to distract myself from the world around me. But Jonas's irritation was clear.

"Fine. Well, Beth, in that case — would you write down your new address for me?"

"What?" Nina said. "She's not going anywhere."

Jonas pulled a face. "Well, I doubt she'll be happy to stay here much longer if you keep treating her like this."

My heart jumped erratically. How was Nina going to react?

She turned slowly and stared at me. It was probably the first time she'd looked me directly in the eye since I told her I'd pretended to be her for her grandfather's visit.

"I honestly don't want to take your place," I said meekly. "I never meant to —"

She gulped, and then she flung her arms around me.

"I know," she sobbed. "And I don't want you to leave. I've been really horrible. I was

140

jealous of you getting to meet my grandfather, but I know it wasn't your fault. It wasn't anyone's fault. I'm sorry, Beth. I'm sorry."

Jonas sighed loudly. "Girls." He raised his eyebrows. "Are we going swimming, then, or what?"

Nina and I wiped away our tears, and we ran upstairs to change into our swimsuits. She was extra nice to me for the rest of the day, but I was conscious that our reconciliation was down to Jonas, and I watched him more closely than usual as the three of us messed around in the shallows. When Nina floated out into deeper water, I seized my chance and thanked him privately.

"Well, I had to do something," he said, holding my gaze. "I'd hate to see you go. I like you, Beth."

In that brief moment, I forgot about all my worries.

"I like you too," I said.

"Do you think maybe, one day —" he began. But Nina was splashing toward us, shouting that she'd seen a giant pike, that it had nibbled at her toes. Our moment of intimacy was over, but I smiled to myself each time I thought about his words. *I like you, Beth.* Things weren't so bad at Raven Hall, after all.

SADIE

The next course looks intriguing, Sadie thinks. Thick lamb chops, a medley of green vegetables, and something round, stodgy, and golden brown. She prods it with her fork; it's larger than the palm of her hand, and it's clearly been fried, but she can't work out what it is.

"Puffball mushroom," Nazleen says, with more than a trace of unease.

"Ah, yes, lovely," Everett says, and he tucks in with gusto, giving Sadie the confidence to nibble a tiny piece of hers. Not bad. She slices into her lamb, and a thin, bloody liquid oozes instantly across her plate. _It's a good job there are so many courses,_ she thinks, _because at this rate, I won't finish any of them._ She takes another sip of her wine.

The guests continue to ask one another questions while they pick at their food, and

142

Sadie tries to keep track of the replies in her head, wishing she could jot down some notes. She's confident she's drawing closer to identifying the guilty party, but she keeps changing her mind, and the alcohol isn't helping . . . Which guest swore they came downstairs empty-handed? Which clue has she overlooked? As people begin to set down their cutlery, Nazleen appears to remember something.

"Oh."

Nazleen reaches for the game cards, and she takes a sip of water before she begins her next speech, and Sadie realizes with a jolt of surprise that Nazleen hasn't been drinking wine like everyone else. Perhaps it's Nazleen's choice, or perhaps it's a condition of the hostess role; the rest of them have been plied with drinks all evening, but maybe the company felt one person should remain sober and in charge.

"It was Nazleen," Zach whispers at Sadie's side. "Don't you think? I'm pretty sure Lady Nightingale murdered her own husband . . ."

Nazleen raises her voice. "Ladies and gentlemen, I have a card here for each of you which will provide you with details of the last conversation *you* had with Lord Nightingale. This will be new information for you, and something you will now want to question one another about."

Mrs. Shrew closes her eyes as if she's in pain, but Genevieve gives Nazleen a bright smile and helps her to hand around the small envelopes.

"Please keep your own cards private," Nazleen says. "And remember, you must answer all questions truthfully."

Sadie tears open her envelope and pulls out a square card. *Miss Lamb,* it reads, *In your last conversation with Lord Nightingale, he told you he used to be a friend of your mother's.* Sadie blinks and reads on. *He said you must have been a great disappointment to your mother, turning up at grand houses in the hope of employment, unable to hold down a job.*

Sadie's pulse races. She knows this is about her character, but it feels disturbingly close to home — to her recent sacking from the shop, and to her belief that she was a disappointment to her own mother. It's unnerving. She glances at the serious expressions of the other guests as they each read their private cards. Everett rips his into quarters and posts them in the empty gravy boat in front of him with a snort of disgust.

Sadie drops her gaze back to her own card and reads the second paragraph. *Lord Night-*

*ingale told you there would never be a place
for you at Raven Hall.* "Over his dead body"
*was the phrase he used. He felt the same way
as your mother — he knew you'd never
amount to anything.*

Sadie's vision blurs. This is just a game,
so why does it feel so personal — so *nasty*?
At her side, Zach folds his card carefully in
half and slides it into his jeans pocket.

"Is yours . . ." Sadie's not sure what she
wants to ask him. "Is yours what you expected? Does it — you know. Does it make
sense, for your character?"

Zach frowns, hesitating, as if suspicious
she might be cheating. "I think I'm close to
working it out. Is there a prize, do you
know, if we get the right answer?"

His oblique reply only disconcerts her
more. Across the table, Joe, too, seems to
have disposed of his card entirely. Genevieve has rolled hers into a tube, and she
looks mildly bored. Mrs. Shrew's envelope
sits unopened next to her plate, and an
uncomfortable silence hangs heavily in the
room. Nazleen looks like she wants to say
something, but she can't seem to find the
words needed to reignite their enthusiasm
for the game.

Feeling distinctly uneasy, Sadie slides her
card back into its envelope, the word *disap-*

145

pointment rolling around in her mind like a marble in a jar. She's never had a problem keeping a character's story separate from her own life before, but this has touched a nerve.

"Oh, for goodness' sake!" Sadie draws herself up as everyone stares at her. She's determined to regain her former good spirits, to stop being so oversensitive, and to move the game along now. "Come on, then. Who's going to go first? The answer must be here somewhere." She catches Joe's eye. "Right, Colonel Otter, tell me . . ."

The group fires questions and answers across the table for a few minutes. Sadie suspects Genevieve at first, and then Everett. Zach acts as though he suspects her. Joe accuses Nazleen, who in turn accuses Zach. Apart from Mrs. Shrew, they're all smiling, all making an effort . . . But somehow it still isn't enough, and eventually the questions tail off. Sadie's gaze rises to the portrait hanging at the head of the table, and she has the uncomfortable sensation that the stern man is glaring back down at her, rigid with disapproval.

"It's all red herrings anyway," Everett grumbles, leaning back in his chair. "They won't give us all the information until tomorrow morning, will they? They can't

146

have the game solved before breakfast; that would never do."

"Oh," Sadie says, strangely comforted by this thought, "I suppose that's true."

On her other side, Zach gives a heavy sigh. "I'm sure I've almost got it. If I could just work out who . . ."

While the waiter clears their plates, Sadie drains her water glass and refills it, vowing not to drink any more wine. She has an odd, hollow feeling in her head, and a prickling sensation that the unseen clue writer knows too much about her. If that were true and they thought poorly of her, why would they have hired her? They wouldn't. She's being ridiculous. The waiter bustles out of the room, but he quickly returns with the dessert trolley, and all eyes swivel to the elegant glass dishes.

"Tropical fruit pavlova," Nazleen murmurs.

Sadie wishes it were something simpler — what's wrong with plain English strawberries and cream? The waiter sets down her bowl in front of her, and her throat closes; a peeled lychee, resembling nothing more than a ghostly eyeball, stares back at her from its bed of meringue. Her stomach churns, and she can't tell whether it's panic, but in that brief clammy moment, she's seized by the overwhelming conviction that someone *has* been watching her . . .

She shoves her chair back, desperate to get away from the table, away from these strangers. She thinks she might faint if she stands up, but she lurches to her feet anyway.

"Are you okay?" Nazleen half stands, but Sadie composes herself and gestures for Nazleen to sit down again.

"Yeah, I'm just —" Sadie tries to keep her body language calm as she heads toward the door; she's a little unwell, that's all, and she can't bear any fuss. "I just need some fresh air. Just give me a few minutes."

It's much cooler in the hall.

She stands in front of a huge gilt-framed mirror and rests her fingertips on the polished wood of the table beneath it. Slowly her heart rate settles, and the panic-inducing flashes of heat and cold on her skin ease. Perhaps it was something she ate. Perhaps it was just too warm in the dining room. She studies her reflection and gives herself a rueful grin: fancy seeing eyeballs in her pudding; how embarrassing. She feels well enough to go back and join the group now, but she's struck with the idea of sending Wendy a quick text about this — it'll make her laugh.

A clattering of pans somewhere at the back of the house jolts her into action — she's supposed to be a sophisticated dinner guest; she doesn't want to be caught lurking out here, pulling faces in the mirror. She hurries up the stairs, relieved to have a clear head again, but when she reaches her bedroom, she discovers that, just like Genevieve's phone, hers has no reception.

Oh well. The humorous text to Wendy will have to wait.

Back out in the corridor, Sadie eyes up the other bedroom doors. She's curious about her fellow guests. She's learned all sorts of details about their game characters, but next to nothing about them as real people, and the chances are, she'll never see them again after this weekend. She'll probably never stay in such a grand house again either. In a couple of days' time, she'll be slumped on the sofa in her flat, browsing uninspiring job adverts and waiting for that big-break phone call from Wendy that never comes. But tonight, she has a chance to explore this mansion and to peek into the lives of the strangers she's sharing it with.

It's not spying. It's just harmless curiosity. A quick look into their bedrooms, that's all, and then she'll rejoin the dinner party downstairs.

The first room is clearly Nazleen's. Two long green dresses are draped over the bed, and the dressing table is scattered with creams and makeup. A small framed wedding photo sits rather endearingly on the bedside table, and Sadie smiles to see a younger-looking Nazleen arm in arm with her red-haired wife. She closes the door gently.

The room on the other side of Sadie's is blatantly Mrs. Shrew's. Deep blue items are still folded neatly in the open suitcase, and a feather brooch lies discarded on the bedside table. No photographs in this room; nothing particularly personal at all. A faint floral scent hangs in the air, and Sadie closes the door softly and moves on to the next room.

This one's owner is harder to identify. The suitcase is closed, so Sadie tiptoes across the layered rugs and lifts the lid. An array of sickly yellow items brings a faint smile to her face — poor Joe. A darker color would have suited him better — racing green perhaps, or a navy blue. A pair of trainers and a running kit are tucked in at one end of the case, and she smiles at his optimism — presumably planning a run before breakfast tomorrow, despite the freezing weather and the excesses of tonight.

After Joe's room comes a large old-fashioned and fully tiled bathroom, and beyond that is a door set into the end wall of the corridor. Sadie pulls this open and peers up a rising spiral staircase. This must be inside the tower. She glances at her watch and hesitates; it's tempting. But if she doesn't return to the others soon, one of them is bound to come up looking for her, and she'd rather not be caught prying. The door falls shut with a clunk.

She moves more quickly as she works her way back down the corridor. The first bedroom is less luxuriously furnished than the others. Thinner curtains, a single bed, a slinky red dress puddled on the floor. Poor Genevieve has been given a lower-grade room, it seems. Perhaps because she was a last-minute hire.

Another, rather chilly, bathroom, and then a room with no company vintage suitcase in sight, just a sports bag dumped by the bed. Sadie frowns, and then her brow clears; this may well be Zach's room — he of the *"nearly didn't come,"* couldn't-be-bothered-to-dress-up attitude. She closes the door softly and moves along to the last room on this side of the staircase.

And yes, her hunch about Zach's bedroom was right, because this one clearly belongs to Everett. Purple fabric bulges from the open suitcase, and she spots an invitation card poking out from among the clothes. She can't resist; she tiptoes across the room and draws the card out to read the personal message in its loopy blue handwriting. *Hendrik will appreciate your support.* She pulls a face and slides the card back under a soft mauve sweater. Perhaps Hendrik is the owner of the murder mystery company. She can see how such a message would have appealed to Everett's sense of self-importance.

When she is out on the landing again, a faint thud makes her glance beyond the staircase to the opposite end of the corridor — the fire-damaged end, as she thinks of it. Did someone follow her up here? Suddenly, she feels acutely aware of the house around her. So many rooms. So many nooks and corners and potential hiding places . . . The hairs on her arms rise, and before she can tear her gaze from the double row of identical doors, an odd yelping sound comes from behind one of them, like a laugh morphing into a cry.

She races for the stairs, hurtles down them, and almost slips in her heels before she reaches the bottom, only just saving herself in time.

As before, the hall is deserted. She stands

at its center, trying to catch her breath, and when she stares, wide-eyed, back up the staircase, there's nothing to be seen. No ghost, no sinister, shadowy figure . . . *What on earth was I thinking?* A rumble of conversation drifts from the dining room; dishes clank in the kitchen. She presses her hand against her chest and waits for her heart rate to settle.

It was probably an animal, that's all. A fox, maybe, or a bird, that found a route into the once-abandoned house and returns to scavenge now. She draws herself up, trying to summon her former confidence, her sense of amused appreciation at finding herself in this privileged situation. But as she reaches for the dining room door handle, she glances over her shoulder at the door of the dusty study that she and Nazleen discovered earlier. She's as sure as she can be that it was shut when she went upstairs. And now it's ajar.

BETH

Summer 1988 to Spring 1989

Jonas may have given me a new reason to feel happy at Raven Hall, but I never saw him alone — Nina and I did almost everything together. As the summer holidays drew to an end, Jonas asked me again whether I'd be joining him at the high school in September, and I felt embarrassed that I couldn't give him a definite answer. The prospect of being at the same school appealed to me, although I'd be in the year below him, so I probably wouldn't see him all that much. I asked Nina if she knew what the plan was, but she merely shrugged and suggested we ask her parents that evening.

It seemed Leonora and Markus hadn't given any thought to my ongoing education either, but they quickly came up with a suggestion.

"Not the local high school, no," Leonora said, "but let's go and look at this other place." She glanced at Nina. "Perhaps you both might like to try it there."

Nina was surprisingly agreeable, and three weeks later we were both enrolled at a small and very welcoming private school. The other girls there were friendly, and I hit it off with my new violin tutor straightaway. The only downside was the school was miles from Raven Hall. We left in a taxi early in the morning and got home late, but Nina was cheerful about it, so I was determined to be happy too.

At first, I fretted every time money was mentioned at school — why were Leonora and Markus insisting on paying for my education, and what would happen if they stopped? I still felt I had to be careful not to antagonize Nina. Not that she ever referred to the "game" again or said anything pointed, but I knew that if she asked her parents to send me away, they would — they'd always put her first, and quite rightly too. So I stayed alert for any sign that the family might be preparing to send me back to the children's home. But as the months passed, and my school life grew more absorbing, I began to relax.

Caroline came for a short visit in October, staying for barely an hour, during which time we made polite conversation in the drawing room and I ate a lot of biscuits to fill the awkward silences. She said she'd see me again before Christmas, but in the end, she sent a parcel and her apologies — she'd been assigned work in South America for six weeks. Eventually, at the end of January, she made a second visit to check on my welfare.

"You seem very settled," she said.

She'd been in the house hardly two minutes. Leonora, Markus, and Nina had retreated promptly, leaving us to chat privately by the fire that crackled in the black marble fireplace, a tea tray placed on the coffee table between us. I scrutinized her expression, sensing that she was, more than anything, relieved that I was no longer her problem. I was tempted to make a snide retort. *Yes, how convenient for you, Aunt Caroline.* But as ever, I masked my resentment of her.

"They're nice people," I said. "It does feel like home now, I have to admit."

"Hmm." She looked as though she might say something disparaging, but she must have thought better of it. "Well, that's good. It all worked out for the best, then."

She reached forward for her teacup, and there was something about her profile — the line of her jaw, the lowering of her

156

eyelashes — that reminded me suddenly, quite overwhelmingly, of my mother, her sister. Raven Hall had gradually softened my grief, like a layer of new life growing over a raw tree stump. Caroline's unwelcome presence ripped that protective layer away and reminded me forcefully of the life I'd lost. In that moment, I hated her for it. I'd rather have been left completely alone in the world, I thought, than have *her* as my aunt.

I grabbed my own teacup and made an effort to bring my emotions under control. Caroline was grieving too, I reminded myself. Although she'd never been particularly interested in my brother and me, I'd seen photos of her and my mum together when they were growing up — they must have been close at some point.

"You've spilled tea on your skirt." She eyed me sternly. "I do hope you're behaving yourself here, Beth. The last thing I need is to hear they don't want you anymore."

Heat rose to my cheeks, but I met her gaze without flinching. "They seem to like me well enough. They say I'm part of the family now."

It was Caroline who looked away, then, although whether her conscience pricked her or she was merely growing bored, I couldn't tell. I waved her off soon afterward, but the weight of her words added to the usual pressure I'd grown used to: I was still an outsider. I had to be on my best behavior, all the time.

It was a few weeks after my birthday, when I'd been living at Raven Hall for eight months, that something changed my perception of my position there. It came about because Nina got a part in the school play, and her rehearsals went on well into the evening as the performance night drew closer. Leonora and Markus took pity on me and offered to send two taxis for us, just for those few dates. So I was back at Raven Hall, without Nina, when Jonas knocked on the door late one afternoon.

We strolled around the lake, talking about everything and nothing. I glanced sideways at him frequently, wondering what was going through his mind. Would he tell me again that he liked me? Should I tell him that I liked him? A short way past the old tree stump, he came to a sudden halt by a little stone beach, and I carried on for a couple of steps before swinging around to face him.

"What?"

"Let's swim."

I laughed. "No way, Jonas. It's not even

April yet. It'll be freezing."

He gestured at his short-sleeved T-shirt. "It's fine. Practically summer."

"You're crazy." But I followed him down to the water's edge, and I watched him undress, my pulse jumping.

"Come on, scaredy cat," he said, and he plunged into the green-black water, splashing wildly and yelling at the shock of it. My heart raced. Could I bear it? But could I bear not to join him? Quickly, I tugged off my school skirt and jumper, and I took a running leap.

I was swallowed into a different world. I hung there, staring sightlessly into the water, unable to move. No air in my lungs, no gentle spring sunshine on my skin, no background chirrup and rustle of life. I waited for something to happen as the tightness in my chest grew.

"Beth!" Jonas was shaking me, and suddenly the sky had returned, and I could breathe again. "Bloody hell, are you okay?"

I made a supreme effort to move my fingers, my arms, my legs, and I felt my blood start moving again.

"I hate you," I said to him. And then I laughed. "I *told* you it was too cold." I kicked away from him and felt warmth flood back into my body as I swam clumsily farther away from the shore and then back again.

We clambered out, teeth chattering, and Jonas's face was unusually serious. He insisted on my replacing my own soaked blouse with his dry T-shirt, turning away as I made the switch. Then he wrapped his arms around me.

"I admit," he said, "that was maybe a bit stupid of me."

And then we were kissing, just like that. As if it were the most natural ending to our first swim of the season. As if it were the most natural thing in the world.

Later that evening, when Nina came home, she tapped on my bedroom door. I was already in my pajamas, sitting in my bed. She came in, full of gossip about the rehearsal, her costume, the makeup she was planning to wear. It took her several minutes to ask me how my afternoon alone had been.

I hesitated, and it was in that fraction of a second that I realized — I *wasn't* dependent on Nina for my happiness; I didn't *need* her approval of everything I did. I was fifteen now, and the adult world was within touching distance. Suddenly, I knew I had a future ahead of me, with or without the support of the family at Raven Hall.

"Oh, Jonas called round," I said, "so we just went for a walk around the lake."

Nina stilled. "And?"

I pulled a face. "And nothing."

She went off to her own bedroom soon after that — to her round Rapunzel room in her fairy-tale tower. But as she passed my empty laundry basket on her way out, she glanced into it — so fleetingly, it wouldn't have registered if I hadn't had a guilty conscience.

I waited until the next morning — until the last minute, as our taxi was turning onto the driveway and heading toward us — to scurry back up to my room, claiming I'd forgotten my math homework. I snatched my damp clothes from under my mattress and dropped them into the laundry basket, hoping the daily cleaner wouldn't comment on their state. Jonas's T-shirt I'd already washed by hand in the bathroom next door and dried on my bedroom radiator. I sat in the taxi and plotted how soon I could return his T-shirt and see him again.

I did feel guilty about keeping a secret from Nina, when up until now we'd shared everything, but I also felt — powerful. Independent. Strong. For the first time in my life.

Unfortunately, that feeling didn't last.

161

Events at Raven Hall had no regard for my blossoming love life. It was only a few weeks later, on a Saturday, when I was skipping into the house after a brief secret rendezvous with Jonas, that Leonora called me into the drawing room.

"Oh, Beth," she said. "There you are. I'm afraid I need to ask you a favor."

I hovered in the doorway, my heart sinking. "Yes?"

Her gaze ran over my hair and down to my new sandals, and I stiffened — had I failed to straighten my clothes after kissing Jonas so passionately just now? How much did Leonora know? But I discovered her mind was on another subject entirely.

"Markus's father has announced a surprise visit, Beth. He'll be here in a few hours. And poor old Nina's feeling unwell again, and — well, now that he's met you, it would be so hard to explain anyway, and . . . Beth, we need you to play the game again."

SADIE

January 2019

Sadie is ridiculously relieved to find the other guests still sitting around the dining table as if nothing has happened. *Nothing has happened,* she reminds herself sternly. *It's an old, creaky house; you have to expect odd noises now and then.* She returns to her seat, and Nazleen breaks off midsentence to ask her if she's feeling better. Sadie nods briskly, and as she picks up her spoon, Zach leans closer.

"You missed the speech about the evening's clues being at an end," he murmurs.

"Uh-huh." Sadie pushes her lychee aside and scoops up a spoonful of mango and cream.

"And now we're getting the legend of Raven Hall," he says. "It's very rich, isn't it?"

It takes Sadie a moment to realize his second statement refers to her pudding. She nods and sets her spoon back down.

"Ah, perfect timing," Nazleen says. "Here comes the coffee."

The trolley clatters and clanks as the waiter wheels it into the room, and the rich aroma lifts Sadie's mood instantly. She sits up straighter, admiring the tall coffee jugs and the dainty china cups and saucers. The waiter turns and nods stiffly at the photographer, like a prearranged signal, and the photographer approaches Nazleen discreetly and dips her head. She murmurs something about the roads icing over, and Nazleen waves a gracious hand.

"Of course," Nazleen says to her. "I'll take it from here."

As the two staff members hurry away, Nazleen stands and pours coffee for all of them. Sadie declines cream, but she drops a granular brown-sugar cube into her cup; she doesn't normally take sugar, but this evening, she feels a need for it.

"So," Nazleen says, taking her seat again. "Yes. The legend of Raven Hall. Let me begin by asking you, ladies and gentlemen — have you ever felt desperately, horribly, painfully *lonely*?"

The gentle noises of the room — clinks of spoons against china, soft coughs, slurps of coffee, and murmurs of appreciation — all fade to silence. Sadie focuses on the delicate handle of the espresso cup in front of her, sensing that the others, too, are avoiding eye contact. She curls her fingers around the cup, using the heat from the china to drive away the ache she feels from missing her mother. When Nazleen speaks again, her voice is lower, as if she knows for certain she has their full attention.

"Well, pity the poor spirit in my tale, then. It's just a shadow now, a faint shimmer in the corner of your eye, a haze of memories and longing and loneliness . . . but it's real."

Sadie lifts her gaze to Nazleen. Their hostess has a printed sheet of text in front of her, but she doesn't appear to be reading directly from it; she must have rehearsed this thoroughly. Sadie tries to focus on the professionalism of the delivery, rather than the pathos of the story. But despite her determination to remember this is all just part of a game, she leans forward over the table, willing Nazleen to continue and wanting to know more about this supposed ghost.

"This poor spirit is all that's left," Nazleen says softly, "of a once-happy family that lived here at Raven Hall a long time ago. But betrayal struck at the very heart of the family, and it was torn apart, ripped apart . . ."

Sadie holds her breath. How much truth is behind this tale? Does it relate to the reason the house was abandoned in the late 1980s?

Nazleen gestures toward the curtained windows. "If you take a stroll around the lake here, around Avermere, you might just glimpse this spirit. But only ever at dusk, in those eerie few minutes when the sun is slipping behind the horizon, and the world is shifting into darkness. That's when it appears." Her voice grows louder. "It rises out of the lake, out of Avermere. And it drifts up to Raven Hall, slowly, slowly. And it presses itself against the windows, like a breath of mist against the cold glass, peering in with its hollow eyes, peering . . . peering . . . desperate for one last glimpse of its lost, destroyed family . . ."

Sadie's heart races. *And then what happens? Is the ghost inside the house, now? Roaming around upstairs, watching guests explore where they shouldn't?*

"But," Nazleen says sharply, "here it meets the ultimate betrayal. Raven Hall refuses our poor spirit entry. No matter how desperately it scratches at the windows, rattles the mail slot, moans down the chimneys . . . Raven Hall is heartless; it won't let our spirit

166

in. And so it continues, night after night, rising at dusk, roaming around the stone walls, searching, searching for a crack or a gap it can enter through — listen!"

Sadie strains her ears, certain that the other guests must be doing the same, but the noise that erupts isn't outside the window; it's across the table. Mrs. Shrew is stifling a cough — or could it even be a sob? — with her napkin.

Joe shoves his chair backward sharply. "Okay, that's enough!" He makes a visible effort to compose himself. "I think we've heard enough for one night, thank you. Shall we take our coffees through to the drawing room, and . . ." He glances at Nazleen, and his expression slides from apology to concern. "Are you okay?"

Nazleen doesn't look okay; if anything, she looks more distressed than Mrs. Shrew. For a moment, Sadie wonders if Joe's interruption has offended her, but then Nazleen moans quietly and curls forward over the table, until strands of her dark hair rest in her almost-empty dessert bowl. Joe starts toward her, and Sadie and Everett both rise to join him, but Nazleen straightens again and waves them away.

"I'm so sorry." Nazleen sounds embarrassed. "I actually don't feel very well at all.

I think I'll go up to my room, if you don't mind." She stands without help, but she looks a little hunched as she walks to the door, as if in pain. Before she leaves the room, she turns back to them with a strained smile. "Please, do take your coffees through and sit by the fire. Breakfast at eight, don't forget. I'll see you in the morning."

The six guests gaze wide-eyed at one another as Nazleen's footsteps fade up the stairs. Then Sadie grabs her coffee cup and indicates the door.

"Shall we?"

Zach accompanies her across the hall and into the drawing room. Everett shuffles close behind, and Sadie doesn't begrudge him grabbing the armchair nearest the fire. He's certainly the oldest in the group, and he's looking pretty tired. Mrs. Shrew comes in soon afterward, and she heads to the far corner of the room, where she perches on a chaise longue as if not planning on staying for very long.

"It was probably the pudding," Zach says to Sadie in a low tone. "Don't you think? Nazleen ate all of hers. It was very rich. I didn't eat all of mine . . ."

Sadie pulls a noncommittal face; she's watching the door, straining her ears for the other two guests. Where have Joe and Genevieve got to? She feels unsettled without Nazleen's presence, as if the whole evening might unravel now that their hostess is feeling ill.

A minute later, Joe makes his entrance. He carries a glass of water, and he takes it straight to Mrs. Shrew. Zach spots a deck of cards on one of the many occasional tables, and he asks Sadie if she wants a game, but she shakes her head.

"I might just sit for a bit," she says, her hand drifting to her abdomen, "and let my food settle." Her stomach feels delicate again, and she's growing increasingly convinced that something she's eaten tonight has disagreed with her. Each time the nausea stirs, she thinks uneasily of the story line of the game — the toxic substance that supposedly killed their host. She sinks onto a velvet armchair and wonders how soon she can head up to bed.

Finally, Genevieve appears in the doorway, and she looks upset — her face is pale, her dark eyes enormous. She clutches a long fur coat against her chest, and she doesn't come into the room. Sadie glances at Joe — did he say something to her out there to distress her? But Joe looks just as surprised and concerned as the rest of them. Genevieve clutches the fur coat tighter against herself,

169

and she rushes to give her own explanation.

"I don't feel very well either, I'm afraid. I'm, erm — I might go outside and get some fresh air."

Zach sounds triumphant. "I *told* you it was the pudding. She ate a lot of hers too." The others ignore him.

"Do you want me to come with you?" Sadie asks, but she's relieved when Genevieve shakes her head.

"No, no." Genevieve forces a smile. "I'll be fine. It's freezing out there; you stay indoors."

They listen as her heels clack away down the hall, and the front door slams.

"And then there were five . . . ," Zach says.

"Please be quiet, Zach." Sadie hurries to the window and pulls back the curtain, and she watches Genevieve, now wearing the coat, march away — across the little pool of light on the gravel and into the darkness. Her further progress is indicated only by a thin beam of white light from the torch on her phone. Behind Sadie, Joe clears his throat, and he joins her at the window, peering over her shoulder just as Genevieve's phone light flicks off and a tiny orange glow appears.

"She's on the dock," he says. "A quick cigarette and she'll be straight back in; don't worry. It's bitter out there."

Sadie lets the curtain fall back. "I'm not worried. Who says I was worried?"

Joe makes a placatory gesture. "I just meant —"

Sadie turns away, and she sees that Zach is shaking Everett's arm.

"Dad? Dad!"

Everett blinks awake, and he mumbles a denial.

"Everyone's feeling ill, Dad," Zach says, and he adds in a smaller voice, "Even me."

Everett sits forward and glares at Sadie and Joe, as if it might be their fault. Sadie's tempted to suggest Zach's symptoms might be alcohol related, but she bites her tongue.

"Well," Everett says. "Not vomiting? No? Milk of magnesia, then, and sleep it off." He eases back in his chair and pats his stomach through his purple waistcoat. "Too much of the fine stuff." He chuckles. "It was worth it, though."

Mrs. Shrew rises without even glancing in Everett's direction.

"I shall retire to bed myself," she says, "and hope we all feel better in the morning."

She waves away Joe's offer of help and leaves the room. Sadie looks at her remaining three companions, and a sudden thought makes her return to the window.

"Both the cars are gone," she says.

"What?" snaps Everett. "Has that young filly driven off and left us?"

"Not Genevieve," Sadie says. "They were already gone when she went out."

Joe's tone is tense. "They must have been the staff's cars. The chef and the waiter and the photographer — they all went home a while ago, didn't they?"

Sadie fails to suppress a swell of panic. The seven of them arrived in chauffeur-driven luxury. Now they're stuck out here, in the middle of nowhere, with no phone signal, no transport, and they're all feeling unwell . . . And then her heart lurches with a greater shock, and she leans closer to the glass, searching for, and failing to find, either a white light or an orange glow.

"Where's Genevieve?"

BETH

May 1989

Leonora gave me a different dress to put on for Markus's father's second visit — it was also blue, but in a more adult style, so it was a little more comfortable to wear. I'd grown taller since I'd moved to Raven Hall, and I was slimmer and fitter from all the outdoor exercise I'd had. I studied my reflection in the big cheval mirror in my bedroom, and my mind churned with questions.

The details didn't make sense; I must be missing something. I didn't mind helping Leonora and Markus out — I didn't even mind too much if Nina's grandfather shouted at me again. I just couldn't understand the way it had all happened.

Surely Nina's falling ill *again,* just before her grandfather's visit, was a remarkable coincidence? But I couldn't believe she was faking it — certainly not last time, when she'd looked so washed out and weak. Was it psychological — was she so terrified of meeting her grandfather, it brought on physical symptoms? But, despite her mother's apparent fear of germs, Nina was one of the toughest, bravest people I knew.

Besides which, since Markus's father now believed *I* was Nina, of course it made sense for me to play her again for this second visit. There was no alternative — Nina could hardly go skipping in and claim to be the same child he first met ten months ago. So perhaps Nina's current illness really was just a coincidence. I frowned at my reflection. I just didn't know. But something didn't feel right.

"I think — yes, I think we'll plait your hair again," Leonora said, eyeing me critically in the drawing room. "I'm sure he won't stay long, Beth. It'll all be over soon."

I closed my eyes as she tugged the brush through my hair, and this time I thought not about my parents, but about Jonas.

Jonas was in favor of our breaking the news to Nina that we were an item, but I'd asked him to wait. I worried that Nina would be hurt, and I felt guilty that my friendship with her had loosened in the last few weeks while I was sneaking around meeting Jonas in private. What if Nina became angry? What if she asked her parents to send me away from Raven Hall?

A little voice whispered in my head: *They can't very well send me away now — what if Nina's grandfather comes back for another visit?* But Leonora's heavy strokes with the hairbrush reminded me of how determined she was. She'd find a way around any obstacle; I knew it. I couldn't trust in my own importance. I had to keep Nina — and Leonora — happy.

"There," Leonora said, standing back. "Perfect."

I felt detached from my surroundings as I sat in the drawing room with Leonora and Markus, waiting for Markus's father to arrive. My thoughts meandered up two flights of stairs, to the turret room, where Nina lay. I should have rushed up to see her when Leonora told me she was ill, but instead, I'd spent too long staring at my own reflection in that stupid mirror, puzzling over another odd aspect of this game. *Why the plaits?* Nina never wore plaits. I considered asking the question aloud, but I thought better of it.

"He's here," Leonora said tightly, from her position at the window. I smoothed down my skirt. I would do this calmly and properly, for Leonora and Markus's sake, and for Nina's.

This time, when Leonora tried to hold me back in the hall, Markus's father snapped at her. "Let the girl come in with us."

I followed him into the drawing room and took a seat next to Markus on the sofa. The two men ignored me for the first few minutes, and I didn't pay too much attention to their conversation. Markus's father grumbled about wanting Markus to help him run his business in the States, but I knew Markus would never do it — Leonora and Markus would never agree to leave Raven Hall. And I, as Nina, was ready to back up that sentiment.

Leonora brought in the tea tray more promptly than on the last visit, and once we'd finished our tea and cake, Markus's father turned to me.

"So, Nina, will you humor an old man and play for me again today?"

I'd never shared Nina's love of drama lessons at school, but I felt a strange calmness slide through my veins as I drew the role of Nina over myself this time, as if I were stepping inside her skin. I knew Nina inside out; she was almost a sister to me now, and in that moment, I almost believed I *was* her.

"Of course," I said, rising to take my violin from Leonora's trembling hands. "I'd be happy to."

I played for him — much better than last time, thanks to the months of teaching that Markus and Leonora kindly paid for at my school. This time, I didn't turn my back on him, and he smiled at me through his tears. When I finished, I sat down next to him, and his expression seemed genuinely apologetic.

"I'm sorry I raised my voice at you last time." He patted my hand awkwardly. "Your playing brings back so many memories, I may have become a little . . ."

"Emotional?" I met his gaze straight on.

He blinked. "Well, that's a strong word, but —"

I laughed then, and he gave me a puzzled smile in return. He wasn't scary at all, I realized. He just didn't know how to deal with his feelings. I felt suddenly, surprisingly, sorry for him, and for the trick we were playing on him.

"So," he said, clearing his throat, "have you thought any more about my offer?"

In my peripheral vision, I saw Leonora reach for Markus's hand; their faces were tense. I almost smiled at how easy it would be to say yes — *Yes, please, Grandfather, take me back to America with you.* But instead, I frowned gently.

"I appreciate the offer," I said. "I really do. But you know — my life is here; my friends are here; I have exams at school next year . . ."

He bowed his head. "I understand. But" — when he looked up again, his eyes were glittering fiercely — "I won't stop asking you."

I smiled. "Okay. 'Til next time, then."

After his chauffeur had driven him away, Leonora and Markus seemed unnerved, casting me odd, anxious looks.

"Did I do all right?" I asked, suddenly worried I'd messed it up.

Leonora said nothing, merely staring at me, but Markus pulled himself together and patted me on the back.

"You were great," he said. "You kept him happy; you clearly know how to handle him." As he headed for the door, he gave Leonora a pointed look that I was unable to decipher. She turned away. I unraveled my plaits with my fingers and headed up to see Nina.

"You don't need to hide it," Nina said.

I was pouring her a fresh glass of water from a jug on her bedside table, and the handle slipped, sloshing liquid onto the wooden surface. I hurried to dry it with a tissue, hoping my cheeks weren't growing as red as they felt. Was she talking about her grandfather's visit or about Jonas?

"Your dress," she said sadly. "And your hair's all wavy. Did Mum plait it again? What was he like?"

I sank back onto her bed. "You know I couldn't say no, don't you? I mean, after doing it last time . . ." I sighed. "He was here less than an hour. He's — he's grumpy, I suppose, but underneath that, he's quite nice, I think. He goes back to the States tomorrow."

Her dark eyes were enormous. "Did he like you?"

"Why do they do it, Nina?" I searched her gaze, desperate to find an answer. "Why didn't they just tell him the first time that you were ill? It's just — I don't understand . . ."

A tear slipped down her cheek. "I don't know. How am I ever going to meet him now, if he thinks you're me? My own grandfather . . ."

My heart squeezed with sympathy, and I leaned forward and hugged her, despite the risk of germs.

"I'm sorry," I said. "I'm so sorry about everything."

But she didn't reply to that. She merely

asked me to leave so she could go back to sleep.

Remembering the cautious air of celebration after Markus's father's last visit, I went back downstairs, half expecting to find Leonora and Markus drinking wine, but they were nowhere in sight. I carried Nina's empty water jug into the kitchen and set it down next to a couple of mugs by the sink. I was already thinking of Jonas again, wondering whether I might ring him at his mum's B and B — I felt bad for thinking it, but Nina's illness was an ideal opportunity for Jonas and me to spend a whole evening alone together. I don't know what made me notice the mugs — perhaps the novelty of the faint chocolate aroma, as we hadn't drunk hot chocolate since the end of the winter. I almost moved away, and then I leaned back over them.

One mug was the standard Raven Hall china, and the other was Nina's own — a custom-made, satisfyingly chunky mug with her name painted on. Both had the usual thick chocolate dregs at the bottom. But Nina's held an extra layer — a thin, oily layer that didn't look like anything I'd ever seen before. I picked up the mug tentatively and tilted it to the light, and my skin prickled. There was definitely something unusual in there. What on earth was it?

Suddenly, the mug handle seemed to be burning my fingers. I set it down quickly and glanced behind me to the door. Had something been added to Nina's drink? Was this why she was sick? The idea was shocking, but the more I tried to come up with an alternative explanation, the faster my heart raced.

Poison.

I backed away from the sink and retreated up the stairs to my bedroom as quietly as I could. Who could I ask about this? Who could I go to for advice?

It would be appallingly disloyal to mention this to anyone outside of the family. And what might the repercussions be if I mentioned it to Leonora, or to Markus, or to Nina? What if I was wrong? They'd be hurt, offended — outraged, even. It didn't bear thinking about.

My only option was to keep it a secret.

I crawled into my bed and pulled my sheet and blanket over my head, and a single word rolled around and around in my mind.

Poison. Poison. Poison.

I thought back to earlier that morning when Raven Hall had felt like a safe place. Now I wasn't so sure.

She spreads her meager picnic around her on the grass and sighs. She spent all of last Saturday roaming Avermere without managing to bump into the tall, kind-eyed horticulture student. It took her three hours to hitchhike to Raven Hall again this morning, and so far, her luck hasn't picked up.

Where is he?

There were several cars parked in front of the stable block again today, but she's never been good with car makes. She recognizes the young doctor's Ford Capri — mink blue, he told her it was, once; his pride and joy — but other types are just a blur, and she couldn't begin to work out whether the student's car was here this morning. She imagines him at home in London instead — perhaps his long-haired girlfriend has gone to visit him there.

She's brought her sketchbook with her, and she tries to distract herself by drawing her view of the lake and its little island, but her heart's not in it. She closes the book with a snap. Then, just as she's packing away her uneaten food and preparing to leave, along he comes, striding down the trail with a long stick in his hand, like an overgrown schoolboy. She scrambles to her feet, her heart booming.

"Aha!" he says. "Hallo. I was hoping I might bump into you." He eyes the flattened patch of grass and her crumpled clothes, and he narrows his eyes. "You don't live out here, do you? In a little burrow by the lake, or something?"

She laughs, delighted. "I wish I did."

"I've got some tea, in a flask . . ." He pulls a face as he swings his rucksack from his shoulder. "Sounds boring, I know, but . . ."

She shakes her head. "It sounds lovely."

They make themselves comfortable on the grass, and the student pulls out more than just a flask — he has a Tupperware container packed with perfectly ripe strawberries, and two generous slices of treacle tart wrapped in brown paper. She discovers she is hungry after all.

"They're from the garden," he tells her as she bites into her first strawberry. "At Raven Hall. They're good, aren't they?"

She closes her eyes and pretends to be savoring the taste while she squashes down

183

memories of nurturing those strawberry plants with her mother, years before.

"They're gorgeous," she manages to say at last. "What's it like, then, studying horticulture in London?" Really, she wants to ask him whether his *girlfriend* minds him taking picnics out into the countryside to share with a girl he barely knows. But she's worried what the answer might be — that he feels sorry for her, or that any old companion would do. If either of those is the case, then she'd rather not know.

He gives an exaggerated sigh, then grins at her. "It's harder than people think, actually. I've just finished a load of exams, and there's never enough time to do what I want . . ."

"Isn't this what you want?"

"Well, yes, what I mean is — I feel guilty about doing nice things like this, when I should be . . ."

"Working?"

"Yeah . . ." He tosses a strawberry husk into the undergrowth. "And my mum's not very well, so I feel like I should spend as much time with her as I can."

"Oh," she says. "I'm sorry. My mum was ill, too, for a long time."

He squints at her, and then he sits up straight and gives her a concerned look. "Do you mean . . ."

"She died, a few years ago. I —" She shakes her head, not sure what she wants to say. "I miss her so much, every day."

"Oh." Tentatively, he reaches out and touches the back of her hand. "I'm really sorry. If I'd known, I wouldn't have . . ."

"It's fine," she says. "It's just — I suppose I might know a bit more how you feel. Than other people do, I mean. Luckier people." She's thinking of the long-haired girlfriend in the orange crop top.

He nods slowly. "We don't actually know what's wrong with my mum. The doctors can't work it out . . . She's a medical mystery." He tries to smile. "But they're trying different treatments. And, you know, we're lucky in other ways. Mustn't take stuff like this for granted." He gestures at the tangled weeds behind them. "When you think of what other people go through — did you know the poor family who lived at Raven Hall before? They had a daughter about your age —"

"No," she says abruptly. "I never knew them."

They sit in silence for a minute, watching a swallowtail butterfly explore a patch of thistles.

"Well . . ." The student crumples his treacle tart paper into a ball and drops it into his rucksack. "You're right. We should talk about happier things, before I have to get back. Did you meet up with your friend the other day?"

She stares at him, trying to get past the phrase *"before I have to get back."* Has he grown bored with her already? Is he missing his girlfriend? And what friend does he mean? Oh, of course — the young doctor.

"No, I didn't bother seeing him, in the end," she says. She drains her tea and hands the cup back to him. "I need to get going myself, actually."

They don't speak as they gather their belongings together and brush crumbs from their clothes, but once they're ready to go their separate ways, the man stretches out his hand.

"I'm Markus, by the way," he says. "It was nice talking to you, and — thanks, you know, for understanding about my mum."

She nods. "I'm . . ." But the tip of her tongue hesitates on the roof of her mouth as his earlier words rattle through her head: *"the poor family who lived at Raven Hall before."* She lifts her chin. "Lara," she says. "I'm Lara. I'll look out for you again next weekend."

186

BETH

My thoughts were haunted by that oily gleam in Nina's hot-chocolate mug.

For days, I tried to find an innocent explanation. I scoured the pantry for vitamins or medicines that might account for it, with no success. When the others were occupied elsewhere in the house, I experimented furtively with marshmallows and other sweet ingredients, attempting to dissolve them in boiling water, then letting them cool. But I failed to re-create the strange-looking shiny layer.

I kept replaying the night before Nina's grandfather's first visit: Markus popping his head into the tree house and saying, *"Come on, sleepyheads . . . Mum's making you hot chocolate indoors to warm you up . . ."*

Twice, Nina had fallen ill just before her grandfather's visits, and each time she'd drunk hot chocolate in the hours before-

187

hand. Hot chocolate that, on the second occasion, looked to have had something unusual added to it. Hot chocolate that, on the first occasion at least, Leonora had made for her.

But why on earth would Leonora want to poison her own daughter?

I withdrew into myself, telling Jonas I needed space and telling Nina I needed to concentrate on my schoolwork. I sat in my bedroom for hours, flicking through prospectuses for higher education courses that provided accommodation, wondering whether I should apply for one the following year to give me an escape route from Raven Hall. When I wasn't worrying about poison, I was brooding on my lost family, wondering what my brother, Ricky, would be doing now if he were still alive. I longed to ask my parents for advice. I resented not having Ricky here as a role model.

Meanwhile, Nina bounced back to full health, and the rest of my life rumbled along in its normal routine; as the weeks passed, my anxiety about the possibility of poison eased, and my melancholy mood gradually lifted. I stayed alert for any recurrence of illness in Nina, or any sign of odd behavior in Leonora, but nothing happened to raise my suspicions. Eventually, I decided I might have been mistaken. Perhaps I hadn't seen anything strange in the mug after all.

By the time Nina's birthday came around in June, I'd made a conscious decision to put the whole strange episode out of my mind. If anything, the memory of my initial reaction to it made me feel guilty — how could I have leaped to such a dreadful conclusion about Leonora, when she was never anything but kind to both me and Nina? As if to reinforce my guilt, Leonora and Markus took us to a West End show for Nina's birthday and showered both of us with all manner of treats and gifts. Life seemed good again. The long summer holiday was fast approaching. And I felt secure enough in my position at Raven Hall to switch my focus back to trying to see more of Jonas.

But it was as difficult as ever to meet up with Jonas alone during the holidays. Nina and I ate breakfast together, chose our daily activities together — we did almost everything together. Finally, at the dinner table one evening, Leonora reminded Nina she had an optician's appointment the following day — miles away, over near Cambridge — and I sensed an opportunity. When I trudged down to the dining room for breakfast the following morning, I complained of a thumping headache.

"I think I might have to go back to bed," I said. I kept my eyes narrowed, as if the bright sunlight streaming through the window were hurting them. "If that's all right with you? You don't need me to go with you today, do you?"

Leonora frowned and came over to feel my forehead. "Have you been drinking enough water? Do you want some paracetamol?"

I told her I'd already taken some, and I plodded back upstairs with a guilty conscience. My head was fine; I'd taken nothing. I cracked open my bedroom window and got back into bed, waiting to hear them leave.

As soon as Leonora's car had disappeared down the driveway, I ran downstairs and phoned Jonas at the B and B. Then I strolled out to the kitchen garden and picked a bowlful of luscious strawberries; I ate them out in the front, sitting on the stone steps in the sunshine and reveling in having the whole house to myself while I waited for Jonas to arrive.

"Let's get away from this place," Jonas said before he'd even kissed me.

I pulled a face. "I don't know. I'm supposed to be ill. I don't want them to come back and find me gone . . ."

"You can say you went for a walk to clear your head, can't you?" He hooked his fingers into mine and drew me closer, his smile widening. "Come on, grab your bike, and let's go into the village. I can introduce you to my mates, or we can go back to mine . . ."

"No." Reluctantly, I pulled my hands from his. "I can't. I'm not allowed . . ."

He sighed. "Okay. So — what then? Are you going to invite me in? First time for everything."

It took a moment for the significance of his words to sink in.

"You mean you've never been inside the house?"

He shrugged. "Nope."

"That's weird."

"Well, yeah. But it's probably the least weird thing about this place, don't you think?" He searched my gaze. "C'mon, Beth. What would *you* like to do? Don't you fancy getting away for a bit?"

"I —" I shook my head. How could I tell him the truth? That I was scared to break the rules, too frightened of what Leonora might say if she discovered I'd snuck off into the village as soon as her back was turned. "Actually, I — my head doesn't feel that great . . ."

Jonas's gaze slid past me to the shadowy interior of the hall, and he took a step back. "Okay. Well, it's up to you."

"I'm sorry," I said. "I've wasted your time."

"You know what I think?" His expression was tight. "This isn't right. Not being allowed to go anywhere or see anyone. I think you should ring your aunt Caroline and ask her to take you away from here, find somewhere more normal to live. That's what I think."

"Wait." I followed him down the steps and across the gravel to his bike. "I know what you're saying, Jonas, but they're still nice people. I like it here. It's my home, now. So I have to follow their rules, you know? Does that make sense?"

He scowled. "Yeah. I get it."

"Look, why don't you come in? I'll make us a drink. We can sit in the garden . . ."

For a moment, I thought he might say yes. We leaned toward each other, and we kissed with his bike jammed between us. But he'd already made up his mind.

"I'm just not sure I can keep doing this." He frowned down at his handlebars. "You won't tell Nina about us. You're not allowed to come round to my house. Every time I come up here, I've got to pretend we're just . . ." He bit back the rest of his sentence. "It's not really working, is it?" He swung himself onto his saddle and put one foot on a pedal.

"But —" I said. "You'll still come back, won't you? You'll come swimming with us . . ."

"I don't know, Beth." He squinted at me. "Just ring me, okay? If anything happens. If you need me. For anything."

I returned slowly to the top step and watched him cycle away until he was out of sight. Then, with a sense of wounded irony, I went back inside to find some painkillers — I really did have a headache now. I couldn't see a way of keeping everyone happy. Leonora, Markus, Nina, Jonas. And as much as I liked Jonas, I *had* to keep Nina and Leonora happy if I didn't want to jeopardize my position at Raven Hall.

So Nina and I swam without Jonas that summer, and whenever she grumbled about his absence, I tried to look innocent and changed the subject. And unsurprisingly, Nina invented new ways of entertaining us. She decided she would throw a party for me at the end of the holiday, to belatedly celebrate the anniversary of my arrival at

Raven Hall.

To my surprise, Leonora agreed to the plan, and it kept Nina and me busy for a couple of weeks. We drew up a guest list of school friends for Leonora's approval, and we baked a huge cake and ordered sparklers, and we arranged for an up-and-coming band from London to perform in the garden. On the evening of the party, Jonas joined us for a while, and he pecked me on the cheek in front of the other guests, which made me blush. But when I looked for him a while later, hoping to grab a few minutes alone with him, he'd already set off on his bike for home.

September, and the new school year, came around quickly, and my sadness about the situation with Jonas was replaced with worries about coursework and exams. In the middle of October, Markus went off to Malaysia on a six-week diving trip, and not long after this, Leonora called Nina and me into the drawing room one evening with a glint of excitement in her eyes.

"I was thinking," she said, "now you're both getting older, maybe I should take you on a shopping trip. We could go into London next Saturday, have a day of trying on clothes — what do you say?"

Nina and I were thrilled. Up until now,

Leonora had ordered all our clothes for us from a catalog, but my jeans were becoming too short, and I fancied something a little more elegant anyway. In the end, not only did we go on a huge and successful shopping spree; I also got my hair cut at a posh salon, and Nina persuaded Leonora to let her have her ears pierced. I knew we were being spoiled, but there was no point resisting it, and both Nina and I were very pleased with the outcome: we felt much more grown up.

It was only days later that Jonas paid us a surprise visit at Raven Hall. He greeted both Nina and me with equal friendliness, and he asked us casually — out of earshot of Leonora — whether we fancied sneaking out that weekend, to go to a party in the village with him. I kept my expression neutral, and he didn't stay long — he said he'd leave us to talk it over.

"Oh, go on," I begged Nina, after we'd gone up to her turret bedroom to discuss it in private. "What harm can it do? Your mum'll be none the wiser, and we'll have a great time." I was already imagining myself wrapped in Jonas's arms, swaying to dreamy music, with Nina conveniently distracted by some other good-looking village boy.

But Nina gnawed at her fingernail. "I just

don't think we can, when my dad's not here. If Mum *did* realize we were missing, and she was here all by herself . . ."

I flexed my fingers, frustrated. "How's that different from both of them finding us missing? And she'd guess what we were doing, wouldn't she? It's hardly the crime of the century, is it? It's just a party."

But Nina shook her head. "If Dad was here, he'd come into the village to look for us, but Mum by herself . . . She'd be distraught. I can't risk it."

"Oh, for God's sake." I glared at her. "This is ridiculous. I'll go by myself then."

"You won't." Her eyes glittered. "You wouldn't dare."

I wanted to cry with frustration. But I couldn't risk disobeying Nina. I could feel all my old insecurities returning, sliding along my skin, slipping into my pores, and creeping around my body. I stomped away down the spiral staircase and slammed my own bedroom door behind me. I loved Nina like a sister, but sometimes I hated her too. I couldn't sneak out without her, in case she told Leonora. Despite my sometimes ambiguous feelings about Raven Hall, I still didn't want to be sent away.

We didn't go to the party.

■ ■ ■ ■

I was still in a bad mood with Nina when Markus returned from his trip abroad. Nina and I stood side by side on the top step as Leonora hugged him on the gravel, and Markus laughed as he swung his suitcases from the car boot.

"These are twice as heavy as when I left; I've stuffed them with so many presents for you."

But as Nina trotted down the steps and launched herself into his arms, his gaze slid over her head and landed on me, and his taken-aback expression made me feel acutely self-conscious. Had he forgotten I lived with them now? Or perhaps he hated my new look? I tucked my hair behind my ear and waited for Nina to let him go, and by the time he came up to greet me, his face was friendly again.

"How're things, Beth?" he said. "You've both been growing up again, I see."

I trailed after them — Leonora hanging on to one of his arms, and Nina on the other — and I knew they all noticed my quietness at the welcome-home dinner that Leonora had prepared for him. But I didn't know how to hide this painful loneliness that gnawed at me in spite of the warm chatter around me, and as soon as I could, I slipped away and went to play my violin in my bedroom. I missed my parents and Ricky as if it were only three weeks they'd been gone instead of three years.

It was a sign of how much of an outsider I was feeling that I even began to look forward to Caroline's dutiful Christmas visit. She might be cold and selfish, but at least she was my real family.

SADIE

January 2019

"Where's Genevieve?" Sadie says again, this time more loudly, as if she might somehow have missed a reply in the hush of the drawing room. But Zach merely shakes his head, one hand pressed against his abdomen, while a bleary-eyed Everett blinks at her from his armchair by the fire.

"What?" the old man mutters. "What's the silly girl playing at?"

Joe joins Sadie at the window, and he, too, peers into the darkness.

"She was right there," Sadie says. "She hasn't come back in — we'd have heard her."

"She might have her back to us," Joe says. "Shielding her cigarette . . ." But he heads for the door, and Sadie hurries after him. "Let's call her in."

They grab a couple of coats from the cloakroom and go outside, down the stone steps, and across the gravel. Joe switches on his phone torch as he calls out Genevieve's name, and Sadie curses her lack of pockets, which made her leave her own phone upstairs. It's freezing out here, and despite the lamps on either side of the front door, they're plunged into darkness before they're even halfway across the parking area. But Joe seems confident about his bearings, and, sure enough, after hurrying down a gentle slope of grass by the light of his phone, they reach a little dock, nestled in among the reeds. At its far end, the lake gleams oily black in the feeble torchlight, and a small rowing boat scrapes gently against a wooden post as if inviting them to climb in. There's no sign of a young woman in a fur coat.

"Genevieve!" Sadie calls. And again, more frantically, "Genevie-e-eve!" She's shivering, and she can hear the note of panic in her voice.

The only reply is the soft lapping of the lake water and the rustling of reeds.

Joe casts his thin beam of light around until it picks out a pale object on the wooden planks. A half-smoked cigarette, with bright crimson lipstick marks still on it. He swivels the light in every direction, but it doesn't penetrate the darkness far enough to make out more than reeds and grass and the cold reflection of the water.

Sadie nudges the cigarette butt with her toe. "What shall we do?"

"Maybe," Joe says slowly, "she did go back inside, and we just didn't hear her."

"Let's go and check," Sadie says. "I think I know which room she was given." She tries to push away the memory of that unearthly cry from the other end of the corridor.

They dash back into the warmth of the house and try calling Genevieve from the hallway, with no success. Zach hovers in the drawing room doorway, looking concerned, but he has no helpful suggestions.

"Okay, I'll check down here," Joe says. "She might have come in the back door, maybe. Do you mind checking her bedroom?"

"Sure," Sadie says, although she's far from thrilled at the prospect of making her way up those stairs again by herself. "And what if she's not there?"

Joe's face creases with doubt. "Well, we'll have to disturb Nazleen, I suppose. She's the company's representative, isn't she? I still can't believe they didn't reconnect the phone line . . ."

Sadie tries to look more confident than she feels. "We'll find her. Just — shout if you find her first, okay?"

Joe starts trying the doors on one side of the hall, and Sadie heads upstairs. The corridor is empty, as before; all the doors on either side are closed, except for one halfway down the smoke-damaged end. Before she can change her mind, she marches down to it and peers inside. It's a junk room: boxes are stacked high on the floor and on the dark wooden furniture. The walls are painted a fresh cream, but Sadie's fairly sure this is the room that had the blackening around its window in the photo, and when she sniffs the air, she's sure she detects a faint scent of soot. For a second, she imagines someone, ducked down behind the boxes, breathing and watching her. She shakes her head and hurries out, closing the door behind her with a bang.

At the other end of the corridor, Genevieve's room is unoccupied. The red dress still lies puddled on the rug, and the curtains are partly open. Sadie crosses to the window and peers down into Raven Hall's walled back garden, but there's little to be seen beyond the weak yellow light from the rear windows downstairs. Faintly, she hears Joe calling, "Genevie-e-eve!"

Sadie doesn't need to guess at Nazleen's room; she taps sharply on the door.

"Nazleen? I'm sorry." Slowly, Sadie turns

the handle. "But it's important. I'm coming in."

Nazleen, looking frightened, is already swinging her legs out of bed and fumbling with her dressing gown.

"Listen," Sadie says. "Genevieve went out for a cigarette, and she — we can't find her. We've looked for her outside, and we're hoping she came back in again, but —"

Nazleen stares at her, wide-eyed. "Well, where is she?"

"That's what I'm saying. We don't know."

"Shit." Nazleen stumbles to the dressing table and jabs at buttons on her phone. "Still no signal. This bloody house . . ." She turns to Sadie with a hopeful expression. "Maybe she's with one of the others?"

"Zach and his dad are downstairs, and so is Joe. They've no idea. It's only Mrs. Shrew we haven't asked . . ." Sadie swings around. "Come on."

Nazleen hangs back in the corridor as Sadie raps loudly on Mrs. Shrew's door, and if Nazleen wonders how Sadie knows which room to try, she doesn't show it.

"It's me," Sadie calls out, her knuckles still resting on the painted wood. "Sadie. Or Miss Lamb, whatever. I need to talk to you." She turns the door handle slowly. "I'm coming in."

"What on *earth* do you think you're doing?"

Mrs. Shrew is still fully dressed. She stands in the center of the room, and her expression is furious.

"Mrs. — uh." Sadie remembers it isn't the woman's real name, and she feels unbalanced. "Um, the young woman in red — Miss Mouse, you know — we can't find her. She went outside for a cigarette and —"

Mrs. Shrew's shoulders relax a fraction. "Oh, is that all? There's no need to panic. She told me she was thinking of walking into the village and spending the night there. I suppose that's what she's done."

"But" — Sadie stares at her — "when did she say that?"

"When we were leaving the dining room. We spoke in the hall for a moment."

"But why would she? It's freezing out there. And she won't —" Just in time, Sadie stops herself from saying, *She won't get paid.* Mrs. Shrew would no doubt find that terribly vulgar.

"Who knows what goes on in the minds of young people these days?" Mrs. Shrew says primly. "Perhaps she wasn't enjoying the company. I can't say I blame her."

Sadie frowns. "Okay, well. I think — we might just check around the place anyway, just in case . . ."

"Very wise, I'm sure." Mrs. Shrew turns away dismissively.

Back out in the corridor, Nazleen huddles deeper into her dressing gown, gazing at Sadie with wide brown eyes.

"Do you think that's what she did?" Nazleen whispers.

"Walked to the village?" Sadie considers the idea. "I suppose it's possible. There's a B and B, isn't there?" She remembers the way Genevieve hovered at the entrance to the drawing room, clutching her coat against her chest. The young woman certainly had her phone and cigarettes with her by then, and she was the last guest to enter the drawing room by several minutes. What else might she have been hiding under that coat — a night bag, perhaps? A pair of trainers, for the walk into the village? Sadie sighs. "Maybe she did get fed up with us. She felt a bit out of place, I think."

Nazleen nods, as if trying to convince herself. "Or maybe she just thought the house was too spooky . . ."

Sadie gives her a sharp look. "Or she realized she had a lower-grade bedroom than the rest of us."

Nazleen looks surprised. "Does she? That's nothing to do with me."

Footsteps thump up the stairs, and Zach appears. He looks hopefully at Sadie.

"Any sign?"

Sadie shakes her head. "Mrs. Shrew thinks she might have walked into the village."

Zach raises his eyebrows. "Seriously? That's a good half-hour walk."

"Look — why don't you check the rooms up at that end?" Sadie indicates the fire-damaged end of the corridor with a twinge of guilt. "And, Nazleen, you check the rest of the rooms at this end. And I'll go and look in the — er." She frowns at the end door. "In the tower. And then we'll meet downstairs in the hall if we don't find anything."

"Okay." Zach's already turning away. Nazleen opens the door to Sadie's room, calling Genevieve's name. Sadie hurries to the end of the corridor, and this time she heads straight up the spiral staircase before she can change her mind.

BETH

December 1989
Caroline's Christmas visit fell early in December, because she was much too busy to fit me in later in the month. I'd bought her a silk scarf from my allowance, and she gave me some sheet music for my violin that she told me she enjoyed playing herself. I almost asked her if it was a joint Christmas and early birthday present, since she'd missed my birthday entirely the previous February, but I knew that would be rude, and in fact, the music was perfect — a genuinely welcome gift from one violinist to another. But when I went to give her a grateful hug, she flinched away, as usual.

After fifteen minutes of stilted conversation in the drawing room, Markus suggested Caroline might like a little walk by the lake before she headed home. Caroline looked so relieved at the word *home,* she sprang up immediately, and Markus winked at the rest of us behind her back.

"Leonora might be best staying indoors, actually," he said. "She's brewing up a bit of a cold, I think."

Leonora gave him a faint relieved smile, and we left her behind, although I didn't really believe she was coming down with anything. Once we reached the lakeshore, Markus told Nina and me to go ahead and take the boat out, if we were brave enough.

"The lake'll freeze soon, with a bit of luck," he said, "and then there won't be any rowing 'til it thaws."

Relieved to have an excuse to escape Caroline's strained attempts at friendliness, I followed Nina onto the dock, and we leaped down into the boat. Nina grinned at me as she took the oars, and I was reminded forcefully of the fun we'd had during my first summer at Raven Hall. I smiled back at her, and suddenly the day seemed a whole lot brighter.

Nina waited until we were past the island before she set the oars down.

"So, what's going on between you and Jonas?"

"Nothing." I knew I'd answered too quickly. "I mean, why do you even ask? You know Jonas and I are just —"

She tilted her head. "Friends?"

I nodded, frowning. "Friends. Exactly."

"I wish . . ."

"What?"

"I just wish you'd be honest with me, Beth. I wish you'd tell me what you're thinking. You go around all wrapped up in your own thoughts all the time. It's like sometimes you think" — she hesitated, gazing at me earnestly — "that I'm your enemy. Like you don't trust me. Or Mum and Dad either."

"That's not true." I tried to laugh. "Of course I trust you." But a series of memories pulsed in my mind: Leonora thrusting the blue checked dress into my hands; Markus's wary expression when he came back from his diving trip a few weeks ago; the oily film at the bottom of Nina's hot-chocolate mug. I blinked them away. "You know I'm very happy here."

"Are you?" Nina said quietly. "Are you really?"

I shifted uncomfortably. "Ah, come on, can we stop this now? I just want us to be friends. All of us. Jonas too."

She scrambled forward and indicated for me to switch places. "Fine. Your turn to row, then."

I seized the oars, glad of the opportunity to use my muscles. I took us on a circuit

209

around the island, and it was a while before I looked across to the dock and saw that Markus and Caroline had left us to it. By the time Nina and I returned to the house, Caroline had already set off for home.

Markus was right about two things. Leonora *was* coming down with something. She spent days locked away in her bedroom until she felt well enough to rejoin us downstairs, and even then, she remained pale and withdrawn. And the lake *did* freeze over the following week.

Markus announced he was taking the rest of the month off as holiday. He checked the ice obsessively each morning, drilling bore-holes, checking air and water temperatures, and goodness knows what else. His excitement radiated through the house.

"We've been getting fewer and fewer properly cold winters," he told me. "Last year was terrible, but this year" — he beamed at me — "with a bit of luck, we'll be out there on our skates before New Year's Eve. You'll love it, Beth. A proper Fenland tradition. And you're a proper Fens girl now, aren't you?"

I laughed, slightly unsettled by the intensity of his gaze. "I suppose so."

"You can come out with me tomorrow,"

he said, "if you like. I'll show you how I check the ice depth . . ."

"Oh, leave the poor child alone," Leonora said from the doorway. "Beth, Jonas is on the phone for you."

I was relieved to escape to the hall, and I pressed the phone to my ear. "Hello?"

"Beth? It's Jonas."

I smiled. "I know."

"Have you got plans for Christmas Eve? 'Cause my mum's having a little party here, and I wondered . . ."

"What does he want?" Nina's voice from the staircase was sharp. I turned to look at her. She held my gaze.

"Nina's here too," I said into the mouth-piece.

"Well," Jonas said, "she's invited, too, of course."

I tilted the phone away slightly. "Jonas's mum is having a little party on Christmas Eve. He wants to know if we'd like to go."

"Mu-um!" Nina called.

A moment later, a cross-looking Leonora appeared in the hall. "What, darling? There's no need to bellow for me. You should come and find me."

"Jonas's mum is inviting us to a party at his place on Christmas Eve," Nina said.

From the phone by my ear, I heard Jonas groan.

Leonora fixed me with a stern look. "Tell him it's kind of him, but no, Beth. Anyway, we do our own thing here on Christmas Eve." She took stock of my disappointed face, and her tone softened slightly. "It's nice of Stephanie to invite us, but we just can't make it. Do thank them, all the same."

I waited for her to return to the drawing room, and then I said to Jonas, "Did you get that?"

"Bloody Averells," he said.

I glanced up to where Nina still hovered, watching me.

"Funny you should say that," I said sweetly. "I was thinking the same thing."

When I hung up, Nina hurried down to the hall and caught both my hands in hers. "I'm sorry. That was mean of me. I'm really sorry, Beth. If you want to go — or maybe we could both sneak out and go . . ."

But it was hardly the sort of party I wanted to go to anyway — a boring adult affair in the middle of the day at the village B and B. I wanted loud music and dim lights and sweet cider and Jonas's arms around me.

"It doesn't matter." I gave her a weary look. "Honestly. I'm sure we'll have a nice time here."

Nina was very childish, sometimes. I pitied her. But underneath that, I felt a sort of protectiveness toward her. She'd grown up in this strange, isolated bubble at Raven Hall, and she didn't know any different — it wasn't her fault. Perhaps, when I eventually left, I'd persuade her to come with me.

On Christmas Eve, the family had a tradition of exchanging one small present after dinner to kick-start the festive celebrations. I'd bought my offerings on our shopping trip with Leonora in November, and I'd wrapped them carefully: rose-scented hand cream for Leonora, a bag of his favorite toffees for Markus, and a notebook with daisies on the cover for Nina. I was looking forward to seeing them opened.

Nina gave out her presents first, and then I gave out mine. We all cooed over our gifts and held them up for one another to admire. Then Leonora looked at Markus.

"Dad did the Christmas Eve shopping this year," Leonora said, raising her eyebrows in mock alarm.

"Uh-oh," Nina said, and both she and I giggled.

"Just you wait," Markus said, and with a flourish, he produced two identically wrapped boxes. He switched them between his hands with a show of consternation. "Which one's which? How to tell?" He held one out to each of us. "Luckily, they're both the same."

We tore into the paper, eyeing each other's as much as our own and laughing in our competition to see which of us could reveal the contents first.

"Oh," I said.

"Wow," Nina said.

We both tilted our boxes toward Leonora to show her. Inside each was a delicate gold charm bracelet twinkling with reflections from the dining room lights.

We lifted them out and helped each other to fasten them around our wrists.

"They're beautiful," I said.

"Thanks, Dad." Nina ran around the table to give Markus a hug.

"The charms represent the wildlife around the lake." Markus's voice was gruff with a sudden shyness. "There's a flag iris, a grey-lag goose, a reed warbler . . ." He cleared his throat. "Anyway, I'm glad you like them. And for my beloved wife —" He produced a third box, which turned out to hold a beautiful necklace, the same shade of gold as our bracelets.

"These aren't small presents," Leonora

said quietly.

Markus looked uncomfortable. "I know, but" — he turned to Nina and me — "I thought they'll always remind you of Raven Hall, when you're grown up. And you know, maybe you'll want to pass them on to your own daughters, for their sixteenth birthdays, say. I just thought it was a nice idea . . ."

He turned back to Leonora and helped her fasten the necklace under her hair. She didn't look as happy with her gift as I thought she ought to, but that was Leonora for you. She wasn't like normal people. I knew that by now.

She's in love.

This is nothing like the childish feelings she had for the young doctor. What she feels for Markus is real love. Proper, soul-mate, meeting-of-minds, forever-and-ever love.

It took her a while to hitch a lift to anywhere even vaguely close to Raven Hall today. She's now taking the field route around the village rather than risking being recognized walking down the high street. Not that she doesn't have every right to be here — it's a free country, isn't it? But she can't bear the thought of questions — or worse, pity — from the people she used to feel mildly sorry for because they all live so clustered together in the village instead of somewhere proud and magnificent like Raven Hall.

But she doesn't mind taking the long route; she's content to be alone with her thoughts. The sun is high, and her T-shirt sticks to her skin, but she smiles to herself as she strolls along. She's thinking of Markus.

On their third meeting by the lake, she told him an edited version of her life story — that her father had died last year; that she now lodges with a distant relative of her mother's, who barely speaks to her from one week to the next.

"I feel like my whole life was stolen from me," she blurted out, in an unguarded moment as they watched a hobby catching dragonflies above the lake. "Mum, then Dad, then my home . . ." She bit the rest of the sentence back; this was dangerous territory. What would Markus do if he discovered she was the "poor girl" who'd been turfed out of Raven Hall when his girlfriend's parents bought the place? Would his sympathy be replaced by awkwardness? Would he feel obliged to tell his girlfriend's parents he'd found this strange, traumatized young woman roaming around their property? And what would they do then? Prosecute her for trespassing? Or worse — offer her pity and fake condolences?

Markus tried to comfort her. "I expect things will look brighter next year. If you do apply to art college . . ."

But he inadvertently touched on her greatest fear, and a tear slid down her cheek.

"What if things never look brighter, though?

What if I can't ever move on? I'm just so *angry* at the man who did this to us."

Markus looked surprised. "Who?"

She wiped at her cheeks. "The Backstabber. That's what my dad used to call him. He was supposed to be my dad's friend, but after Mum died, he accused my dad of making mistakes at work, of being drunk." It was a relief to say it out loud, to feel listened to. "He got my dad sacked, in the end. And he — he —"

"What, Lara? What did he do?"

"He kept trying to buy our house from us. That's what he was after, all along . . ." She covered her face with her hands, forcing herself to stop talking before she blurted out anything more incriminating — that that was why she was here, the day she and Markus first met: she had been spying on her beloved former home, to see whether it was the Backstabber who'd finally succeeded in buying it.

"Hey." Markus shuffled closer to her, and even that single word managed to comfort her. He touched her lightly on her arm. "You can always come and stay with me, you know. In London. If your mum's cousin, or whatever she is, doesn't mind . . ."

And so, the following weekend, she told her mother's relative she was going to meet up with an old friend, and she took the train to

London. Markus cooked for her in his student flat, and he made her laugh, until she forgot about her sadness for the first time since her father died.

And a couple of weeks later, when she went back for a second visit, Markus opened the door with a charmingly sheepish expression.

"What is it?" she said. (She can tell when his emotions are high, even when he tries to hide it. She knows this is a sign they're meant to be together.)

He waited until the door was shut, and then he blurted it out.

"I've broken up with Kat."

"Oh, that's — I'm so sorry." She tried to look sympathetic, but her heart swelled with a joy that felt tainted — like relief mixed with triumph. The young woman in the orange crop top still had Raven Hall, but she'd lost Markus; perhaps there was some fairness in the world after all. "Why?" she asked. "What happened?"

"Ah." Markus scrunched up his face. "We weren't that well suited, really. We wanted different things in life . . ." He hesitated, as though tempted to say more, and she leaned closer to him.

"I think," she said, "we're well suited. You and I. Don't you think?"

"Lara." There was an apology in his smile. "I

really like you, but if we're going to do this, we have to take it slowly. I'm four years older than you. You've been through a tough few years, a lot of trauma. I don't want to . . ."

She tried to kiss him then, but he held her back gently.

"Seriously," he said. "I mean it. Slowly."

"But I'm eighteen."

"I just . . ." He searched her gaze. "I feel like there are things you're not telling me."

Her heart lurched. He knew. She didn't try to deny it. In fact, she almost blurted it all out, then and there: that her name wasn't really Lara; that the home she'd lost was Raven Hall.

"There is something I haven't told you . . . ," she began.

But he drew her into his arms, as if she were some injured creature he'd found by the shore of the lake. "It's okay. There's no rush. I won't ask you any more questions. Let's just get to know each other, until you're ready, okay?" He'd stroked her hair softly. "I'm not going anywhere."

While he cooked them dinner that evening, she pottered around his flat and cleared away all evidence of the former girlfriend. Hair bands, magazines, a silver earring, an alarming pair of black lacy knickers, and — worst of all — a photo of Markus and Kat together, sitting in the garden at Raven Hall. She collected it all into a carrier bag, and, when Markus wasn't looking, she stuffed the whole lot into the kitchen bin.

That was two months ago, and she's spent almost every weekend with Markus since. And he's been true to his word — he hasn't asked her any more questions. But as she cuts across the field now in the baking afternoon sun, she smiles to herself. She's going to tell him everything next weekend. She trusts him completely; she knows he'll understand why she lied.

She was planning to do it this weekend, but he rang her a couple of days ago, full of apologies. His mum's health is deteriorating, so he's gone to visit his parents instead. She doesn't mind. She completely understands, but the prospect of an empty weekend unsettled her, so she decided to pay one last visit to Raven Hall. Mostly, she wants to say a final goodbye to her beloved home. But it's true; she wouldn't mind catching a glimpse of the girl in the orange crop top looking just a little bit miserable.

She jumps across a ditch and pushes through a hedgerow, and she's back on the road, just beyond the village. It's still a fair old walk to Raven Hall from here, and she glances over her shoulder at the sprawling yellow-brick house at the tail end of the village. It's the local B and B, and she remembers that the owner used to spruce up old bicycles, ready for guests who wanted to explore the flat Fenland countryside, or just to cycle to the pub. She'll save herself a lot of time if she can borrow one, and she'll return it within a few hours — they'll never need to know.

She creeps up the B and B's drive, eyeing the collection of battered bikes in the open-fronted bike shed, and she spots one that looks ideal. But as she's easing it out from between its neighbors, she hears the creak of a door, and she swings around to see a young woman with a baby on her hip standing at the side door of the house, clutching a basket and staring at her.

Her heart thumps as she searches her memory. This must be Stephanie Blake — she remembers her vaguely from school. She was a couple of years older, and always seemed a kind, quiet sort.

Stephanie raises her eyebrows as if waiting for an explanation.

"Is it okay if I borrow it?" She tries to smile. "I'll bring it straight back. I promise."

Stephanie nods slowly, and then she tilts an ear to the open door.

From indoors, a man shouts, "Steph? Bring some raspberries in too, will you?"

222

"Okay, Dad." Stephanie gives her one last, assessing look, before hurrying away around the back of the house.

The bike squeaks a little, but it's a lot better than nothing, and Stephanie's kindness stays with her as she pedals away. Is it possible, she wonders, that for every bad person in the world, there's a good person? For every cruel, greedy man like the Backstabber, there's a thoughtful, generous woman like Stephanie? For every spoiled, careless girlfriend like Kat, there's a warmhearted, patient man like Markus? Is there some kind of moral balance in the universe?

She pedals harder, the rubber handlebar grips clammy under her palms. She wants to be a good person too. But frequently, she feels so furious about everything that's been taken from her: her mother, her father, the house that was meant to be her birthright. She knows a good person would accept this fate and walk away, but here she is, sneaking back yet again to spy on her former home, wishing ill on its new owners, and knowing she'd seize any chance to get her house back, no matter what the consequences.

She knows this makes her a bad person. But maybe when she confesses it all to Markus next weekend, he will help her to change, to improve, to become more like him.

Meanwhile, she wants just one last look at Raven Hall. It won't alter anything, and she's so close now, she can feel it calling to her. Just one last look, that's all she wants, and then she'll try her best to put it all behind her.

BETH

December 1989

It was the day before New Year's Eve. Nina, Leonora, and I were in the dining room, eating croissants and admiring the patterns of frost on the windows, when Markus came charging up from the lake, waving his arms and shouting.

"It's ready!" he declared as he burst through the door. "The ice is thick enough. Come on, sleepyheads." He beamed at the three of us, still sitting there in our dressing gowns and staring at him. "Get your skates on!"

We scrambled upstairs to get dressed, and then Nina and I went out to the stable block to rummage through a huge box of skates. Most were of a similar design: leather lace-up boots with long metal blades underneath that jutted out front and back. As we pulled them out, searching for a good fit, I held up a pair that looked quite different:

225

simple wooden-base sections with straps and blades attached.

"Those are Fen runners," Nina said. "They were my grandparents' and great-grandparents'. They used to have big skating parties here, when it froze like this — races with prizes. And people came from not just the village, but from miles around, and they had big feasts in the evening. I wish . . ." She gazed out toward the lake. "I wish I could have seen it."

"It sounds amazing." I ducked my head as an unexpected sadness washed over me. Not about the bygone era of skating parties on Avermere, but about the sensitive subjects I wasn't supposed to ask Nina about — the mysteries and secrets at Raven Hall I'd learned not to query. I wanted to ask: *Which grandparents — the Meyers or the Averells? Why are people from the village no longer invited to events here? Why aren't you allowed to show your face at the rare parties your parents do hold?* But instead, I frowned down into the box and pulled out another pair of skates.

The rumble of a car engine made us both scramble to our feet. Jonas had recently passed his driving test, and he was roaring down the driveway in his mum's old Volvo. I stayed where I was and watched Nina jog across the gravel to meet him, her breath rising in puffs of steam, her arms hugging her body against the cold. More and more, I felt pulled in two directions these days. Did I want Nina's friendship, and a stable family life at Raven Hall? Or did I want Jonas? I couldn't have both.

Oh, snap out of it, I told myself. *You're seeing problems where there are none, as usual.*

I started forward to join them. Nina held on to Jonas's arm, chattering excitedly about the first time he'd walked here by himself to skate on Avermere — did he remember? — and how many times they'd fallen over, and how fast they'd gone, and how much fun it all was. Jonas nodded as he listened, but his gaze slipped around her to me before his smile widened. Suddenly, I desperately wanted him to give Nina the full attention she deserved, so I turned away.

Markus and Leonora were striding down from the house, all wrapped up and bright-eyed.

"Have you ever skated before?" Markus asked me.

"Yeah, a bit." I'd been to the indoor ice rink in Peterborough a few times when I was younger, and I'd considered myself a pretty decent skater back then. But now that I was contemplating stepping out onto the surface of a real lake, I saw it had a different look entirely, and I slowed my pace as we approached the edge.

Nina and Jonas glided out onto the frozen lake first, and Markus and Leonora quickly followed. I stepped onto it hesitantly. Under my skate blades, the ice was translucent, but when I gazed out across the expanse of frozen water, it looked like a mottled mirror, reflecting the clouds and sky above. And I knew how deep the water was under that six-inch crust.

Nina and Jonas whooped as they shot across the ice, leaving swooping lines scored into the surface behind them. I stood still and watched. She went left, and he right, and then they looped around toward each other and picked up speed, the ice crackling and snapping around them.

I held my breath. They were going to collide.

Nina barreled into Jonas. He caught her, and they spun around and around, both laughing. I felt like a terrible person suddenly, inserting myself into Nina's family and interfering with this beautiful friendship she had with Jonas. I tore my gaze away from them and scraped my skate blades against the ice, my heart still jumping.

Seconds later, they were in front of me,

Nina flushed and beaming, Jonas stretching a hand toward me.

"Hey," Jonas said. "Come on, we'll help you."

I allowed him to take my right hand, and Nina my left, and together, the three of us slid away from the reeds and out onto the milky expanse. I lifted my chin, not wanting to look at the ice directly beneath my feet.

"There," Nina said. "You see? You can do it."

I found my balance, and we picked up a bit of speed. It felt surprisingly good, having the three of us linked together. Maybe everything would work out, after all. I lifted my face to the bright, pale sky, and I laughed, and Nina and Jonas joined in with me.

"Okay," Jonas said. "Now try by yourself."

They let go of me, and I mimicked their body posture, leaning forward and clasping my hands behind my back. We peeled apart, heading in three different directions, and I realized with a surge of delight that I no longer felt afraid. The ice was hard under my blades, and the surface was pitted, but I pushed myself to go faster, curving to the right and then to the left. I felt weightless, as if I could carry on gliding forever, leaving all my problems behind me. With a smile, I turned and swooped closer to the others, then away again, relishing the wind in my hair and the sudden warmth of the sun on my face. It was exhilarating.

"Okay," Markus called out from the shore. "Now the races begin."

He and Leonora proceeded to roll two wooden barrels onto the ice, and they stood them upright a good distance apart. I joined Nina and Jonas by the first barrel, and our breath mingled overhead in a cloud.

"Right," Leonora said. "One lap, Nina and Jonas first, start on my whistle."

I hung back next to Markus, watching entranced as Nina positioned herself on one side of the barrel, and Jonas on the other. They were both serious-faced, poised to set off. Leonora raised her hand, then dropped it sharply while making a noise like a whistle.

Nina set off faster, but as they raced toward the far barrel, Jonas overtook her on his side of the ice. He was first to spin around the second barrel, and first to return, flying past Leonora and Markus and me, his arms raised in jubilation. Nina came to a stop by grabbing the barrel at our end, and her eyes were shining. I felt a surge of excitement. I wanted a turn.

"Okay, winner against Beth," Leonora

said, laughing. "No chance to get your breath back, Jonas."

Jonas beat me, of course. Leonora almost beat Jonas. Leonora beat Markus, and Nina and Markus were neck and neck. When I raced against Markus, I won, but only because he let me.

It was intoxicating: the speed, the brilliant sunlight glinting on the ice, the good-natured teasing. When I wasn't breathless from racing, my chest filled with an unfamiliar sense of no-strings-attached joy. Nothing else mattered that morning on the frozen lake. All my private worries about Nina's isolation, my secret relationship with Jonas, that oily residue I'd seen in Nina's mug — all were scorched away by the dazzling winter sun and the adrenaline in my blood.

I wanted the morning to go on forever. But eventually, we staggered back up the slope to Raven Hall, our stomachs rumbling, our legs suddenly wobbly at having to lift our clumsy feet against gravity for every step. I wondered briefly whether Leonora and Markus might invite Jonas into the house for lunch, but Jonas glanced at his watch and said he'd promised to go home and eat with his mum.

I should have said good-bye to him then. I should have followed the others into the house. But Jonas had a certain expression — raised eyebrows, eyes sparkling — that I could never resist, and I hung back and waited for the front door to close before I went to him.

"Hey, you," he said, pulling me even closer to him. "Am I allowed to kiss you, now?"

For the next few seconds, I was aware only of him — but as we pulled apart, I realized belatedly that the front door had reopened. Nina stood on the top step, watching us.

"Oh," I said. "Nina, I —"

Her voice was flat. "Maybe you should go and have lunch at Jonas's house, Beth."

I stared at her. "I can't —"

"Mum!" she bellowed back into the hall. "Beth says she's going to eat at Jonas's house instead."

I tensed, waiting for Leonora to come scurrying out, to tell me this wasn't allowed, to drag me back into Raven Hall. But instead, Leonora's voice floated calmly down the hall.

"Okay, that's fine. Come inside, then, Nina, and close the door."

It was like the sun burning through winter cloud: the truth hung there, clear and shocking, in front of me. Why had I never realized it before? I could leave whenever I liked; I could go wherever I liked. It was

Nina who was banned from the village, not me. Nina who was kept here in a little bubble. Not me.

"But I don't want to —" I began.

Nina's voice was tight. "A bit late for that, don't you think?" She retreated into the house, slamming the door behind her.

I turned to Jonas, my heart rattling.

"What do I do?"

He gave me a cautiously optimistic smile. "Come home with me?"

I felt dazed as I walked to his car, not sure what I was committing to — not in regard to Jonas, but in terms of leaving Raven Hall, and walking away from Nina. Would the family — would Nina — definitely allow me to go back? I sat in silence on the short drive to the village, gazing sightlessly through the windscreen. Jonas cast me concerned glances, but he didn't speak again until he'd turned onto the B and B's driveway and parked by the bicycle shed.

"My mum'll be pleased to see you, you know," he said. "Delirious, actually. I mean, I'm downplaying it, if anything. You really don't need to worry."

"It's not that," I said.

He studied me. "I'm worried about you, you know. That family. It's like you hide your feelings all the time, in case they don't approve, but — it's not right. You shouldn't have to pretend to be something you're not . . ."

I gulped, thinking of the two occasions I'd tricked Nina's grandfather into believing I was Nina.

"I shouldn't have left," I said. "I need to get back. It feels disloyal . . ."

"Beth." He took my icy fingers in his and tried to rub some warmth back into my hands. "Look, you're almost sixteen. You can leave Raven Hall if you want to. Talk to your aunt Caroline. Come and live here, with me. I mean, it doesn't have to be — Mum would happily put you up, as a friend of mine; I promise you. And then we'd be . . ." He squeezed my fingers gently. "You can be yourself, here. And we could see each other whenever we like."

I shook my head slowly, feeling like the worst person in the world.

"But that's not what I want."

Jonas blinked a few times. "What isn't? Being with me — ?"

I pulled my fingers free of his, and I indicated the yellow-brick house in front of us. "It's such a nice offer, but it's not —"

"Nice?" Now he sounded insulted.

I twisted in my seat to face him, trying to find the right words. "It's just that — I'd

234

still be so close to Raven Hall, and — I can't even think it all through. They'd stop paying my school fees, wouldn't they, if I left? And for me to move just down the road would seem so . . . rude, somehow. But you're so close to your mum, and the business, and this whole place — the village, everything. I can't expect you to leave that behind and —"

"What do you mean?" He searched my expression. "Move somewhere else, together, you mean?"

I shook my head. "You can't. You can't leave this place; you belong here. And I can't just leave Raven Hall but stay nearby. I'd need to make a proper break, a clean break." I sat back in my seat, then, and turned my head to the side window. "Which I'm not ready to do. So." I took a deep breath. "I need to go back."

"You're really not making sense," he said.

I curled my fingers around the door handle, feeling dizzy, as though I were teetering on the edge of the dock back at Raven Hall, unsure whether to fall one way or the other. All I knew was, I couldn't have it both ways: I couldn't have Jonas *and* my life at Raven Hall. I had to decide between them. And there was no point in trying to explain that to Jonas, because there was nothing he could do about it. He'd be better off without me. I couldn't give him the happy, carefree, *normal* relationship that he was looking for, or that he deserved.

"I'm sorry," I said. "Look, I'll walk back. You go in. Your mum's waiting for you."

The hurt in his voice was clear. "Fine. Go running back to them, then. But things won't get any better, you know. Markus's dad's coming back again, and Mum says he's determined to sell the house this time; did you know that? He has an appointment with an estate agent while he's here. He's desperate to get Markus and Nina to the States with him, with or without Leonora, and Mum reckons he won't accept any more stalling . . ."

My mouth fell open, and I grabbed his sleeve. "When? When's he coming? Why didn't you tell me before?"

Jonas looked taken aback. "I didn't think of it. I only heard this morning. Mum said his secretary rang late last night, asking for a last-minute room. He's arriving tomorrow, just staying the one night, apparently . . ."

My breath scraped in my throat. What did it mean? Could this be good news for me? They'd *need* me back at Raven Hall now, to play the role of Nina, wouldn't they? But an image of the hot-chocolate mug shimmered in my mind, and I felt paralyzed.

"It's so little notice, for New Year's Eve," Jonas grumbled. "Mum could do without the hassle, really, but she doesn't like to turn people away. I don't know if he's trying to make it a surprise visit, but Mum'll ring and tell Leonora, like she did before — to give her a bit of time to prepare, you know . . ."

With a supreme effort, I found my voice again.

"Do you think your mum's already rung her?"

Jonas frowned. "I've no idea. Mum went out first thing. And Leonora was skating with us all morning, wasn't she? Mum could be ringing her right now, for all I know."

"Please, Jonas." I gripped his fingers in mine, this time. "Please, *please,* will you drive me back?"

"Why?" He stared at me with growing concern. "Beth? What is it?"

"I can't —" I squeezed my eyes shut, thinking of that oily residue in the hot-chocolate mug, and Nina's sickness. The word was back, hissing in my ears, pulsing through my body: *poison, poison, poison.* "I need to check on Nina. Please, Jonas. Take me back to Raven Hall."

The B and B's bike makes her journey so much quicker. Raven Hall soon comes into view, and she keeps her gaze fixed on it as she pedals: the welcoming gray stone frontage, the familiar chimneys, the proud turret. She feels bolder today, and she cycles down the center of the driveway with her back straight and her chin up — what's the worst that can happen?

Instead of cutting across to the garden wall as on previous visits, she leaves her bike on the verge and strolls closer to the front of the house, pulled like a magnet to the drawing room window. Is this where the long-haired Kat will be sitting, weeping into her hands, comforted by her slow-moving mother? She can't resist — she walks right up to the glass and peers in. If anyone challenges her, she'll say she's collecting money for charity.

The drawing room is unoccupied. But the familiar contents make her heart squeeze painfully. The black marble fireplace is still there, of course, but she's surprised to see so much of her parents' furniture, too, and her old piano. Was it all sold as one lot, together with the house? Nobody consulted her. Even her mother's painting of Raven Hall still hangs above the old polished bureau. She grips the windowsill tighter and cranes her neck to see more.

"Oi! What do you think you're doing?"

She whirls around. A tall man is striding up the grass from the dock. She opens her mouth to begin her charity-collecting excuse, but the words shrivel in her throat; she knows this man. Her stomach lurches, and she crashes back against the stone wall.

It's the Backstabber. Daddy's so-called friend; the man who stole Daddy's job and got him sacked; the man she blames for Daddy's death. It's her father's murderer.

"Well?" the man snaps. "What do you want? You're trespassing."

She struggles to accept the evidence in front of her: Can the Backstabber really be the new owner of Raven Hall? She didn't think he had a daughter, but she must be wrong. Can he really be the husband of the slow-moving woman she saw on the veranda; the father of Markus's ex-girlfriend, Kat?

"Are you just going to stand there?" he says.

"Come on, clear off, or I'll set the dog on you."

It's his hollow bluster — an image of that fluffy white dog trying to chase her down the driveway — that jolts her out of her terror.

"You don't even recognize me, do you?" Her voice grows louder. "You forced my dad out of his job. You made him drink himself to death. And you stole our house. You took everything from me. And you've got the gall to say *I'm* trespassing?"

The man's brow lowers. "Who the hell are you?"

Her voice slides up in pitch. "Isn't it obvious? How many men have you done that to? You must be so proud of yourself, tearing families apart . . ." A sob overtakes her.

"My God," he says. "You're Charles's daughter, aren't you? Look, you clearly don't have the right information, young lady — I tried to help your father, many, many times . . ."

"You destroyed him," she snarls. "You killed him."

The man narrows his eyes. "There's no point in our having this conversation if you're not going to listen to me. I can see you're just as obstinate as your father, and I'll tell you one thing for free. If your old man had agreed to let me buy this place when I first offered, he'd still be alive today."

She gasps. "No."

"I don't even like this bloody house. My wife took a shine to it, and I knew it would solve your father's financial problems, so I made him an offer. You could have moved somewhere smaller together; he could have got help with his drinking . . ."

"No," she whispers.

"And he'd have cleared all his debts instantly, instead of descending into bankruptcy." The man gives her a surprisingly sympathetic look. "It was your father's obsession with keeping hold of this house that killed him; you must be able to see that. He should have put your welfare before his attachment to his bloody ancestral home — I told him that, but he wouldn't listen . . ."

"That's not true," she says. And again, louder. "That's not true! You just wanted to get your hands on Raven Hall; you didn't care who you hurt. You never thought about me while you were taking away my home, my memories of my parents . . ." She curls her fists and fights back a sob. "You don't even remember my name, do you?"

In her peripheral vision, she sees the front door swing open. A large figure in a billowing dress shuffles forward onto the top step.

"Hendrik?" the woman says. "What's going on?"

But neither of them glances up at her. They

hold each other's gaze, and he scowls as though he's searching his memory, desperate to recall this trespasser's name and prove her wrong. And somehow, on top of all the very real harm he's done her, this feels like the ultimate insult.

"I'm Leonora Averell," she says, "and Raven Hall should be mine." She steps forward, but before she can say any more, a single word punctures her fury.

"Lara?"

It's like ice-cold water sluicing over her skin.

She spins around on the gravel and — it's quite inexplicable. On the far side of the large pale-faced woman, supporting her on his arm, is Markus. And Leonora looks from Markus's straw-colored hair to the Backstabber's; from the Backstabber's tall, broad-shouldered frame back to Markus. The facts stir and re-arrange themselves like autumn leaves picked up by the breeze, and they settle with deceptive gentleness into a new explanation.

This never was the home of the girl in the orange crop top. Markus wasn't visiting his girlfriend, Kat, here. He and Kat came together to visit his parents.

She can see it, now. She can't believe how stupid she's been. Markus is the Backstabber's son.

She runs for her bicycle and flees.

BETH

December 1989

I leaped out onto the gravel in front of Raven Hall, and I forced myself to dip my head to say something to Jonas before slamming the door on him.

"Thanks for bringing me back," I said. "But please, just go now. I'll explain everything later."

"Well, when?" he said. "Tonight? Will you ring me?"

The prospect of trying to explain any of this on the phone from Raven Hall, where I might be overheard, made me shake my head quickly. But I was afraid Jonas would refuse to leave if I didn't suggest an alternative, and I feared it would make everything worse if I burst back into Raven Hall with an inquisitive Jonas hard on my heels.

"Tomorrow," I said. "Wait for Markus's dad to get back to the B and B after he visits us, and then" — I glanced at the frozen lake

243

— "just — park up on the road, so they don't know you're here, okay? Walk across the ice to the island, and I'll sneak out and meet you there."

Jonas muttered a few words of annoyance, clearly thinking my caution was over-the-top, but he put the car into gear and left me to it.

I was more than a little relieved to find the front door of Raven Hall wasn't locked against me. I hurried inside, straining my ears for any sound of the family's where-abouts. The drawing room and dining room were empty, but in the kitchen, I found Nina, perched on a breakfast stool and finishing off a mince pie, with an empty mug beside her. Enticing savory aromas drifted from the oven — they hadn't eaten lunch yet.

"Back already?" she said, sounding more wounded than hostile. "Didn't you like the food at Jonas's?" Then her tone sharpened. "Hey, what are you doing?"

I grabbed her mug and tilted it toward the feeble light from the window, but there was nothing unusual to be seen. Just tea dregs. No oily residue. I eyed her plate, my pulse still jumping.

"How many mince pies have you had?"

She opened her mouth, but it took her

several seconds to answer. "What the hell's got into you?"

"Nina, seriously. How many have you had?"

"Two — I was starving, and lunch'll be another half hour. Is that okay with you?"

"Are they —" I snatched the remnant from her fingers and examined it in the palm of my hand. "Are these the ones your mum made? Who gave them to you?"

"Beth, you're scaring me." She slipped off the stool, gazing at me, wide-eyed. "Mum gave them to me, just a few minutes ago. She warmed some up for all three of us. Why are you being so dramatic about it?"

"I think —" But suddenly, I didn't know what to say. What if the substance in the hot chocolate really was something innocuous? How could I blurt out the word *poison* without making my position here completely impossible? How could I expect Nina to ever forgive me if I wrongly accused her mother of deliberately making her ill?

I set the fragment of pastry back on the plate, thinking frantically.

"How are you feeling?" I asked her. "Do you feel sick? Do you feel okay?"

Nina glanced over my shoulder toward the door, and I heard light footsteps come in behind me.

"Ah, Beth," Leonora said. "Back already?" She hesitated, glancing at Nina and back to me. "Is something wrong?"

I shook my head stiffly.

Leonora smiled. "Well, not to worry. You can eat with us, then, after all." She gestured to the oven. "Would you like me to warm you up a mince pie?"

I shook my head and circled around her, stumbling backward toward the door. "Thanks, no, I'm — did Jonas's mum ring, while I was out?"

Markus's voice behind me made me jump. "Stephanie? Yeah, she did, but it wasn't about you. Why, did you and Jonas have an argument or something?"

All three of them watched me with frowns on their faces.

"No, I —" I raised a trembling hand to my cheek. "Actually, I'm just very tired. I'm going to go and have a . . ." I made a vague gesture.

"Nap?" Leonora suggested, after a moment of silence. "Don't you want any lunch?"

"No. Thanks." I escaped from the room, and none of them followed me, but even after I'd shut myself in my bedroom, my skin still prickled from their bemused stares, and I pressed my fingers to my burning

246

cheeks. *What must they think of me?*

I forced myself to take several deep breaths.

Concentrate on the facts. Nina's grandfather is coming back to Raven Hall tomorrow, for a third visit. Stephanie Blake did ring a little while ago, almost certainly to warn Leonora and Markus about the visit. In which case, Leonora will ask me to pretend to be Nina again. Of course she will. She has no choice.

I am the powerful one in this situation, I tried to insist to myself. But it didn't feel like it. I sank onto my bed and waited for Leonora to knock.

But when the knock eventually came, I knew straightaway it wasn't Leonora's. Nina slipped into my room, and she hovered by my bed, her face painfully, distressingly pale.

"I don't feel very well," she whispered. "What's going on? You've got to tell me."

All those months of worrying, yet I had no idea how I could possibly articulate what my fear was. In the end, I patted the bed and waited for her to sit down beside me, and my heart wouldn't stop drumming.

"First of all," I said, my voice barely above a whisper, "I don't have any answers. And you're not going to like what I'm going to say. So you can change your mind right now, if you want to, and walk away. I

247

wouldn't blame you."

"You're scaring me, Beth."

"I'm scared myself. That's the trouble."

She thought for a moment. "Okay. You have to tell me. Just say it."

"You know I don't want to hurt you?"

She nodded. "Just say it, whatever it is."

"How many times have you felt sick like this, since I started living here?"

She barely paused. "This is the third time."

"And what happened the first and second time — who came to visit?"

Her voice was quiet. "My grandfather."

I swallowed hard and nodded. "Well, Jonas just told me your grandfather's flying back for a third visit. He's on his way right now. I'd guess he's likely to turn up here tomorrow afternoon, if what Jonas says is true."

"That's what Stephanie was ringing Mum about?"

I jerked my shoulders stiffly. "That's what I'm guessing. Jonas said she would."

Nina frowned. "But why did you — how did you know I was going to be — what were you looking for in my mug?"

I ground my teeth, hoping she'd work it out herself. But her frown only deepened.

"Tell me, Beth, for God's sake. What were

you *looking* for in my mug and my mince pie?"

"Okay. The thing is, I saw something odd, in your hot-chocolate mug, after your grandfather's last visit. You must have drunk it just a few hours before he arrived, and it had a — like an oily substance at the bottom. And you felt sick after drinking it."

She gazed at me. "And . . . ?"

"Well, I don't know, Nina." I felt angry with her suddenly. "You tell me. Why would you get sick every time, if it isn't just some weird, huge coincidence?"

Her eyes were enormous. "I don't know."

"Well, maybe — maybe —" I had to force the words out. "Maybe someone put something in your drink. Or your food. To make you sick. That's all I'm saying."

Nina shook her head slowly. "No, that can't be it. Who would? And why would they? You're making this up. I don't believe you."

"How are you feeling right now?"

She frowned down at her lap, and when she eventually replied, her voice was small.

"Sick. Nauseated. Like I want to throw up, but I can't."

"Well, let's go and see a doctor. They'll know . . ."

"No!" She looked horrified. "I'm not allowed. Mum would never . . ."

I leaned forward. "Come on, Nina. You can do it if you want to. I'll ring Jonas. He'll pick us up, take us to the surgery in the village . . ."

"I'm not allowed," she repeated, but this time her tone was blank, and I sensed she wasn't to be persuaded.

Slowly, I leaned back against my headboard. My muscles were already aching from the morning's skating, and a wave of tiredness crashed over me.

"I told you I didn't have any answers," I said.

She gave me one last, long look, and then she left, closing the door softly behind her. I curled into a ball on my bedspread and waited for another knock. Whether it came this afternoon, or tomorrow morning, I knew Leonora would seek me out and ask me to play the role of Nina again.

I was sure it wasn't my imagination. Leonora seemed much warier of me as we waited for Markus's father to arrive this time than she had on the previous visits.

"Don't forget," she said, "you can be short with him. Make it clear there's no question of you ever wanting to join him in America."

I nodded stiffly.

"Tell him again what you said the first time," Leonora said, "about never wanting to leave Raven Hall or it would break your heart."

"Got it," I said. "I'll remember. Don't worry."

I twisted my bracelet around my wrist, squeezing each charm in turn between finger and thumb. "Flag iris," I whispered. "Greylag goose. Reed warbler." As if the chanted words might somehow bring me luck. Leonora watched me from the corner of her eye, and I wished she'd focus on the driveway like she had on the previous visits. Did she know what I'd said to Nina yesterday afternoon? An image of Leonora eavesdropping on that conversation sprang up in my mind, and my skin felt cold.

I had to concentrate on getting through this visit, and making sure Nina recovered properly. What else could I do? If I told anyone outside the family that I was worried Nina had been poisoned, they'd never believe me. I wasn't sure I even believed it myself. The whole thing seemed so unlikely. I was beginning to think it more likely there was something wrong with *me*.

"Here he comes," Leonora said, finally.

I fought back déjà vu and trudged after her to wait in the hall while Markus went

251

out to meet the car. Earlier that morning, I'd dragged the cheval mirror out of my bedroom and left it in a room at the far end of the corridor. Now I turned my back on the hall mirror for the same reason. I couldn't bear to see my reflection any longer — the juvenile plaits, the uncomfortable high-necked dress. *Hurry up, old man,* I thought. *Let's get this stupid game over and done with.*

"Ms. Averell," he said as he stalked into the hall.

"Hendrik." Leonora nodded stiffly by my side.

The old man's expression softened as he turned to me. "Well now, Nina. This is a quick visit, but I'm very interested to hear your views on a little proposal I have for you . . ."

He turned toward the drawing room, clearly expecting me to follow. Leonora reached out and pinched my arm as I moved away from her. A silent reminder of what I was supposed to tell him. She hurried away to the kitchen then to fetch the tea tray.

Markus's father settled on the sofa nearest the fire, and I perched next to him. Markus took a seat opposite me, and his smile was surprisingly relaxed.

"It's great to see you, Dad," Markus said. "Really good."

I frowned at him. I doubted Leonora would be pleased to hear him sound so sincere about his father's visit, but she was still out in the kitchen.

"I'll cut to the chase," my supposed grandfather said. "I want you to come back with me, Markus. I've got a position all lined up for you, and in five years you'll take over the company. It'll be the best thing for Nina. And for you, too, of course. I won't hear any argument. This place is going on the market next week."

Markus's mouth gaped like a startled fish's.

His father turned to me. "What do you say, Nina? You can take a few months off, switch schools, and pick up where you left off, no problem. Are you ready to make a fresh start?"

Teacups rattled in the doorway behind me, and I knew Leonora must be standing there, hastily grabbed tray in hand. I gazed into the older man's eyes, and I tried to communicate my real feelings to him, even as I opened my mouth to parrot Leonora's words.

"I couldn't bear to leave Raven Hall, Grandfather," I said mechanically. "Please

253

don't make me go. It would break my heart."

His blue eyes looked beyond mine into my skull, into my soul, and my skin tingled with the certainty that he knew I was acting — that he saw the real me underneath. And I *wanted* him to see me. I kept my gaze fixed firmly on his, and I pleaded silently with him, with all my might. *Help me. Get me out of here.*

"I understand," he said slowly. He reached into his pocket and pulled out a handkerchief. And then, in one swift movement, he caught hold of my hand, as if to give it a conciliatory squeeze, and he slipped a small rectangular card into my palm. "I'm sure we can sort everything out," he said, without breaking our eye contact. "I'll do whatever it takes to make sure you're happy."

The clink of china came nearer, and Leonora set the tray down on the coffee table.

"Tea?" she said brightly.

But Hendrik was already rising. "No, thank you." He frowned at Markus. "I meant what I said. I won't put up with this any longer. Let me know Nina's exam dates, and I'll take that into account. But this house has been a curse on our family, and it's going to be sold, whether you like it or not."

He stalked from the room, and as Markus and Leonora hurried after him, I dropped my gaze to the small rectangular card in my hand. It was a business card, with HENDRIK MEYER printed across the center, and several phone numbers. I now had the means to contact my supposed grandfather whenever I wanted.

I was still sitting there, feeling dazed, when I heard a new note of urgency in the voices from the hall.

"Is that smoke?" Hendrik said. "What's going on?"

"My God!" Markus said, his voice rising to a shout. "Something's on fire!"

I ran out to the hall. Thick gray smoke obscured the landing and billowed down the stairs. Markus was already disappearing into it, his arm held across his nose and mouth, and I couldn't see whether he turned left or right at the top. A sharp, acrid smell filled my nostrils, and a moment later, I began to cough.

"For God's sake," Hendrik bellowed at a frozen-looking Leonora. "Phone the fire brigade. We could lose the whole house!"

Hendrik started up the stairs after Markus, calling his name. Leonora turned to me, white-faced.

"Nina," she whispered, and the sound of her own voice seemed to snap her into action. Ignoring Hendrik's instruction, she, too, ran up the stairs and was swallowed by the smoke.

The sound of crackling flames reached my ears, and I heard a choked shout from Markus, followed by a prolonged bout of coughing that could have come from any of them. My heart battered in my chest like a bird trapped in a chimney. Nina was up there, sick or asleep in her turret bedroom — and what if she couldn't get out? Before I could change my mind, I held my sleeve over my own nose and mouth, and I ran up after them.

She didn't know she had so many tears saved up inside her. She pedals furiously toward the village, feeling her heart shattering into thousands of tiny jagged-edged pieces. The Backstabber is Raven Hall's new owner. And Markus is the Backstabber's son.

She's lost everything. Her parents, her home, and now Markus. All gone.

She swipes angrily at her eyes and swerves closer to the grass shoulder as a car approaches from behind. It slows, and she's horrified to see Markus's concerned face glide alongside her. The Backstabber himself is in the driver's seat — she remembers, now, that his name is Hendrik. That's what Daddy used to call him before Daddy started drinking, before everything went so horribly, terribly wrong.

"Lara, please," Markus says, "let us give you a lift somewhere, at least . . ."

"Go away!" she shouts. "I don't need you!

Leave me alone, or I'll —"

She looks around wildly, wondering if she should discard the bike and run into the fields, but a car is approaching from the other direction, and she feels a glimmer of triumph.

"I'll flag these people down," she shouts, glaring through the open window at both of the men. "I'll tell them you're trying to kidnap me."

"Oh, this is ridiculous," Hendrik says loudly, and a moment later he accelerates away.

The second car whizzes past, and she focuses on the road ahead and continues pedaling. But Hendrik must have swung his car around in the farm track farther along; he and Markus are heading toward her again, this time on the other side of the road.

Markus leans across Hendrik and calls out, "Please, Lara . . . Leonora . . ."

She doesn't even look at him. And a second later, they're gone, heading back to the house they stole from her.

She cycles on toward the village, knowing she's entirely alone now. There's no one left in the world who cares about her anymore.

Her tears have run dry by the time the village finally comes into sight, and she hops off the bike in front of the B and B. As she slots it back into the bike shed, Stephanie appears at the side door again, frowning.

"Are you okay?" Stephanie asks.

She draws herself up, forces herself to smile. "Yeah, I'm fine." She nods at the baby on Stephanie's hip. "Is he yours?"

Stephanie presses her lips into the child's chestnut hair. "He sure is."

"He's gorgeous. Thank you for the loan of the bike." She turns away.

"Do you need help with anything else?" Stephanie calls out.

But a familiar car is drawing to a halt in front of the bungalow next door — a mink-blue Ford Capri — and her heart lifts.

"No, thanks." She doesn't glance back.

It's fate. It must be.

She hurries toward the car, a tentative smile forming as she sees the young doctor spring out from the driver's seat. He never misled her, she thinks. She always knew exactly who he was, and where he lived, and who his family was.

"Leonora?" The man's startled gaze runs over her tearstained face, her sweat-soaked T-shirt, and the rip in her skirt where she caught it on the roadside brambles. "What on earth are you doing here? Are you hurt?"

She shakes her head, her pulse jumping as she takes in his familiar sharp-jawed face, his wiry frame, the doctor's bag in his hand. She glances at the bungalow behind him.

"Are you on a visit?" she says.

"I am." He tilts his head. "How about you? I haven't seen you since . . ."

They blink at each other, remembering that awful scene in her father's study.

"Oh," she says, "I'm — I'm living with a kind of aunt now. But she doesn't care where I am. No one cares . . ."

He glances up the road behind her. "Ah. Boyfriend jilted you, has he?"

Leonora's knees feel weak — he knows her. The young doctor knows her. He can read her emotions, just like she thought she could Markus's.

Stop thinking about Markus.

"Could I —" She lifts her chin, tries to smooth her skirt. "Is there any chance you could drive me back to my aunt's place tonight? I hitchhiked here, but —" She gestures down the road. "It's been an awful day, and I'm just so tired . . ."

The man studies her thoughtfully. "I can't tonight," he says slowly. "But maybe in the morning. If your aunt won't worry . . ."

"Oh, thank you, Roy. Thank you." She hurls herself into his arms, almost knocking the bag from his grip. He glances across the road to the B and B, and he pushes her gently away, but he's smiling.

"Wait in my car while I just get this visit

done. We'll have a nice evening together, then, okay? We fit rather well together, I think, you and me."

SADIE

January 2019

Sadie pauses at the top of the spiral staircase and listens outside the door for a moment.

"Genevieve?"

There's no reply. She can hear Nazleen's and Zach's voices calling out the same name on the floor below, and it gives her a moderate amount of reassurance. Gently, she pushes open the door and feels around on the wall for a light switch; her fingers find it easily.

The room is circular — *of course it is* — and it must once have belonged to a child. There are children's books mixed in with classics in the bookcase, and collections of dusty feathers and pinecones and bead necklaces scattered over a long, curved dressing table. Cobwebs drape from the high ceiling, and the air smells musty, but when Sadie studies the bed, she thinks it looks recently slept in. The pillow has a dent at its center, and the covers are thrown back, and there's a glass of clear water on the bedside table.

Slowly, Sadie turns, and she almost screams when she sees a whole bank of glassy eyes staring back at her. Dusty carnivorous creatures wearing human clothing; their malevolent glares bore right through her skin. She presses her hand over her thudding heart.

"Genevieve?" she murmurs. "Where are you?" But the room remains silent, and there's no obvious hiding place. Still feeling uneasy, she hurries back down the spiral staircase.

When she emerges in the corridor, she hears Zach and Nazleen talking on the floor below, so she goes down to join them in the hall. Joe is with them, swinging a heavy torch in one hand, and he gives Sadie a tight smile that holds no trace of amusement.

"You'll come out with me, won't you?" Joe says to Sadie. "Make sure I'm not seeing things."

Zach grumbles at him. "I said I'd come, didn't I? I just don't feel very well . . ."

Nazleen tightens her dressing gown belt and waits for Sadie to answer.

"What have you found?" Sadie asks, but Joe merely indicates the front door. They leave Zach and Nazleen behind, and they make their way back out into the freezing darkness.

"Come on, what is it?" she says. They crunch across the gravel. Joe's torch gives a much broader, brighter beam, but for some reason it makes Sadie feel more rather than less anxious.

Joe shakes his head. "You have a look first. See what you think."

Her heart pounds as they approach the dock for a second time. The reeds are a ghostly silver, swaying and rustling, as if trying to escape the darkness behind them. The black surface of the lake rumples gently like oil. A sudden flurry to one side makes her cry out.

"Hey." Joe touches her arm briefly. "It's just a bird. We woke it up, that's all." He swings the torch beam away from the dock to the frosty grass beside it, and he slides the light left and right. "What do you make of these?"

At first, Sadie can't see anything but white-tinged grass. She peers closer. Actually, there *is* something — a faint trail of impressions — two different sizes of indentations in the frost, half of them round-cornered triangles and half of them small circles. She straightens slowly.

"You think they're Genevieve's foot-prints?"

Joe nods and swings the beam away in the direction of the driveway. "High heels, don't you think? And they join the drive just over there. And there're no other tracks next to them."

"Except yours." Sadie blinks at him. "Presumably? If you followed the trail . . ."

"Well, yes, I meant —"

Sadie turns toward the house and gazes at the yellow glow seeping around the drawing room and dining room curtains. She's not sure she can trust anybody here. But sometimes you have to trust somebody.

"Mrs. Shrew thinks Genevieve was planning to walk to the village. To stay at the B and B instead."

"Yeah, Zach told me." Joe rubs his mouth. "I suppose that must be what she did, then."

Sadie peers at him in the gloom. "Do you know her? Mrs. Shrew."

He takes his time replying. "I used to, when I was young. I grew up round here."

Sadie considers this. Mrs. Shrew said she'd traveled a long way to get here this evening, but it doesn't surprise Sadie that she, too, used to be local — it fits, somehow, with her uptight behavior and reactions tonight.

"Do you trust her?" Sadie asks. "She just seems a bit . . ."

He frowns, as though trying to weigh up the evidence to give Sadie a fair answer. "I feel sorry for her, mainly. And I don't trust her, particularly, no. But equally — I can't see why she'd lie about this."

Sadie hates feeling so powerless; they ought to be *doing* something. "Well, we can't phone anyone, can we? And we don't have a car. Do you think one of us should walk to the B and B to check that Genevieve got there okay?" She tries to suppress a sudden conviction that the company won't pay her if she ends up following Genevieve into the village and spending the night at the B and B. And all because the selfish young woman couldn't be bothered to let them know what she was planning to do.

But Joe doesn't need any more of a hint. "I'll go. I know the route."

"No!" Sadie grabs his sleeve. "Actually, no, you're the only one here I can rely on. You can't leave me with that lot." She jerks her head toward the house, picturing the four remaining guests — self-centered Everett, arrogant Mrs. Shrew, cowardly Zach, and indecisive Nazleen. *And how would they describe me?* she thinks, cringing inwardly. *A pathetic, desperate actor who*

266

puts money before her own safety?

Joe searches her expression in the torch-light, frowning, and she waits for him to re-assure her, to tell her she's overreacting. But instead, he tilts his head as if more confused than ever.

"You know, it's been niggling at me all evening," he says. "You really do remind me of someone. Do you mind me asking — what's your mother's name?"

BETH

December 1989

I hesitated at the top of the stairs, coughing with every other breath, blinded by the thick gray smoke.

"Where are you?" I shouted. "Where is everyone?"

Someone crashed into me in the gloom. It was Leonora. And she pulled a frightened-looking Nina behind her.

"Get downstairs!" Leonora said. "We need to get out."

We stumbled down the stairs, and as Leonora yanked open the front door, Markus and Hendrik emerged from the smoke behind us. Markus's eyes were red-rimmed and streaming. Hendrik, coughing and wheezing, was bent double, gripping Markus's arm for support.

Leonora tugged Nina and me across the threshold, and we all gasped in lungfuls of cold, fresh air.

"I've shut the door on the flames," Markus shouted. The smoke in the hall was thinning, now that the front door was open. "It'll buy us some time; the fire's contained. Did anyone ring 999?" When nobody answered, he peered around and reached for the phone. He dialed the number, then turned to Hendrik. "Get outside, Dad. Go with Leonora. I'll follow in a second."

I tried to move back into the hall, wanting to help Hendrik, who was struggling to breathe and pressing his fingers and thumb against his streaming eyes. But Leonora's grip on my arm was strong, and she shoved Nina and me down the steps ahead of her, as if she couldn't get away from Hendrik fast enough.

"Leave him. He'll be fine." Her voice was surprisingly bitter. "He always is."

"What happened?" I said. "Where's the fire?"

Leonora's fierce stare made me shrink inside my skin. "It's in your bedroom, Beth. Were you burning a candle in there?"

I shook my head, appalled. "No, I —"

"Did you leave something switched on? Your hair dryer?"

"No!"

Leonora made a sound of disgust, but she cut it off sharply and checked over her shoulder. Hendrik still hadn't emerged from the house. Leonora glanced across to the stable block with a calculating expression on her face. It was dusk; in another few minutes, it would be completely dark.

"Go and sit on the wall," she said, gesturing toward the shadowy end of the stable block. She dropped her voice to a hiss. "Whatever happens, he mustn't see there are two of you."

Wordlessly, Nina and I linked hands, and we stumbled away across the gravel together. My chest ached from the smoke I'd inhaled, but also from something else — this confirmation that the deception of Hendrik had never been a game at all. It was something far more serious.

Before Nina and I reached the stable block, a crash of shattering glass made us look up to see flames bursting out through my bedroom window. Clutching at Nina, I staggered backward, my heart racing. How had this happened? It wasn't really my fault — was it?

When I turned away from the bright flames, the surroundings seemed even darker in comparison. I could just about make out Hendrik sitting on the gravel beyond the steps, batting away his chauffeur's attempt to get him up on his feet, with one hand shielding his eyes. Leonora and Markus stood side by side a little closer to us, their upturned faces bathed in the angry red light from the flames at my bedroom window.

A sudden thought stopped my breath. They were going to blame me for this, weren't they? It was my bedroom; of course they'd blame me. My throat tightened at the injustice of it; I dropped Nina's arm and stepped away from her. It *wasn't* my fault. I was sure it wasn't my fault. But what difference would that make? I wasn't really part of their family; I'd only ever been a guest.

Nina was still transfixed by the fire, and I took the opportunity to turn away and scan the frozen lake in the gloom, desperately hoping to catch a glimpse of Jonas. Might he have come over early? Might he already be waiting for me on the island? The idea of moving in with him and his mum was suddenly vastly more appealing.

I tried to creep away across the gravel, but before I reached the lakeshore, I heard Nina close behind me.

"What are you doing?" Her voice was heavy with bewildered hostility.

"I'm just —" I peered again toward the island, but dusk was rapidly giving way to night, and it was impossible to see more than hazy shapes. There was no gleam from a torch, no sign of Jonas.

"Did you start the fire?" Nina said. Her face was a smudge in the gloom, her dark eyes glittering. "Did you put something in my food to make me sick? Was it you?"

"No!" I stared at her, aghast. "How can you even say that?"

"Well, you think it was my mum — how can *you* even say *that*?"

"I don't know, Nina. I don't know!" I stepped onto the ice in the brand-new pixie boots I'd been so proud of yesterday. "Please. Just go back."

Nina's tone changed as she followed me onto the slippery surface. "I'm sorry. I don't know what to think. Don't leave me, Beth, please. I need you."

I turned to face her, skidding a little. "No, Nina. Go back to your parents."

"I'm not supposed to show my face to my grandfather, remember?" She sounded close to tears. "Where are you going? You can't leave me here."

I shook my head and half walked, half slid away from her as fast as I could. A new, thin layer of powdery snow covered the ice, and I swung my arms as I plowed ahead, trying to generate some speed to widen the gap between us. But it wasn't long before I realized she was still following me.

"Beth," she sobbed, "please don't go. I need you." Her voice rose in pitch. "Take me with you."

I almost laughed at that, and I swung around, unable to see her expression in the darkness now, even from just a few meters away.

"I can't even look after myself," I said. "Just look behind you." I waved an arm at the glow from the upstairs window in the distance. The faint wail of sirens reached us across the fields.

"But where are you going?" Her voice was a wail. "You're going to see Jonas, aren't you?"

My heart squeezed with sympathy for her, but what choice did I have? "You know you can't come with me, Nina." I began to slip-slide away from her again. "Go back to your parents."

This time, there was no sound of her attempting to follow, and for once I was grateful for Leonora's rules. I veered away from the island slightly, no longer believing Jonas might be there waiting for me — he'd have joined me by now. Instead, I planned to skirt around the island, cross the lake, and walk up past Milner's Drain to the main road. I'd lived at Raven Hall for eighteen months; I felt confident I could find my way in the dark — perhaps Markus was right about me becoming a proper Fenland girl. While the fire engines battled the blaze in my Raven Hall bedroom, I'd be marching down to the village to seek refuge with Jonas.

But then a shout flew across the frozen lake. "Girls!" It was Markus's voice from somewhere near the dock. "Nina! Beth! Where are you?"

I hesitated, and in that moment, I heard Nina's breaths, short and sharp, moving toward me again. I swung around, trying to make out her shape in the darkness.

"Go back, Nina!"

"No!" She crashed into me and grabbed my hands in her icy fingers. "I'm coming with you."

Markus's voice boomed out again, and it sounded closer. "Girls! Please! Where are you? Come back!"

"Let go of me." I freed my hands from her grip and stumbled away, no longer sure of my bearings.

"Wait!" she called out. "Hang on. Dad drilled his holes on this side. He said we mustn't skate beyond the island."

Nice try, Nina, I thought. "I'm not skating."

274

She was still coming closer. "But it might not be strong enough . . ."

"Well, go back, then!" I turned in a circle and caught her outline in my peripheral vision. "I'm trying to get away from *you* too — can't you understand that?"

And that's when it happened. A loud snap, like the crack of a whip. A strange, slow-motion shift of the ice beneath my feet. And we were both slipping and tipping. And no matter how far I clawed my fingers onto the ice in front of me, my feet and calves and thighs slid down, down, down into the cold, deadly water. I couldn't breathe. And I couldn't move. The world closed in around me.

SADIE

"What's your mother's name?"

Joe's question hangs in the frosty air between them, and Sadie stares at him as if not understanding it. Eventually, she clears her throat.

"Perhaps you could tell me exactly who *you* are, first."

Joe looks startled, but he gives her a small apologetic nod. "Yes, of course. I'm Jonas Blake. I grew up in the village. My mum still runs the B and B there. I used to be friends with —" His gaze slides toward the lake, as if the rest of his sentence has been sucked away across the black water.

She waits for a couple of seconds. "Friends with who?"

"There were two girls who used to live here. Nina and Beth."

Sadie's heart is a drum. Is she finally going to hear the story her mother would

276

never tell her?

"What happened to them?" she whispers.

He eyes her warily. "Surely you'd know that if you're Beth's daughter?"

She shakes her head. "Mum never told me anything about her childhood. Seriously, virtually nothing. I mean, I know she had a brother, Ricky, and he and her parents were killed in a road accident, but apart from that . . ."

Joe's pupils are enormous in the torch-light. "You didn't know she lived here?"

"No. How old was she then?"

"Fourteen, fifteen. Didn't she mention the family, even? Leonora and Markus and Nina?"

"No, I told you. I wasn't allowed to ask her anything. Little things could set her off. If she was reminded of the past, she'd withdraw from everything, shut herself away, didn't want to talk about it. So in the end, I stopped asking."

Joe looks horrified. "I tried to find her, afterward, but she literally" — he swings the torch in a helpless gesture — "disappeared."

Sadie thinks of the charity her mother always insisted on supporting. "She was homeless for a while. I don't know much more than that. She lived on the streets 'til she got pregnant with me, and then she got some support, and things got a bit better."

"Good grief." Joe shakes his head heavily. "I'm so sorry."

"Just tell me what happened here. Please."

"It was an accident," he says slowly. "There was a fire, in the house. And while they were waiting for help to arrive, Beth and Nina went out onto the frozen lake, and they —"

"What?" Sadie says.

"The ice broke. They fell through. Into the water . . ."

Sadie hugs herself, thinking of all the times she complained of her mother's heating being turned up too high, and her mother saying it was what her cold bones needed.

"The fire brigade had just got here," Joe continues. "They managed to pull both girls out, but —"

Sadie remembers the line from the ramblers' group blog: *"Raven Hall has been abandoned and uncared for since a tragedy befell a local family in the late 1980s."* She takes a step backward and glances at the gentle glow from the drawing room window, no longer wanting to hear the rest of the story. What if her mother was responsible for the other girl's death? Is that what happened? Beth and Nina went out onto the ice, but only Beth came back?

Joe catches at her sleeve, and his voice cracks. "It was my fault; that's the trouble. I promised Beth I'd meet her on the island, but I wasn't there — I was still at home. I hadn't even set off. If I'd been here . . ." He gives Sadie a pleading look. "Where is she now? I'd love to see her again, to explain . . ."

Sadie gives a short laugh. "That'll be tricky."

"Why?" His eyes widen. "She's not —"

"Dead?" Sadie pulls a face. "No, but she's not exactly easy to get hold of. She quit her job a few months ago, gave away all her stuff, left me to sort out the tedious bits while she went off to join some cult in the wilderness."

"Cult?" Joe says.

"Well, they call it a retreat. It's in the Scottish Highlands. They do talking therapies, that kind of thing, and she's convinced it'll help her, but they're really strict. No phones allowed, no visitors for the first six months, only one letter a month, things like that. She just went and joined them. I couldn't talk her out of it."

"It does sound a bit cultish."

"That's what I told her." Beth drops her

gaze, and she sighs. "But she thought I'd be better off if she left for a while. She thought I was too dependent on her, that because we saw each other all the time, she was stopping me from taking responsibility for myself . . ."

Joe hesitates. "And was that true?"

"No!" Sadie looks out over the black water. "At least, well . . . I did use to go round there a lot and let her go through the job adverts for me, you know, and cook me meals and stuff, but —" She shakes her head. "I miss her."

"So . . ." Joe sounds confused. "How did you get invited here tonight if . . ."

"I don't know." Sadie rubs her arms. She pictures her mother falling through the ice with that other girl, Nina, and a thought slams into her, sending a shiver from her fingertips all the way up to her neck. *What if I wasn't picked for this job at random? What if someone invited me here because of the connection between this house and my mother?*

Back in the drawing room, Sadie and Joe describe the footprints they saw heading down the driveway. The relief in the remaining guests' voices is clear.

"It makes sense," Zach says. "It's not that long a walk to the B and B. I'm quite tempted myself."

"Thought she was too good for us," Everett grumbles.

"Oh, I wouldn't go that far," Nazleen says.

Sadie is still reeling from the discovery that her mother once lived in this house, and she eyes the other guests curiously. So, Joe was once a friend of her mother's, but what about the others? Everett would have been in his forties back then, she guesses, and Zach just a small child.

"Have you been here before?" she asks Nazleen abruptly.

"To this house?" Nazleen frowns. "No. Why do you ask?"

Sadie shakes her head. "No reason."

But if Sadie's presence here isn't a co-incidence — if someone at the company knows that her mother used to live here — why did they invite her here without explaining the connection? And who are they, anyway? Sadie frowns, thinking of the other names Joe mentioned outside — Leonora and Markus. Could it be one of them?

"Well, I'm going to bed." Zach hauls himself up off the sofa. "Remind me not to do this sort of thing again, Dad, won't you?"

Sadie wanders across to the window, wanting one last look outside before she, too, heads up. She feels self-conscious as she parts the curtains — imagine if Genevieve was back out there on the dock, smoking another cigarette and laughing at them. But it's something far stranger — Sadie blinks and turns her head from side to side, trying to catch it in her peripheral vision. Tiny bluish lights flicker and jump in the darkness; with nothing else visible, it's impossible to judge how far away they are.

"There's something —" she says, and she can hear the fear in her voice, but she can't hide it. The others hurry toward her — even Everett, who a moment ago was heaving himself out of his chair as if he barely had the energy to stand. They crowd round her, peering into the black night.

"There are tiny lights — look." She turns a stricken face to Joe. "You don't think Genevieve — ?"

The others watch for a moment, and then Zach laughs.

"They're will-o'-the-wisps," he says. "Have you never seen them before?"

"It's just marsh gas," Joe says to Sadie, more kindly. "It's a natural phenomenon. Nothing to do with Genevieve."

"Oh." Sadie lets the curtain drop back.

"Perfectly normal to see them . . . ," Everett begins.

"In the Fens." Nazleen sounds weary. "We

know; we know. Well, it's lucky we've seen them tonight, 'cause I, for one, certainly won't be coming back."

Sadie grinds her teeth against the thought that she ever contemplated trying to get the hostess job here for herself. Certainly not one of her better ideas. Especially now she knows of the connection between this house and her mother's painful past.

The guests exchange muted good-nights at the top of the stairs, and as soon as Sadie is alone in her room, she kicks off her shoes and collapses with a groan onto the bed. Her eyes close instantly, and she's tempted to sleep where she is, fully dressed — but a worrisome thought gnaws at the edge of her consciousness. She shouldn't be feeling *this* tired; it's not even midnight yet . . .

She hauls herself up and prepares for bed properly, trudging down the corridor to the bathroom to brush her teeth, relieved to get back to her room without bumping into any of her fellow guests. Her thoughts are sluggish, as if her mind were operating underwater. What was she thinking as she climbed the stairs? Something about the job. The hostess job . . .

She flips back the sheet and blankets, and she frowns as a new idea occurs to her. What if Nazleen's wrong? What if there is no long-

283

term hostess job? What if . . . Sadie forces herself to stay on her feet, determined to think this through before she sinks onto the soft mattress and allows her head to touch that oh-so-tempting pillow. *What if this evening's event is a one-off, designed to gather the seven of us together?*

Sadie sways, a hint of her earlier nausea returning. She should have left when she had the chance. She should have volunteered to follow Genevieve's footsteps. She could be tucked up safely in the cozy B and B by now, instead of being stuck here in this huge house with five complete strangers . . .

She lifts her gaze to the door. There's a keyhole, but she hasn't seen a key. She plods barefoot to the big cheval mirror and drags it across to just in front of the door, then stands back to assess the effect. Anyone could force their way in, still, but at least she'd have a warning now.

When she finally falls into bed, she pulls the sheet and blankets right up to her chin and holds them there, while images slide through her kaleidoscope mind. Blue, looping handwriting: *Hendrik will be grateful for your support.* The fair-haired old man in the portrait, looming over them. That fish eye, dead like a circular stagnant pool. The black, ominous surface of the lake, rippling, rippling . . .

Sadie doesn't so much fall into sleep; she's sucked down under its surface.

She dreams of her mother. Arms crossed, warning frown. *"I've told you, Sadie. It's not something I can talk about."* A long sickly yellow hospital corridor, a playroom full of childish plastic toys while her mother talks to a little tortoise of a woman behind a blue door covered in peeling posters. *"I'm okay, Sadie; I promise you."* *"I don't want you to go, Mum."*

She wakes cold and clammy, the blankets thrown aside. Her heart is pounding as if she's just heard something terrifying. The lamp is still on, and she half sits, feeling dizzy. Her gaze jumps to the door; it's still blocked by the mirror. She lets her head fall back to the pillow. *Thank God.* But there it is again — the noise that woke her: a sharp crack-crack on the window.

Perhaps she's still dreaming. She slides out of the bed and curls her toes into the soft rug. It feels real.

Crack! Another rattle at the window. And it's the strangest thing, but she really does think she can hear her mother's voice calling her.

She drags back the curtains, and by the light from the outside lamps, she can just make out a car on the driveway — a mini. This is good news, isn't it? Has someone come to check on them?

"Sadie!" There it is again — her name being called, and someone *is* down there. A woman in a huge coat, standing back, craning her neck to peer at the upstairs windows. Her arm jerks back and upward, and a flurry of stones — gravel? — hits the window of the room next door. Sadie tries to lift the sash window to get a better look at the woman, but it's locked, so she presses her face closer to the glass and waits for the light to catch the woman full in the face.

It doesn't seem possible. Sadie rubs her eyes and peers again. It really *does* look like her mother down there. And then two things happen at the same time. Sadie inhales through her nose and catches a faint scent of smoke. And the woman on the driveway shouts a single word that slices through the glass and sets Sadie's heart pounding.

"Fire!"

■ ■ ■ ■

PART 2

■ ■ ■ ■

Part 2

BETH

January 2019

I hurl another handful of gravel at the window.

What am I doing here?

I vowed I'd never come back. It's painful to remember what happened here thirty years ago. But when Sadie's dutiful monthly letter arrived at the retreat earlier today, a string of words flew out at me like a flock of panicked geese: *I've got an amazing job lined up, a sort of game, at a place called Raven Hall . . .*

I've driven for hours. Too many to count. Red warning lights flashing on the dashboard of the hastily borrowed car, a dreadful grating noise from the engine for the last few miles. I thought Sadie might grow up a bit if I put some distance between us. I never dreamed that in my absence, she'd be in danger from my past.

The doors are locked, as are the downstairs windows. Flames glow menacingly behind the glass above the front door. There's no response to my hammering. No signal on my phone. I think frantically: There are no other cars on the driveway — might the house be empty after all?

I can't risk it.

I hurl more stones at the upstairs windows, and I work my way along, shouting my daughter's name as loudly as I can.

"Sadie! Are you in there? There's a fire! You have to get out!"

SADIE

Sadie drags the cheval mirror aside and lurches out of her bedroom into a haze of throat-tightening smoke, lit by fierce orange flames somewhere near the stairs. She holds her arm across her face and stumbles closer, her eyes stinging. It's on the staircase. The fire is on the staircase.

"Fire!" she yells.

She hammers on each door in turn, unable to remember in that moment which guest should be in which room.

"Wake up! There's a fire!" She opens the door next to hers and finds herself face-to-face with Nazleen.

"What do we do?" Sadie says. "Where's the fire exit? Where are the — the . . ." She gestures wildly, thinking of smoke alarms and sprinklers and extinguishers. Surely the company has a legal obligation?

"Oh my God," Nazleen says. "Oh my God, oh my God."

Sadie swings away and crashes into someone else. It's a dazed-looking Zach.

"How did this happen?" he says. "We need
to get out. What's Joe doing?"

Sadie turns to watch Joe creeping closer
to the flames, as if looking for a way through
them. Sparks shoot past his head, and he
pats frantically at something on his shoulder
and stumbles backward.

Everett's voice booms over Sadie's shoulder. "What in the name of all that's holy . . ."

Sadie tries desperately to think. "My
window's locked. Can any of you get yours
open?" She looks from one guest to another.
"Where's Mrs. Shrew?"

For a moment, they stare at one another
blankly, and then they all hurry into different rooms, and Sadie's left feeling dizzy.
What should she do first? Look for Mrs.
Shrew? Try other windows? Help Joe?

"Sadie!" It's Joe, right in front of her. She
struggles to lift her gaze from a singed patch
of fabric on his shoulder. He takes her by
the arm and steers her out of the worst of
the smoke, into the nearest bedroom —
Nazleen's. He tries the window, but just
like in Sadie's room, it won't open. Joe peers
through the glass, then swivels to face her.

"Who's the woman out there?"

She stares at him. "I thought it was my

mum, but . . ."

He nods, seeming less surprised by the suggestion than she is.

"She'll go for help," he says, "won't she? She's got a car. She'll drive to the village and raise the alarm . . ." He sounds as though he's trying to convince himself more than anything.

Sadie curls her fists, frustrated by the fogginess in her head — she'd blame it on the smoke if it hadn't started hours earlier, around the dinner table. She feels like she's been drugged.

"All the windows are locked." It's Nazleen, breathless. Sadie turns to look at her, wondering if they'll all wake up from this nightmare in a minute.

Zach stumbles in, and his words are punctuated by coughing. "I can't find Mrs. Shrew. Dad won't stop trying his phone. I keep telling him there's no signal. Is there another set of stairs up at the far end?"

Sadie remembers the spiral staircase she climbed earlier. She shakes her head.

"It only goes up, to the top of the tower. Not down."

"Well . . ." Zach looks taken aback. "How do we get out, then?"

Sadie's surprised at how calm her voice sounds. "We'll have to put the fire out, won't we?" She turns to Joe. "We'll need water."

Joe squeezes the bridge of his nose. "Okay, yeah. There's debris on the stairs — it looks like someone piled up wood or something, to get it started. It's spreading up the carpet, and the banister's starting to burn. But" — he gives Sadie a wide-eyed look — "if we can smother it with blankets — wet blankets . . ."

"Everyone," Sadie says, "get the bedding off the beds. Curtains, anything you can find. Run the baths to soak them."

"Will it work?" Zach says.

For a split second, Sadie feels paralyzed by his doubtful expression. Her head buzzes with a host of other questions: Can that really be her mum outside? Who started the fire? Where's Mrs. Shrew?

"For God's sake," Nazleen snaps at Zach. "We've got to try something. Go and fill the baths."

They form a ragged human chain along the corridor, passing sodden sheets and blankets along, and then they surge forward — all but old Everett, who's still punching numbers uselessly into his phone. They take it in turns to dash closer and hurl the dripping items over the flames. It takes almost every item of bedding from eight bedrooms, but the fire is gradually dampened until they can tackle the final patches with less panic.

"I think we've done it," Nazleen says.

But Joe urges caution. "As long as the staircase can still take our weight."

Sadie is the first to make her way down the stairs, her feet squelching on the still-smoking blankets. She runs to the front door and pulls back the lower bolt, but her hands are sore from getting too close to the flames, and the upper bolt is stiff and repeatedly slips in her grasp.

"Who locked us in?" she says, her voice high-pitched, as Everett reaches the ground, puffing loudly.

Halfway down the stairs, Nazleen holds up a big bunch of keys with a confused expression. "Not me. But I do have keys . . ."

"It's the bolt that's stuck." Sadie tries it again, panic rising in her chest like boiling water in a pan. "It's too stiff. Can someone help?"

Zach springs down the last few stairs behind Nazleen, and Joe is close behind him, but as they move toward Sadie, a door creaks open farther down the hall, and they all swing around. A figure hovers in the study doorway, her pale blue dressing gown

lending her a ghostly appearance in the dim
light.

"What's going on?" she says peevishly.
"You woke me up." It's Mrs. Shrew.

Sadie presses a hand over her heart.
"What are you doing down here?"

"I couldn't sleep in that room . . ." Mrs.
Shrew's voice falters as she peers up the
staircase. "What on earth — ?"

"There's been a fire," Joe says, and he
sounds almost apologetic.

Sadie grabs Zach's arm. "Just get the door
open. Please."

Zach yanks back the bolt and tries the
handle. It isn't locked, and the door swings
wide open. Sadie is the first to run out into
the freezing night air. Her attention is immediately caught by the metallic grinding
of a car engine turning over and over and
failing to catch. A moment later, the woman
in the big coat hurtles out of the mini and
sprints toward Sadie.

"Mum?" Sadie says. She falls straight into
the woman's arms.

"Oh, Sadie," her mum cries. "I thought
I'd lost you."

Sadie presses her face into her mum's coat
and hugs her hard, utterly speechless. But
from somewhere behind, she hears the

wonder in Joe's voice as he greets her mother.

"Beth, is that really you?"

Sadie's mum sounds equally amazed. "Jonas?"

And Joe's words trip over one another then. "I thought I'd never see you again. I looked for you for months, Beth. I tried everything I could think of . . . and then tonight — what are you doing here? You woke us up." His voice takes on a new tone of wonder. "You saved our lives."

Sadie pulls away from her mum and studies her face. "You were throwing stones at the windows. But how did you know — ?"

"Your last letter," Beth says. She sounds exhausted. "I tried ringing you from the retreat before I set off, but you didn't answer. I drove all the way down to your flat — I've still got my key. I saw the invitation on the table . . ." Her gaze slips over Beth's shoulder, past Joe, and on to the other guests, and suddenly she rocks backward as if she's been slapped.

"You," she says. "I should have known. This is all *your* doing, isn't it?"

Leonora sways gently from side to side, soothing the baby wrapped against her chest. For the hundredth time, she leans forward and peers around the corner of the stable block, but nothing has changed. The front door still yawns open; the chauffeur continues to leaf through his newspaper, oblivious to her presence. She's tempted — so tempted — to shuffle back a few meters, to let her knees unlock, to sink into the warm, damp grass and close her eyes . . . She hasn't slept for more than two hours at a time since the baby was born. But the one thing she desires even more than sleep is to see Hendrik leave Raven Hall for good.

Finally, voices float from the hall, and here is Hendrik stepping out, closely followed by Markus. Hendrik's chauffeur springs up the steps to take a box from Hendrik's arms, and all three men descend to the gravel with somber faces.

She shrinks back against the sun-warmed wall, unseen, but listening intently.

"I'll keep the job open for you anyway," Hendrik says. "For when you change your mind."

"Dad." Markus sounds weary. "Will you stop saying that? I want to live here . . ."

Hendrik makes a scathing noise. "She wants to live here, you mean." His voice softens. "She's taking advantage of you, Son. Can't you see that?"

"Dad, stop it, please. I love her. I told you."

The silence stretches. She stands very still. When the baby stirs, she kisses the top of her head softly. *Stay asleep a little longer, Nina.*

"Well, like I said . . ." The car door clunks open, and Hendrik's voice grows muffled. "You can join me as soon as you're ready."

It takes all her willpower to stay hidden until the engine noise has faded beyond the top of the driveway. When she finally emerges, Hendrik's car is out of sight, and Markus is already on the top step, about to retreat indoors.

"Leonora!" He's shocked; he thought she was staying at her lodgings until tomorrow. "Is Nina okay? What are you doing here?"

For one awful moment, she's convinced he's been persuaded by Hendrik's words after all; he's changed his mind; she's come this close, and now she's going to have to leave again. But he hurries down to her, his eyes glowing with concern, his arms wide open.

"I couldn't stay away," she says. "I had to come — I couldn't bear to be away for even one more night."

He pulls her into his arms, the baby sandwiched between them. "I'm glad you came. I couldn't bear to be away from the two of you either." They stand like that, the three of them locked in an embrace, until the baby begins to wriggle.

Then, as he leads her up the steps and into the house, she dips her head and whispers into her daughter's hair, "This is your home, Nina. This is where you belong. I'll do whatever it takes to make sure it's yours forever."

BETH

I stare at the silver-haired woman in the pale blue dressing gown. It's almost thirty years since I last saw her, but her eyes glitter just as brightly now, in the freezing night air, as they did that long-ago summer's day when I first arrived at Raven Hall.

"Leonora," I say. "My God. I should have known."

Her eyes widen, and she pulls her flimsy dressing gown closer around herself. "Beth? Is that really you?"

I pull Sadie tighter against me. What the hell did Leonora want with my daughter? I'd disappeared, changed my name, done everything I could to leave this place behind. I thought I'd be free of Raven Hall forever, so long as I never mentioned it again; I had no reason to suspect that Leonora might track me down — why would she? But it seems I've been so focused on burying the past, and on trying to ensure Sadie's life turns out better than my own, that I've deprived Sadie of the very knowledge that might have kept her safe.

Leonora lured me here once and made me play her game. How could I have gone away and left Sadie so vulnerable?

My eyes are gritty with exhaustion. My knuckles are bleeding from hammering on windows and doors. My limbs are weak from the adrenaline that's been pumping through my arteries for too long. But Leonora's expression of faux innocence drives all this from my mind and replaces it with a cold, sharp-edged fury.

I give Sadie one last squeeze and let her go, moving around her on the gravel to advance on Leonora.

"What's *wrong* with you?" As I move toward her, Leonora retreats up the stone steps. I pause, still on the gravel, and I curl my fists. "I don't know what kind of sick game you're playing this time, but I won't let you get away with it again; I promise you. My daughter could have been *killed* in there."

Leonora shakes her head with that same wounded expression. "Your daughter?" Her gaze slides to Sadie. "I had no idea she was your daughter."

My laugh hurts my throat. "Really?"

"No —" Incredibly, Leonora manages to look tearful. "We were introduced as Miss Lamb and" — she gestures to herself — "Mrs. Shrew. If I'd known she was your daughter . . ."

I want to accuse her of lying, but the guilt that's gnawed away at me for twenty-nine years dries the words in my throat. I'm not blameless here; I can't forget that.

I lift my chin sharply. "Well, it's a remarkable coincidence." I indicate the open front door behind her, the ruined staircase beyond. "I suppose this fire was just an accident too?" I turn to Jonas. "Has someone rung the police? I don't have a signal . . ."

Jonas pulls a face. "The landline's not connected. And, Beth" — he glances around at the other shivering guests — "we're all frozen. We need to get coats on, and then a couple of us can drive to the village for help."

I realize he's gesturing to the ancient mini, its driver's door still hanging open. I shake my head.

"It overheated. I can't get it to start again. I was lucky to get here at all — I'd have gone for help if I could." I peer into the surrounding darkness, but I had a view of the driveway in my headlights as I pulled up, and I know there are no other cars here.

"We'll have to walk . . ." Turning back, I see Leonora has retreated to the top step. "Don't let her back in the house!"

Leonora holds up her hands, and her tone is plaintive. "I was only going to get my coat."

"I'll get everyone's coats," another voice says, and for the first time, I look properly at the three other guests who came bursting out of Raven Hall behind Sadie. The wild-haired and anxious-looking woman hurrying past Leonora into the hall to fetch the coats is a few years older than Sadie. The skinny, dark-haired man standing next to Jonas is rubbing his arms and staring at Leonora. The elderly man has gone to sit on the steps to one side; he's partially turned away from us, peering at his phone. I don't recognize any of them.

The wild-haired woman returns with an armful of coats.

"Thanks, Nazleen," Sadie says as she takes a coat at random from the woman. I help Sadie put it on.

"Someone will have to walk to the village, then," I say, "if there's no other way." I look at Jonas. "Do you think you could . . . ?"

"Of course." Jonas drops his voice as he comes closer. "But be careful while I'm gone."

"I lived with Leonora for a year and a half," I say curtly. "Don't worry. I know what she's capable of."

The rest of the group stops murmuring, and I realize they all heard me.

I look into Sadie's eyes, and I know exactly what she's thinking. *Tell me, Mum. Don't hide the past any longer. Tell me.* And I don't know whether it's the therapy I've been practicing at the retreat, or the shock of seeing Leonora again after all these years, or just the pleading expression in my daughter's eyes, but I feel a sudden surge of strength, as if I were drawing courage directly from the earth beneath my feet.

"Certain things happened here when I was a child." I look pointedly at Leonora. "Not just the fire. Other things too. Nina was poisoned here."

There's a collective intake of breath.

Nazleen glances at Leonora, then back to me. "Who's Nina?"

"Nina was —" For a moment, I don't think I can go on. But Sadie reaches out and catches my hand in hers, and it gives me courage. "Nina was Leonora's daughter," I say. "She was four months younger than me. My best friend. We were almost like sisters." I squeeze Sadie's hand tighter. "And Leonora made her sick, deliberately.

I'm convinced of it. Not just once. Three times, at least."

On the top step, Leonora shakes her head, but her expression is fearful.

The skinny man pipes up. "Wait. I felt sick this evening. Several of us did, didn't we?" He calls out to the old man sitting on the steps. "You did too, didn't you, Dad? And you said you felt really tired, like you'd been drugged or something."

Nazleen says, "Yeah, me too. I felt nauseated, and then dizzy, like I couldn't think straight."

At my side, Sadie nods. "Me too. And I don't think it's worn off yet. My head still feels hollow. And, Joe, didn't you say — ?"

Jonas shuffles his feet. "Yeah, I haven't been feeling that great either."

As we lift our gazes back to Leonora, she lurches toward the open door.

"Stop her!" I shout.

The skinny man throws himself in front of her, blocking her retreat into the house.

"Well done, Zach," Nazleen says.

Leonora pokes the man called Zach in the chest. "Let me pass." Her voice trembles. "This is *my* house . . ."

I move up the steps behind her. "You say that, Leonora, but it's not true, is it? This was never really your house."

306

She turns to glare at me. "How dare you! I took you in, when you had nobody. I was only ever kind to you . . ."

"You made me lie," I say. "You made me pretend to be Nina. You poisoned your own daughter. You started that fire in my bed-room . . . Why? It was all to do with the house, I know, but *why . . . ?*"

Leonora presses her lips together and shakes her head.

"Okay," Jonas says cautiously. "Look, we need to get the police out here. You lot go back inside. I'll grab a torch and run to the village."

Nazleen crosses her arms. "There's no way I'm sitting in a room with *her.*" She jerks her chin at Leonora. "Not if she just tried to kill us."

"How about," Sadie says, "we lock her in the study? There's a key in the door. Can we get on with it? I'm freezing."

Zach stands aside, and Leonora casts a disdainful look over us all.

"Oh, for goodness' sake," she says, but she marches into the house and shuts herself in the study without another word. Zach marches to the door and turns the key. Jonas retrieves a torch from the hall table, but he pauses on the top step next to me as he comes out again.

307

"I'll be as quick as I can." He searches my gaze. "It really is good to see you again, you know."

For a moment, despite my exhaustion, I consider offering to go with him. Anything to avoid setting foot in Raven Hall again. But the sight of Sadie's shivering figure stops me. She needs me to stay here with her; I'm not leaving her again.

I nod at Jonas. "Just hurry."

He sets off down the driveway at a jog, quickly swallowed by the darkness, only the bouncing beam of his torch showing his progress as he heads toward the road.

The old man, who up until now hasn't said a word, hauls himself up from his position on the steps, and he shuffles toward us with a sour expression.

"Come on, then. Let's get back inside," he says. "One of you girls put the kettle on, will you? I'm frozen half to death here. This bloody house."

SADIE

The interior of the house is chilly, the air tainted with lingering, acrid smoke. When Sadie thinks of how warm and welcoming the place felt on her arrival, mere hours ago, it makes her feel off-balance. Let alone the discovery that her mother used to live here with Mrs. Shrew, of all people, who apparently tried to burn them in their beds tonight. Sadie has a thousand questions churning in her mind, and no idea where to start.

She glances at her mother, sensing this isn't the best time to ask her for more information. Beth is pale, wide-eyed; she stands just inside the threshold and wraps her arms around herself as her gaze jumps around the dimly lit hall. The other guests have gone straight through to the drawing room, and Sadie can hear Nazleen and Zach arguing over whether to light a fire in the grate. A moment later, Nazleen reappears in the hall, closing the drawing room door softly behind her.

"Zach's lighting a fire," she says with an artificial brightness. "I'll make some tea." Her gaze comes to rest on Beth's hands, and she frowns. "Are you hurt?"

Beth holds her hands out in front of her and stares at her bleeding knuckles as if they're not hers. "I was knocking on the windows so hard . . ."

Nazleen's tone softens. "Go and sit down. I'm sure Joe won't be long. We'll be out of here soon."

Beth doesn't reply. Nazleen hurries off in the direction of the kitchen, and as soon as she's gone, Beth turns to Sadie.

"I've got to talk to Leonora. I need to know why she did it, why she brought you here. Honestly, Sadie, if I'd had any idea . . ."

"I know, Mum." Sadie gives Beth's hand a gentle squeeze, taking care not to hurt her. "Okay, let's do it. We'll go and talk to her together."

But Beth still doesn't move, and Sadie feels a familiar stir of frustration. This is what she remembers, growing up: this closed, fearful expression on her mum's face. At the first mention of the past — or any other emotionally difficult topic — Beth would retreat into herself, refuse to engage.

With effort, Sadie keeps her voice gentle. "You can't run away from things forever, Mum . . ."

"I know." Beth nods tightly. "You're right." But she trudges toward the study as if she's been summoned there, as if it weren't her own idea at all.

Beth unlocks the door and walks in. Sadie hangs back in the doorway, watching Beth approach the green-topped desk. Leonora sits on the far side of it, her expression one of haughty contempt.

"What do you want?" Leonora snaps.

Beth's voice is strained. "Why did you bring my daughter here? I know you blame me for what happened, but to take it out on my daughter . . ."

Sadie frowns. What's this about blame? What did her mother *do* here, all those years ago?

"I've already told you." Leonora's reply is icy. "I didn't know she was your daughter until just now."

Beth draws in a shaky breath. "What happened to Markus . . . It wasn't my fault . . ."

A loud bang in the hall sends Sadie spinning around, heart pounding. Someone's knocking at the front door, but it's too soon to be Joe returning with the police, surely?

She glances back at Beth and Leonora, but they both seem as startled as she is. Nazleen is still in the kitchen, and the drawing room door is closed, so when the door knocker crashes again, Sadie hurries to answer it.

A woman stands on the top step, her dark hair hanging in front of her shoulders like limp curtains, her face sallow in the yellowish light from the overhead lamps. She stumbles over her words, and Sadie can't tell whether it's from cold or from fear.

"Is everyone okay?" the woman says. "I saw fire, from across the fields, and I was worried —" She glances beyond Sadie, into the hall, and her tone softens. "Oh, I see you're all right . . ."

Bemused, Sadie turns around. Leonora is approaching, her hands outstretched to the woman as if she's half-angry to see her and half pleading with her to go away.

"Yes, we're all fine," Leonora says. "You didn't need to come. You should go now."

But the woman is no longer looking at Leonora. Her gaze has moved past her to fix on Sadie's mother, and her eyes are enormous, her face slack with astonishment.

"Beth?"

BETH

And in an instant, I'm back floundering under the ice.

It's her voice that does it. Despite her stranger's face — harshly lined, bordering on gaunt in the wash of sickly yellow light from above the front door — I know it's her from the way she says my name with such wounded disbelief.

Nina.

I haven't seen her for almost three decades. My last memory of her is a hazy one — rough hands tugging me to the surface, Nina's dark eyes reflecting my own shock, staring at me, as we're each carried away toward the swirl of blue lights on Raven Hall's drive . . .

"Nina." My voice is a croak.

Somehow, I close the gap between us, but my heart is pounding, because — what will she say to me? I ran away from the hospital the next day; I never went back. I left her there, with Leonora. I didn't take her with me.

I stop in front of her, and we gaze at each other.

"Is it really you?" she whispers.

I try to smile. "How are you?"

Something flickers in her expression, and I prepare myself for an accusation, but instead, she reaches out tentatively for me.

"Oh, Beth." She touches me lightly, as if to check I'm real, and then she flings her arms around me. "It really is you. I'm so happy to see you."

I return her hug, feeling dizzy. "What are you doing here?"

Finally, she lets go of me, and she steps back, and then she gives a small laugh. "I might ask the same of you. What's going on?" She glances at Leonora, and then at the fire-ravaged staircase. "Seriously. Tell me what happened. Is anyone hurt? Have you called the police?"

"Someone's gone for help on foot," Sadie says cautiously, as if not quite sure whether she believes her own words. "They'll call the police when they get to the village."

I reach for my daughter's hand. "Sadie, this is Nina. She was —" I hesitate, weighing my delight at being reunited with Nina against my long-term sense of guilt at leaving her behind. "She was like a sister to me . . ."

Sadie says nothing, merely staring at Nina. I don't notice Leonora drawing closer until her voice cuts across us.

"A sister?" Leonora snaps. "How dare you? After what you did to our family. After what you did to Markus . . ."

My chest tightens. "That wasn't my fault."

"Mum?" Sadie says.

Leonora spits her words out at me. "You took Nina out onto the ice, that night. You knew Markus would follow. You knew the risks, but you lured him out there anyway . . ."

"No," I say. "It wasn't like that . . ."

"He was trying to save you," she says. "And when he fell through . . ." Her voice cracks. "They couldn't save *him.*"

And suddenly I'm back there, in the lake, and I can't breathe. Fingertips clawing at the edge of the ice, fire roaring in my chest . . . When I finally haul my face up into the air, there's a single yell from Markus, somewhere close by. Next to me in the dark, Nina's gasping, coughing. Somewhere in the distance, Leonora is screaming.

And then I'm waking in the hospital, Leonora looming over me, her face gaunt.

"This was all your fault, Beth. Markus died because of you . . ."

I shake my head, forcing myself to return to the present and blinking back tears. "I didn't know the ice would break . . ."

Nina is frowning at Leonora. "Mum, you can't keep blaming Beth. We went out onto the ice together, that night; she didn't drag me out there. I followed her, even after she told me to go back."

I shoot Nina a grateful look. It's true. That *is* what happened. I want Nina to say more, to explain to my daughter that I'm not the terrible person Leonora is accusing me of being. But a door creaks at the back of the house, and a moment later, Nazleen comes into view, carrying a tea tray and looking at us in mild astonishment.

"What's going on?" Nazleen says. She raises her eyebrows at Nina. "Oh, it's you."

Nina draws herself up as if waking from a dream. "Oh, you've made tea. What a good idea. Shall we go and — ?" She indicates the drawing room door.

Sadie and Nazleen look pointedly at me, and I summon my courage.

"Nina, we — actually . . ." I grimace. "We asked Leonora to wait in the study until the police get here. We think she . . ." I glance at the blackened staircase. "We're concerned that she might be responsible for the fire."

Nina begins to smile, and then she seems to realize I'm being serious.

"No way." Her eyes widen, and she turns to Leonora and studies her as if seeing her in a new light. "No, come on. There must be another explanation . . ." But we can all hear the doubt in her voice. Leonora's expression remains closed, tight-lipped.

"She was downstairs," Sadie explains to Nina. "When the fire started. While we were asleep in our beds."

"And someone drugged us," Nazleen adds. "We've all felt ill tonight, and . . ." She glances at me. "Well, Beth told us that Leonora poisoned her own daughter, years ago, so we think . . ."

Nina draws her breath in sharply.

"I'm sorry," I say softly to Nina, acutely aware that Nazleen has no idea Nina *is* Leonora's daughter. Images I've tried to suppress for years are crowding into my mind: the blue checked dress; the oily residue in the mug; Leonora accusing me of starting the fire in my bedroom when I knew it wasn't me . . .

Nina's voice is faint. "How much longer do you think the police will be?"

"Not long," I say.

There's a pause, and then Nina makes a

gesture of defeat. "Well, okay, then. Put her back in the study if you have to. I'll come and wait with you, until the police get here."

Leonora stalks away and shuts herself in the study again. Nazleen turns the key on her this time, and the tension in my shoulders eases slightly as I follow Nina into the once-familiar drawing room, where Zach and the old man are huddled by a modest fire in the grate.

Sadie is safe. The police are on their way. And not only is Nina here, she's chosen to come with me rather than wait with Leonora. Despite everything, Nina still trusts me.

Leonora rarely visits their local market town — they have everything they need delivered to Raven Hall, after all — but she does enjoy these occasional trips out. Perhaps she should do this more often.

She buys herself a necklace that catches her fancy. A new shirt for Markus. A Cabbage Patch doll for Nina's upcoming ninth birthday. Then she pauses in front of the bakery window and eyes up the cakes. She'll buy three doughnuts. Markus and Nina will be waiting for her to return home for lunch. They can eat these out on the veranda afterward, where Nina can scatter sugar to her heart's content.

Tucking the paper bag in with her other purchases, she strolls back to the car park, and that's when she sees it: the mink-blue Ford Capri.

Outwardly, she freezes, but inside, her heart is pounding, her muscles tense and ready to run. She scans the car park twice, three times.

319

There's no sign of the Capri's owner. A young couple passes her, casting her wary looks, and she darts across to her own car, to start the engine with trembling fingers.

She needs to get home. She needs to get back to the safety of Raven Hall. Her shopping lies forgotten in the car park as she escapes the town.

When she reaches the village, she presses her sunglasses more firmly against her nose, and she keeps her gaze fixed on the road ahead, her fingers rigid on the steering wheel, until she emerges on the other side. And then, out on the lane, a good few hundred yards from the top of Raven Hall's driveway, she sees Nina whizzing toward her on her little blue bike. Leonora slams on her brakes. She leaps out, into the middle of the road.

"What are you doing?" She grabs her daughter by the arm and shoves her into the back seat of the car.

"Mummy, my bike —"

"You mustn't leave Raven Hall," she shouts at her. "You must never come this far, not by yourself."

"But I was coming to meet you —"

"What if someone saw you?" She shakes Nina's arm to make sure she's listening. "Do you hear me? You stay close to home, okay? You mustn't come this far again."

By the time they pull up outside the house, Nina is sobbing hysterically. Markus gives Leonora a despairing look.

"Did you have to be so hard on her?"

She reaches out and tries to stroke her daughter's hair, but Nina flinches away from her.

"Daddy will go back and get your bike," she says, her voice soft now with guilt. "I'm sorry, Nina. I was frightened. You could have been hit by a car; anything could have happened . . ."

Markus scoops the little girl out of the back seat. "It's okay, sweetie. Mummy didn't mean to scare you."

Leonora reaches out to touch Nina again as Markus carries her up the steps in his arms, and this time Nina doesn't turn away. She gazes back at Leonora, watching her shut the front door firmly behind them, watching her lean back against it with a sigh of relief. Even after Markus has set Nina down, wiped her tearstained cheeks, and gone to fetch her a chocolate biscuit, her eyes are still fixed on her mother.

"You just have to remember," Leonora tells her, as gently as she can. "It's very important, Nina. You must never leave Raven Hall without us. It isn't safe."

SADIE

Sadie still has that hollow feeling in her head, but she's convinced there's something else wrong with her too. Her body is on full alert, as if an invisible threat were constantly behind her, ducking out of sight each time she glances over her shoulder. She frowns at the back of Beth's head as she follows her into the drawing room.

Zach gazes at Nina as they take their seats, and his expression slides from bemusement to surprise.

"Oh, hi," he says to Nina. "I thought you'd left."

Sadie knows she's missed something. She was so thrown to discover the stranger at the door was Nina — the woman her mother describes as once being like a *sister* to her — that she'd barely registered that Nina looked vaguely familiar too. She studies her now, trying to work out where she's seen her before.

Nina accepts a cup of tea from Nazleen, and she smiles at Zach.

"Yeah, I was hoping for a good night's sleep, but I had a bad dream, and when I got up for a glass of water, I looked out the window and saw smoke . . ."

Finally, Sadie recognizes her. "You were the photographer last night, weren't you?" Her gaze roams over Nina's hair and face. "You looked different, then. Your hair was covered . . ."

"Keeps it out the way of the lens." Nina gives Sadie a puzzled look. "Didn't you recognize me when you opened the door just now?"

Sadie shakes her head, frustrated by the sluggishness of her thoughts. "Did you drive back?" she asks. "Maybe we could overtake Joe, bring help back sooner . . ."

But Nina sighs. "No, I had a drink when I got back. It helps me sleep, you know. I have nightmares fairly often . . ."

Nina looks distressed for a moment, and Beth reaches across and squeezes her hand. Sadie's surprised to feel a twinge of jealousy. She's never had to share her mother with anyone before.

"So I walked back," Nina says.

"You live that close?"

"Not usually, no. I'm just staying there

tonight, for the photography job, you know. The thing is, when I . . . when we . . . got the chance . . . Well, it's strange but — suddenly I really wanted to come back and see the place . . ." She glances at Beth again.

Sadie nods slowly. "How did they hire you? Did you meet the owner in person?" She looks around at the other guests. "Who *is* the owner of the murder mystery company? Does anyone know?"

She's met with blank expressions.

"Do you think . . . ," Nazleen says. "I mean, if it was Mrs. Shrew who started the fire . . ."

Zach's eyes widen. "You don't think *she's* the owner, do you? I mean, why would she join in as a guest without telling us? And why would she . . . ?"

Sadie feels nauseated again. *Yes, why would Leonora want to hurt them?*

Everett's voice rumbles from the depths of his armchair. "Because she's deranged, that's why. The woman needs locking up."

Nina ducks her head, but not before Sadie catches a flash of emotion in her eyes, and Sadie feels desperately sorry for her suddenly. The others clearly don't know that Nina is Leonora's daughter, and whatever Leonora has done isn't Nina's fault. Does Nina think Leonora is capable of it? Sadie

324

rubs her temples. Her thoughts are like darting fish sparking across her mind and slipping out of reach. Despite the hot tea and the flames in the grate, she still feels cold all over.

Nina gets to her feet. "I need something stronger than tea. Anyone else? I saw whiskey in the pantry earlier." The others sit in silence while she's gone, and she returns quickly with a bottle tucked under her arm and a stack of crystal glasses.

Everett leans forward eagerly. "Good girl."

"Yes," Nazleen says, smiling. "This might warm us up a bit."

Nina clatters the glasses onto the coffee table, and she sloshes generous servings of whiskey into each of them. As Sadie watches, she finally catches hold of one of the questions that have been niggling at her. She takes the glass offered and sits back.

"If you saw the fire," she says slowly to Nina, "from your window . . . why didn't you call the fire brigade?"

Nina's condescending expression reminds Sadie so strongly of Leonora, it's almost amusing. "Well, I tried to, obviously, but you know how the phones can be, out here in the Fens . . . Cheers." Nina knocks back the contents of her glass, tucks her chin into her neck, and shivers. "Gosh, that's good."

She nudges Beth's arm next to her. "Drink up."

Sadie is frowning. "But the landline, surely . . ."

Nina's tone has a distinct coldness in it now. "Well, yes . . . That's a funny story, actually . . ."

Sadie makes eye contact with Beth. *Something's not right here.* But Beth lowers her gaze and stares down into her glass, and Sadie's heart sinks. Yet again, her mother seems to be withdrawing, refusing to engage.

"So, I'll tell it to you from the beginning," Nina says, refilling her glass. "Anyone for a top-up?"

The guests murmur politely and shake their heads; they haven't started on their first servings yet. They settle back in their seats to hear Nina's story, lifting the glasses of golden liquid to their lips.

BETH

"No!" It's out of my mouth almost before I know I'm going to say it. "Don't drink it!"

The others stare at me, their mouths hanging open, and slowly they lower their glasses. All except Everett, who tuts and tips his glass back to swig from it anyway. I spring toward him and knock the glass from his hand, sending it hurtling through the air to smash against the black marble fireplace in an explosion of glittering ice-like shards.

"What the hell are you playing at?" Everett barks.

I'm not sure exactly when I knew something was wrong — perhaps when Sadie's worried gaze hit mine, or when I saw a coldness in Nina's eyes that wasn't there thirty years ago — but I'm as certain as I can be. There is something in that whiskey.

I ignore Everett and swing around to check on Sadie. She looks so young, suddenly. She gives me that same trusting smile she always used to when she was a child, and then she peers down into her own glass.

"There's definitely something in it that shouldn't be there," she says, swirling the contents gently. "Something oily . . ."

Everett is all bluster. "What's going on? Are you saying that Averell woman is trying to poison us, now that she's failed to burn us in our beds?"

I turn to Nina, who's just swallowed a whole glass of the stuff. I'm concerned for her, but I can't help thinking, *How could she not have had something to do with this?* I desperately want to believe, like Everett, that Leonora is wholly responsible. But Leonora is locked in the study, and how would she have known we'd end up drinking the whiskey?

"You just drank it . . . ," I say to her, stupidly.

She gazes back at me. "You were right, you know," she says eventually. "About Mum poisoning me, when I was a child."

The room is utterly silent as the other guests absorb this revelation that the photographer is in fact Nina, Leonora's daughter.

Nina gives a heavy sigh. "I made Mum admit it. After — you know, after Markus died. She said it was" — she mimics Leonora's voice — "*just a gentle herbal prepara-tion, that's all.* Just enough to keep me out of the way when my grandfather visited." Nina's face crumples. "Can you imagine how that *feels*?"

I swallow hard. "But what about now?" I gesture at the whiskey bottle. "How did *this* happen?" I search her gaze, and there's plenty of emotion there — anger, frustra-tion, self-pity — but no surprise, no shock or anxiety at having drunk another dose of her mother's poison. And suddenly, I'm thinking of the last time I was in this house, of the horror and fear on Leonora's face before she ran up into the smoke to look for Nina . . .

"My God," I say. "I always thought it was your mum who started the fire in my bed-room. I was sure I hadn't left anything on. I thought maybe she was creating an excuse to get rid of me, but" — I shake my head — "Leonora loves this house. Too much. Definitely too much to risk burning it down — either then or now. Whereas you . . ."

Nina doesn't take her eyes off me. She says nothing, but even after all these years, I can still read her — her wounded air of always being in the right, no matter what.

I step closer to her, my heart pounding painfully. "You did this, didn't you? Brought

329

these people here. Put something in their food to make them sleepy. Started the fire . . . It was you, wasn't it?"

Nina shakes her head and laughs softly. "Oh, Beth. You're being ridiculous. You must be exhausted." She sits forward, as if that's an end to the conversation, and she pulls a white scrunchie hair band from her pocket, scoops up her hair, gathers and twists it until it's captured in a bun on the back of her head.

Deflated, I glance around at the others. Is Nina right? Is this my exhaustion talking? I'm hoping that Sadie, at least, might offer me some reassurance, but she's staring at Nina with a fascinated expression, and when she blurts out a question of her own, I genuinely believe I've lost my grip on the whole situation.

"What time is it, Nina?" Sadie says, enunciating her words with care.

Nina raises her eyebrows, then draws back the cuff of her coat. "Ten past four."

"Your watch . . . ," Sadie says. I follow her gaze to Nina's white sports watch. Sadie sounds both amazed and triumphant. "You've been sitting in your car outside Mum's house, haven't you? These past few weeks. In a dark gray Audi . . ."

I look from Sadie to Nina, my bewilderment greater than ever. "Is that true? Why? Why would you do that?"

Suddenly, Nina's face collapses into a childlike expression — hurt and resentful, as if she's been the victim of a cruel trick. She glares at me as though it were all my fault, and she can't seem to resist bouncing the blame onto me.

"I rang your old workplace, but they'd only say you didn't work there anymore; they wouldn't tell me anything else. I watched your house for *hours,* Beth, and you never went in or out. All I saw was this sad daughter, and people carting away your furniture . . ." She shakes her head bitterly, as if the whole world has conspired against her. "You never answered your invitation, Beth. You made me think you were dead."

SADIE

Sadie scans her memory. All that post of her mother's that she scooped up and dropped unopened into the cardboard box in the hall . . . Beth had assured her, before she left for the retreat, that all her bills were settled; there'd be nothing that needed Sadie's attention. And, of course, Sadie had believed her; she'd barely glanced at anything in that box. How easily an invitation to a murder mystery weekend might have been lost among the pizza leaflets and charity letters and free newspapers . . .

Beth stares at Nina, and her voice is faint. "You really thought I was dead . . ."

Nina presses her lips together, and Sadie suspects she's regretting her outburst.

"So it was you who sent the invitations," Sadie says to her. "But I saw you watching Mum's house weeks before I got my invite. Was I — ?" She glances at Beth. "Did you invite me here as a replacement for my mum?"

Nina ignores her. She looks utterly exhausted now; she slumps back on the sofa, and her next words are quiet and directed only at Beth.

"What does it matter, now, anyway?" she says. "The whole thing has failed, hasn't it? I concede defeat, Beth. Congratulations. You win again."

Leonora watches Markus and Nina from the kitchen window. Mallets clacking, they're playing croquet on the lawn, Nina shrieking indignantly every time Markus knocks one of her balls out of place. It's a joyful, vicious game.

She glances at the clock; she wishes she could be as relaxed as they are.

It's been three weeks since Stephanie's phone call. "Sorry, Leonora. I thought I should let you know. I've just taken a booking for a Mr. Hendrik Meyer for next month, and his secretary said she was booking an appointment with the local estate agent too . . ."

At first, Leonora had felt hopeless. This was it: Hendrik was coming back to put an end to all her dreams. He'd sell the house, throw them out . . . Markus tried to reassure her, but she had to face the truth: their chances of persuading Hendrik to let them stay at Raven Hall were virtually nil. But then, Markus — her wonderful, kindhearted, clever Markus — had come up with a plan . . .

She glances at the clock again. Their guest will be here in a few minutes. She raps on the kitchen window to summon Markus and Nina in.

By the time the car draws up on the gravel, the three of them are lined up on the top step, and Leonora shoots a quick look at Markus over Nina's head: Can they really pull this off? Are they making a mistake? Is it too late to change their minds?

The car door opens, and out steps the child, blond-haired, round-cheeked, her face a mask of self-protection that Leonora recognizes only too well: the face of a survivor, the face of an orphan. Leonora's heart squeezes with a painful mix of sympathy and terror. This girl is their best chance — their only chance.

Leonora hurries down the steps to greet her.

BETH

"This isn't a game, Nina!" I shake her by the arms, trying to make her look at me. "Why did you do it?"

Nina's expression is closed now; she turns her head away. Sadie moves to the window, to the gap in the curtains, and the relief in her voice makes my heart ache.

"The police are here."

I'm shocked to feel tears welling up. Jonas has called for help. We're going to be okay. I turn back to Nina, but still, she refuses to look at me, and I feel my anger rising.

"What was this all *for*?" I gesture at Sadie and the other guests huddled in their dressing gowns and overcoats; at the abandoned whiskey glasses; at the door that hides the blackened staircase beyond. "Just tell me, will you?"

"Yes, tell us." Nazleen's voice is indignant. "You don't even know me. Why would you want to hurt me?"

"Yeah," Zach chimes in plaintively. "What did we ever do to you?"

Finally, Nina meets my gaze — only for a fraction of a second, but it's enough to make my blood freeze. I stumble backward, away from her, away from the ice-cold fury in her eyes. *I know what some of us did to her.*

Leonora made her sick, hid her from the world and from her own grandfather. Jonas switched his attentions to me when I came on the scene. And as for me, I took her place, pretended to be her, stole her only friend away from her . . .

"There's no point in looking for a rational reason," Everett growls from his armchair. "She's a criminal. She needs locking up."

Nina gets to her feet. Blue light slices through the window and washes over her face. She moves closer to the armchair by the fire.

"Dr. Everett," she says, "I notice *you* haven't asked me why I invited you here."

Everett's tone is aggrieved. "I've never met you before either." He glances around the room nervously. "I had no idea that woman was your mother until just now."

"That woman," Nina says, "has a name. Leonora Averell. Do you remember her? Please tell me you haven't forgotten driving

337

her back to your house, years ago, when she was alone and vulnerable."

Everett's dark eyes widen, and Nina nods as something tightens in his expression.

"I see you do remember," she says.

Blue light fills the room now. Car doors slam outside; boots pound across the gravel.

Everett barks at Zach. "Get them in here, quick. They need to take her away, lock her up."

Nina tilts her head, and she looks him straight in the eye. "Dr. Roy Everett. We haven't properly met. I'm Nina Averell. And I'm your daughter."

SADIE

For a long, breath-holding moment, no one says a word. Nina stares down at Everett, and Everett gazes back at her with mounting horror.

"It's not true, Dad," Zach says. "Is it?"

Everett is saved from having to reply. The front door crashes open in the hall, and a woman's voice shouts, "Police!" Beth leaps to her feet, and Sadie moves to stand next to her.

Two uniformed officers burst into the drawing room, firing questions at the guests, and more than one trembling hand rises to point directly at Nina. The officers converge on her, and they take her to one side to talk.

"I don't understand," Sadie murmurs to Beth after a few minutes have passed. "How did you live with this family for so long? The mother poisoning the daughter, the daughter setting the house on fire. It all sounds . . ."

"It wasn't like that." Beth pulls a face. "I mean, okay, those bits weren't good, but apart from that — most of the time — it was a pretty wonderful place to live . . ."

Sadie remains unconvinced. "But you said they made you pretend to be Nina — why?"

Beth answers slowly. "It was to do with the house. Leonora didn't want to lose the house."

"Well, that turned out well." Sadie mulls it over, frowning. "Do you think they dreamed this up together, then, Nina and Leonora?"

For a long moment, Beth doesn't reply. They both watch as Nina repeatedly shakes her head in response to the police officers' questions, and Sadie thinks perhaps Beth doesn't think it's fair to speculate.

But eventually, Beth sighs. "I just can't imagine Leonora agreeing to anything that would damage this house."

Sadie catches hold of Beth's hand. "*We're* going to be okay, Mum, aren't we?" She searches Beth's gaze, feeling like a child again, desperate for her mother's re-assurance. "Aren't we?"

"Oh, Sadie." Beth draws her into her arms, and she holds her tight. "Of course we are. We've got each other, haven't we? We're definitely going to be okay."

BETH

I hold Sadie close to me as I watch the police officers caution Nina and arrest her.

My poor, damaged friend, Nina.

Nina isn't Markus's daughter. She's the local doctor's daughter. I can hardly believe it. And yet . . . I glance from Nina's slim frame to Zach's, then from Zach's fine dark hair to Nina's. Although her half brother must be a good few years younger than she is, the genetic link between them seems suddenly, glaringly clear.

Finally, after thirty years, the bizarre rules of Nina's childhood begin to make sense. Leonora kept Nina hidden, not just from the village doctor himself, but from anyone local who knew him, who might have put two and two together. Nina looked nothing like Markus, and all it would take would be one nosy neighbor to remark on her similarity to Dr. Everett or his son, and the secret might escape . . . *And what if that secret found its way to Hendrik?*

There was no love lost between Leonora and Hendrik. I'd seen that right from Hendrik's first visit. Would Hendrik have allowed Markus to continue living at Raven Hall with Leonora and Nina for as long as he did if he'd known the truth? Would he have been happy with the idea of Nina eventually inheriting the house? I think not.

It's entirely inappropriate, but I feel a sudden urge to laugh. Anyone else in Leonora's position, wanting to hide the paternity of their baby, would have had an easy option: they'd have moved away from where the father lived. But Leonora's obsession with Raven Hall made that solution impossible.

Then my anger returns. It was one thing for Leonora to hide Nina away from her biological father and the other locals, quite another for her to scour children's homes for a more convincing granddaughter for Hendrik. Whatever terrible things Nina has done here tonight, the ultimate blame lies with Leonora; of that, I'm certain.

Perhaps Nina catches a flash of sympathy in my eyes, because she calls out to me suddenly.

"My mother always loved this house more than she loved me; you know that, don't you?" She suddenly looks desperately sorry for herself. "I'm not obsessed with Raven Hall like them. All I wanted was a tiny bit of justice."

I say nothing in reply. My mind is still reeling. She tried to kill my daughter this evening. But she used to be my best friend — how will I ever come to terms with this?

As the officers lead Nina toward the door, she looks over her shoulder and locks her gaze on mine.

"I just hope the fire did enough damage," she says bitterly. "I hope they have to tear this whole place down."

And then she's gone, led out to an ambulance that spills blue light over the gravel driveway. I'm glad, of course, that she's been taken into custody. But I can't help agreeing with her final words. I, too, hope they tear this whole place down.

SADIE

Sadie watches her mother.

Beth has been sitting by the drawing room window ever since the police led Nina out to the ambulance, and she's barely taken her gaze off the ambulance doors. She says she just wants to know where Nina will be taken — to the hospital, or to a police cell. But Sadie knows she's struggling to process the fact that the woman she was once so close to tried to kill several people tonight.

Including Sadie.

If Mum was emotionally reticent before, what will she be like after this?

The police have been through the drawing room, collecting samples and asking more questions. The guests aren't allowed to leave yet, but a few minutes ago, a pair of officers offered to escort them up the damaged staircase to their bedrooms so they could change out of their nightclothes and pack their bags.

"Do you want to come with me?" Sadie asked Beth.

Beth shook her head. "Not 'til I know what they're doing with Nina."

Sadie turned back to the officers. "I'll wait here a bit longer, if that's okay. I don't want to leave my mum alone."

Outside, the darkness is finally giving way to sunrise. Beyond the band of reeds, the surface of Avermere glints with reflected oranges and pinks and golds. Beth leans closer to the glass and breathes out an "Oh."

Sadie goes to join her, and she peers beyond the emergency vehicles to a civilian car, and a man standing next to it.

"Who's that?" Sadie says. "Is it Joe?"

A moment later, he turns, and she sees that the man is Joe. He walks around to the passenger side and helps a second person climb out of the car — an elderly man, white-haired and slow-moving. The old man doesn't straighten fully once he's out on the gravel. He leans on a stick as he walks, his tall frame stooped, his gait uncertain.

Beth is no longer watching the ambulance; she seems transfixed by the spectacle of Joe and the old man approaching the house.

"Come on," Sadie says, aware that her bright tone sounds false. "Let's go and see if Joe's got any news."

She sets off for the hall, half expecting Beth to stay by the window, but after a short delay, Beth follows her. They wait on the top step as the two men approach at the old man's slow pace. When Joe looks across and spots them, his whole face lights up.

"Wow, Mum," Sadie murmurs. "He sure looks pleased to see you." She's only ever known her mum single; Beth always maintained she wasn't interested in finding a partner while Sadie was growing up. Sadie's pondering her feelings about this, when her attention is caught by the old man again — something about his face as he glances up . . .

"Woah," Sadie says. "That man looks like . . ." She turns to Beth. "He looks like the man in the portrait in the dining room."

Beth doesn't reply. The men reach the bottom of the steps, and the old man leans more heavily on Joe's arm as they begin to climb.

Joe looks up at Beth. "How are you?" Belatedly, he tears his gaze from her and smiles at Sadie too. "And how're you feeling? The police just told us they found sleeping pills ground up in the pantry. That accounts for how dopey we all felt . . ." His smile falters. "They told us about Nina too . . ."

The old man pauses and coughs into his fist, and even with his face tilted down, Sadie can see he looks utterly miserable. She catches Joe's eye and looks pointedly back at the old man.

"Oh yes, sorry," Joe says. "This is Hendrik Meyer. He owns Raven Hall. He was staying at the B and B last night . . . Hendrik, this is Beth and Sadie."

Hendrik barely looks at them but indicates they should all move inside. They make their way into the still-chilly drawing room, and Joe guides Hendrik to the armchair that Roy Everett was sitting in not so long ago. Sadie adds a couple more logs to the fire, and then she joins Joe on the sofa opposite Hendrik. For the first time, she feels self-conscious about wearing nightclothes under her borrowed coat. Amazing how such trivial worries creep right back in, as soon as your life's no longer in danger.

Beth returns to the window, to resume her watch over the ambulance.

Sadie studies Hendrik covertly, strangely entranced by the washed-out blue of his age-clouded eyes. He peers around the room, and his gaze comes to rest on the glass fragments scattered over the black marble hearth. *It looked much nicer in here earlier,* Sadie wants to tell him. *It was quite glamorous and welcoming back then.* But she worries it would sound odd for her to try to cheer up this old man, when she's never met him before. So she stays quiet.

Joe shifts his position to look at Beth. "The police said we've just got to be patient . . ."

Finally, Sadie remembers what she wanted to ask him. "Was Genevieve there, at the B and B?"

"Yes." He gives her a relieved smile. "She was. After all that panic here. Mum said she knocked just after eleven — a young woman with dark hair in a red dress, fur coat. She told Mum she'd been at a house party but got fed up with the other guests — can you believe it?"

Even in her least responsible moments, Sadie would never have walked out of a job, leaving people to worry over her like that. Still, she's relieved they didn't find Genevieve's body at the bottom of the lake . . . With a jolt, she remembers what happened to Hendrik's son, Markus.

"So, yeah," Joe says, "I jogged back to the B and B and rang the police. And then I found Hendrik, still wide awake, having a drink in the lounge. He flew over from the States just yesterday."

"Eight-hour time difference," Hendrik

says gloomily. "It doesn't get any easier as you get older, I tell you."

"I e-mailed Hendrik a few weeks ago," Joe explains. "I kept seeing vehicles coming and going from Raven Hall — carpenters' vans, department store lorries. I thought maybe Hendrik was getting the place tidied up to sell, but he said —"

"I thought it was squatters," Hendrik says. "And I said not to worry. I wanted to come over for one last visit anyway, sort through some stuff here and get the place on the market. But then, when Joe said he'd been invited to an event here, I asked him to go along and see who was behind it." He turns his head away to cough, then turns back. "I suppose, before I called the police, I wanted to make sure it wasn't Nina, come back to her old home. But I never imagined . . ."

"That this was what she had planned," Sadie says.

"Exactly." Hendrik shakes his head morosely. "I'd have let her live here, you know — I'd have given her the house if she wanted it. I did try to stay in touch, after Markus . . ." He pauses, waiting for his throat to settle. "But Leonora cut me off, refused all my offers of money for the child. She took Nina away — to the south coast somewhere."

"I'm sorry," Sadie says. "That must have been difficult."

Hendrik sighs. "I should have tried harder to contact her once she was an adult and out of Leonora's clutches. That's the other reason I flew over. I suppose I was hoping, if I could find Nina, we might talk face-to-face. I've no doubt her mother poisoned her against me, but still — she *is* my grand-daughter."

Sadie holds her breath. *He doesn't know yet.* She glances at Joe, but he wasn't there to hear Nina's final revelation either. And over by the window, Beth remains silent. Should Sadie leave it to the police to tell Hendrik eventually, or would it be kinder to break the news to him herself?

"Oh, Mr. Meyer," she says gently. "I'm so sorry. Right before the police arrived, Nina told us —" She hesitates. She has no idea how he's going to take the news. Will he be devastated — or might he even be relieved?

"What is it?" Joe says.

Sadie swallows. "I'm afraid Nina said she'd found out she wasn't Markus's biological daughter. Roy Everett is her father . . ."

She keeps her eyes trained on the hunched old man in the armchair. He lifts his head and stares straight back at her. He looks

350

neither angry nor surprised, merely confused.

"Come closer, will you?" he says. "What did you say your name was?"

Warily, she approaches his chair, and at a gesture from him, she crouches so that he can get a good look at her face. His brow lowers, and his gaze grows sharper.

"All right," he says. "Enough. Is this some sort of game?" And then he looks up, and Sadie realizes that Beth has come to stand beside her.

"Hendrik," Beth says, "there's a lot more you don't know, I'm afraid."

Hendrik's eyes widen. "Nina? Is that you? But the police said . . ."

Beth shakes her head. "I'm not Nina. I never was. They found me in a children's home, and they brought me here to act the part of Nina, to try to fool you. I suppose it was because she didn't look like Markus . . . Oh, Hendrik, I'm so, so sorry."

Sadie looks in shock from her mother back to Hendrik. He screws up his eyes, and Beth reaches out and touches him tentatively on the shoulder. For an awful moment, Sadie thinks he's about to cry, but when he opens his eyes again, she realizes he's laughing — bewildered, strained laughter, but laughter, nonetheless.

"Let me show you something," he says. "Joe, help me up . . ."

Joe eases Hendrik to his feet, and Hendrik fumbles around in his pockets, eventually pulling out a battered leather wallet.

"Here it is." Hendrik sits back down with a huff, and then he slides a photo from the wallet. It's in color but faded. He passes it to Sadie.

Sadie frowns. "When was this taken?" She peers at it more closely, her heart knocking strangely. *I don't remember sitting for this.* It looks so old-fashioned — was it for an audition? No, there's nothing familiar about it — not the garden setting, not the blue checked dress, not the plaits . . .

She passes the photo to Beth and frowns at Hendrik. "It's not me. Who *is* it?"

"She was my wife," Hendrik says. "Anneliese, Markus's mother. This was taken when she was sixteen, when I first met her. And you're her spitting image, my dear. You look even more like her than your mother did." He eases back in the chair and switches his gaze to Beth. "Now, tell me again about this so-called game."

352

With every minute that Hendrik is in the house, Leonora feels Raven Hall slipping more from her grasp. The way he looks at her with those piercing blue eyes. The way he looks at Beth . . .

"I'm Nina, sir," Beth told him, when he arrived. And now she's playing her violin for him. But Leonora can barely breathe; she's waiting for Hendrik to leap up, to declare the whole performance a sham, to banish them all from this place forever.

She curls her fingers tightly in her lap so Hendrik won't see them shaking. Why did she let Markus talk her into trying this? But then again . . . what other option did they have?

Beth lowers her violin, and — is it possible? — Hendrik is crying. He's genuinely crying.

"That was beautiful, my child," he says. "You remind me so much of your grandmother, Anneliese."

Slowly, slowly, Leonora uncurls her fingers.

Against all the odds, it seems their little game might just have worked.

BETH

I can't tear my eyes from the photo of Anneliese. The blue checked dress . . . the ribbons at the ends of her plaits . . . and her face — so eerily similar to Sadie's. But how can this be? What does it mean?

I'm barely aware of Hendrik rising from his chair again. It's not until he grasps my hand that I finally let the photo fall.

"Look at me," he says, his voice raspy. "You remember the first time we met?"

I expect to see anger or disgust in his eyes, but it's something else entirely — a mixture of confusion and concern. I can't find my voice, but I nod.

"I recognized your outfit," he says. "Markus had a copy of this photo, so Leonora would have seen it. I thought she must be trying to unsettle me, by dressing you up to look like Anneliese. It felt like a cruel trick."

I shake my head. "That wasn't the trick."

"But you want me to believe — what?

355

That you were a stranger? That she picked you at random from a children's home? A blond musical child who might just pass as Anneliese's granddaughter?"

"Yes, so you wouldn't kick them out," I say. "And sell Raven Hall. And it worked, didn't it?"

He stares at me, and then we both drop our gaze to the hearth, where the photo of Anneliese lies surrounded by splinters of glass. I can feel my whole history trembling.

"What does it mean?" I say.

Hendrik shakes his head, frowning. "I don't know. We must be missing something."

"Well, come on, then." Sadie steps forward and picks up the photo. "There's only one person who might be able to explain this. And the way I see it, her daughter nearly killed me a few hours ago, and she, at best, took advantage of you when you were a child, Mum." She looks from me to Hendrik, and her eyes glow with determination. "Leonora owes us some answers."

"Why should I tell you anything?" Leonora snaps.

She sits with her arm touching one of the dining room curtains, in an unsettling mirror image of my earlier position at the drawing room window, and my heart contracts with unexpected sympathy as I follow her gaze through the glass to the ambulance that still hasn't moved from the driveway. Despite everything Nina's done, Leonora still loves her. I'm not convinced Nina loves her back, but my own feelings about the pair of them are too complicated for me to analyze their relationship right now.

"I'm sure if Nina wasn't okay," I say gently, "they'd have taken her to hospital by now."

Leonora gives a tiny nod of acknowledgment.

"It's just . . . ," I say. "I know about Nina's biological father now. But still — I'd really like to understand my part in the — in the game. Why you asked me to pretend to be Nina." I study her closed expression. "You gave me a very happy home here, Leonora." I cross my fingers behind my back before I realize what I'm doing. It's as if asking a favor of Leonora has made me revert to being a child again.

To my surprise, tears well up in her eyes. "I did try . . ."

"Oh, you did." Hurriedly, I drag across one of the heavy dining chairs, and I seat myself next to her. "You were always extremely kind to me."

She searches my gaze. "I never meant to

hurt you, Beth. We were desperate, that's all. When Stephanie told us Hendrik was coming back . . ."

"Stephanie, Jonas's mum?" I manage not to glance toward the half-open door, behind which Sadie, Jonas, and Hendrik are hiding, listening to every word. Thankfully, the police were still questioning Leonora in the study when Hendrik arrived, so she has no idea he's even in the house.

"Stephanie was the only other person who knew about Nina," Leonora says. "She saw me get into Roy Everett's car once, and that was the evening he . . ." She shakes her head as if it were something she cannot bear to remember. "And she was the one who helped Markus and me get back together, a couple of months later. So when Nina was born only seven months after that, and what with her looks and everything . . ."

"Ah." I let this sink in. "But surely Hendrik did the math too?"

"He couldn't have been sure, though. Markus and I had been seeing each other beforehand, so for all Hendrik knew, we might have been sleeping together then. And he never saw Nina as a baby."

For a second, my sense of injustice overwhelms my caution. "But it was none of Hendrik's business anyway! Nina *was* Markus's daughter — okay, not in the biological sense, but in every other sense." It takes all my effort not to glare across at the door. "Why couldn't Hendrik just accept you and Nina as part of his family?"

Leonora gives me a tired look, as if I'm missing the point. "He'd have accepted us if we'd all moved to the States, like he wanted, I'm sure. It wasn't about acceptance. He just . . . He always suspected my motives for staying in this house. If he found out for sure that Nina wasn't Markus's daughter, I was afraid he might . . ."

"What?" I stare at her. "Oh. You thought it would destroy Nina's chances of inheriting the house — is that what you mean?"

She presses her lips together and turns away. I've clearly stumbled into dangerous territory. Frantically, I try to pull the conversation back.

"So, when Stephanie told you Hendrik was coming . . ."

She relaxes slightly and sighs. "We guessed then, he wanted to sell the house, to force us to follow him to the States. But we thought if we could just show him how much Nina needed to stay here . . . Except to do that, we needed him to believe she *was* his granddaughter. And we couldn't change the way she looked, of course. But

Markus had this crazy idea that we could get her intensive music lessons, take advantage of Hendrik's weak spot, because Anneliese used to play the cello. Markus said he'd ask a client of his, a violinist . . ."

I sit up straighter. "Caroline?"

"Exactly." Leonora pulls a face. "But of course, Caroline said Markus was being ridiculous. Nina had no hope of learning enough in three weeks to impress anyone. Caroline told him her own niece had been playing the violin for seven years, and she was still constantly learning and improving . . ."

I swallow hard. *That was me.*

Leonora gazes through the window, lost in her memories now. "But apparently, during this conversation, Caroline mentioned she was trying to adopt her niece. And when Markus got home, he said she'd shown him a photo. And he said, *'It's a shame Nina doesn't look more like Caroline's niece.'* He said, *'She's plump and blond and round-faced, just like my mum's side of the family.'* "

I can hardly breathe. "So you thought . . ."

"Well, that's when we decided to invite you here. It was only meant to be for a week or so. Enough time to trick Hendrik into believing you were Nina, and then you'd go back." Briefly, she meets my gaze, and her expression grows earnest. "But we liked having you here, Beth. *Nina* liked you. And Markus always wanted her to have a brother or sister — he was the one who suggested you stay until Caroline was ready for you . . ."

"And Caroline never was ready for me," I say faintly.

"No." She turns back to the window. "No, Caroline turned out to have been playing a game of her own."

I stare at her, and it takes me a moment to respond. "What do you mean?"

But she's lost in her thoughts now. As the silence stretches, my hope stretches with it, like a strand of toffee about to snap. Then, when she finally begins to talk again, her words come quickly, referring to me in the third person, as if she's forgotten I'm right here next to her. I wonder if the shock of last night has finally caught up with her — and then I forget everything else as I'm drawn into her story.

"Markus said he'd never noticed anything odd about Beth until he got back from his diving trip. But then he saw something, when he was getting his suitcases out of the car. *'She looked just like my mother,'* he said. Not that he told me at the time." She frowns. "No, he kept it quiet. Until Caroline came for her Christmas visit."

I think back to that last visit of Caroline's — the stilted conversation in the drawing room; Markus suggesting we walk around the lake but leave Leonora at home; Markus suggesting that Nina and I take the rowing boat out for what might be the last time before the lake froze over. Markus and Caroline strolling away along the lake path, then, just the two of them . . .

"I watched from the window," Leonora says. "They went all the way around, past the tree stump, out of sight. And when they came back, Caroline looked angry. She left immediately, but —" Her voice turns bitter. "Markus was in a great mood. He wanted to tell the girls the news straightaway, he said, but luckily, I made him tell me first, and then I begged him to wait . . ."

I lean closer. "Tell the girls what news?"

She doesn't seem to hear me. "And then he wanted to buy them matching bracelets . . ."

"What news, Leonora? What was it?"

"Caroline wasn't his *client.*" She spits out the word. "She was his ex-girlfriend. I'd seen her years earlier, from a distance, but she wasn't a hard-faced journalist back then. She was all long hair and denim shorts and orange crop top . . . She used to call herself Kat."

Something stirs in my memory, like sludge shifting at the bottom of the lake. My brother, Ricky, calling our rarely seen aunt Caroline "Aunty Kat." As if he'd once had a closer relationship with her, before I came on the scene.

Leonora's voice drops. "He said he made Caroline tell him the truth, on that walk around the lake. That after they broke up, she found out she was pregnant. She was going to get rid of the baby. But her sister persuaded her . . ."

"No," I whisper.

"Because her sister's son had cystic fibrosis, and she was desperate for another child, but she was scared of it having the same condition . . . So the sister took on Kat's baby."

I shake my head. "No!"

"Markus said it made Nina and Beth practically sisters." She screws up her face in anger. "But that wasn't true! And everything I'd ever planned —"

I stumble to my feet, and Leonora's attention snaps back to the present. She looks horrified for a moment, and then she glares at me accusingly.

"Get out!" She, too, springs to her feet, her voice rising to a shriek. "What are you doing in here? Get out of my house!"

I run from her. But I can't run from the truth.

I'm Markus and Caroline's daughter.

SADIE

Sadie stumbles backward into the hall as Beth flees the dining room.

Beth is white-faced, horrified. She repeats the same words over and over: "I'm not . . . I'm not . . . I'm not . . ." When Sadie tries to go to her, to comfort her, Beth bats her away as if she doesn't recognize her.

Sadie's still struggling to make sense of Leonora's words herself. She barely knows her great-aunt Caroline . . . *My grandmother Caroline,* she thinks with a jolt. But one thing's for sure: Beth has never coped well with even trivial emotional subjects. How can she possibly cope with a revelation of this magnitude?

"Beth, look at me." Somehow, Joe's voice cuts through Beth's panic. "You're going to be okay," Joe tells her. "Everything's going to be fine. I promise."

Beth's breathing gradually slows. "I'm not . . . I'm not who I thought I was . . ."

"You're still my mum, though," Sadie says, and this time she manages to catch hold of Beth's hands. "It doesn't change *us*, does it?"

Beth stares back at her. "I wish I hadn't asked . . . Everything I ever thought . . . I wish I didn't know . . ."

Sadie's heart contracts with guilt, because she was the one who sent Beth to talk to Leonora in the first place.

"I'm so sorry," Sadie says. "I'm really sorry, Mum."

BETH

I'm Markus and Caroline's daughter.

It hits me repeatedly, like waves battering a shore.

Sadie doesn't take her eyes off me. "I'm so sorry, Mum." I want to comfort her, but I don't know how to comfort myself.

"Everything's going to be fine," Jonas says again.

I close my eyes. I'm not the person I thought I was. And on top of that, my biological mother is still alive. But she kept our connection hidden, not just when I had parents who loved me, but after I believed myself orphaned, when I was at my most vulnerable. I'm torn between wanting an explanation from her, and wanting never to see her again. What kind of a mother is she?

And then another question occurs to me: Am I like her? *Am I like Caroline?*

My eyes snap open, and I see the tears on Sadie's cheeks.

"I should never have suggested you talk to Leonora," Sadie says. "I'm so, so sorry."

"No." I straighten up, and I try to smile at her. "I was wrong, when I said I'd rather not know. Of course it's better to know . . ."

"Really?" she says.

"Really."

I draw her into my arms, then, my precious daughter.

I'm nothing like Caroline.

SADIE

A police officer interrupts them to say Nina has been given the all clear by the paramedics. She's been charged with attempted murder, and they're taking her to the police station. The rest of them are free to leave.

Beth feels faint, and Joe guides her to a chair in the hall, where she sits, breathing deeply, her head hanging. After a minute, she glances up at Sadie and smiles weakly.

"It's lack of sleep, that's all. I'll be fine, honestly."

Sadie leaves her with Joe, and she goes to talk to Hendrik. He's the only one who continues to look unruffled by Leonora's revelation — reassured, even.

"Well, well," he says. "So now we know. It all makes sense." He beams at Sadie, and finally she feels a flicker of something like gladness in her heart. She studies him with renewed curiosity.

"So . . . you're my great-grandfather, then?"

"It's marvelous, isn't it?" He grasps her hand. "To find each other, after all this time. But you've got a decision to make now, young lady."

Sadie can't help but smile; if anyone else called her young lady, she'd bite their head off, but somehow, coming from her very own, newly discovered great-grandfather . . .

"What decision?" she says.

"Do you want the house?" Hendrik glances across to Beth, then back to Sadie. "I can't imagine your mother wants it. I was going to sell it, get rid of it once and for all. But if you want it, Sadie . . . well, Raven Hall is yours."

BETH

One month later, February 2019

Caroline's e-mail said she'd be back in London for only a quick forty-eight-hour turnaround, but if it really was that important, she could spare us ten minutes. Outside the apartment, Sadie gives me an encouraging smile. I ring the doorbell and step back, my heart pounding.

The door jerks open almost immediately, and though I'm not sure what I was expecting, it wasn't this. Caroline stands there, glaring at us, and she's holding a card at arm's length, dangled between finger and thumb, as if she's revolted by it.

"If you're here because of this, I'm not interested. It's going straight in the bin, and I don't have time for chitchat."

I stare at her, bemused, and then my gaze slides along her arm to the card: it's another of Nina's invitations.

"Can I see it?" Sadie asks, and she virtually snatches the card from Caroline's hand. She scans it quickly, then gives me a shocked look. "Nina invited Caroline too."

"I've literally just opened it," Caroline snaps. "I've been away for three months. There's no point sending me things like this in the post."

Gingerly, I take the card from Sadie, and I read the blue looping handwriting on the back: *We'd love to see you there!*

"I guess now we know why Genevieve was hired at the last minute," Sadie says to me. "A substitute for Caroline when she didn't reply."

Caroline makes an impatient noise. "Look, could you tell me what this is about? I'm really very busy."

"I know," I say.

She frowns. "What?"

"Everything. About Leonora's game. About Markus. About — you. I know you're my mother."

She rocks back on her heels. After a few seconds of shock, her expression softens into something that looks like regret, and for a moment, I glimpse tears in her eyes. But when she finally speaks, her voice is calm and controlled.

"Who told you?"

No happy relief that the truth is finally

out. Just that sharp question, as if she wanted the answer for one of her articles.

"Leonora," I say. "She told me everything."

Caroline's shoulders sag. Sadie and I are barely across the threshold, the door still wide open behind us. I shift uncomfortably, waiting for her to say something, although I don't know what I'm hoping for — what could she possibly say that would make me feel better? I almost wish I hadn't come, but Sadie takes my hand, and her touch reminds me of my new resolutions. To face the past. To be more open about my feelings.

"I was an idiot," Caroline says eventually, quietly. She looks directly at me. "I thought sending you off to Raven Hall would solve all our problems — mine, yours, *and* theirs. I never thought anyone would guess . . ."

I stare at her. "But what about — before that? When Mum and Dad died, the accident. Didn't you think, then . . . ?"

She shakes her head. "It was too late, by then, to tell you. How could I? And anyway, my work . . ."

Sadie makes a scathing noise, but I squeeze her hand to hush her. I want to hear everything Caroline has to say before we leave. Because I know we're going to leave, and soon.

"Look, I'm sorry, Beth," Caroline says. "I don't know what else you want me to say. Your parents loved you. They're the ones who wanted you. I tried, honestly, but I never could . . ." She drops her gaze. "I'm sorry."

The silence stretches. Eventually, I look at my watch.

"Well, we'll leave you to it," I say.

Sadie gives Caroline a strange, penetrating look. "I feel sorry for you, Caroline."

We leave then, Sadie and I. We walk back out of the apartment, hand in hand. I'm glad I faced Caroline, my mother. But I'm even more glad to be going home with my daughter now.

SADIE

Sadie turned down Hendrik's offer of Raven Hall.

There were too many arguments against it. Not least, the horror on her mother's face when Hendrik first suggested the idea. But also, the awkwardness of accepting such an immense gift from a ninety-year-old great-grandfather she'd only just met; and the responsibilities and lifestyle changes that taking on a house like Raven Hall would entail . . .

"I still think you should have grabbed it with both hands," Wendy says. Sadie has met her former agent for coffee, and they're weaving between tables in a café overlooking the high street, heading for their favorite seats. "God, Sadie, you could have sold it straight on if you didn't want it, kept the money. You'd be a millionaire by now."

Sadie laughs. "It's not like that, though.

Hendrik would buy me a different house if I asked him — he even says he'll find me a job in his company if I want it. But weirdly, it makes me realize —"

Wendy pulls a face as she sits down. "Oh, please. Don't start with the *Love is more powerful than money* stuff."

"No, honestly, it's just a weird situation to be in. I want to take my time, that's all. I actually quite like my life as it is . . ."

"How can you say that? You've already changed loads."

"Yeah, but that was nothing to do with Hendrik," Sadie says. "That was me."

After their ordeal at Raven Hall, Beth finally opened up to Sadie about her past. As well as telling Sadie about her time at Raven Hall, Beth described the months she spent sleeping on the streets afterward, and the homeless charity that helped her — the same charity that she in turn has tried to support ever since. When Sadie spotted the charity's name on a job advert in the local newspaper a few weeks later, she drew a circle around it and rang the number straightaway.

"So, when do you start?" Wendy asks her.

"In three weeks." Sadie can't disguise her excitement. "They'll be training me at first, of course, and I know it'll be hard, but — I really can't wait. To actually feel like I'm making a difference to people . . ."

Wendy sighs. "So no more mermaid auditions?"

"Nope," Sadie says with a grin. "Not for the time being, anyway."

"Oh well." Wendy sips her coffee, then tips in a packet of sugar. "At least your mum sounds happier now. How's her new man working out?"

"Pretty well, actually." Sadie smiles. "I mean, he's not that new, but . . . yeah, I think he's good for her. I really like him."

"Oh, it's no good." Wendy gets to her feet. "I've got to have some of that carrot cake. It's calling me."

Sadie watches Wendy weave between tables to reach the counter, and then she drops her gaze to the charm bracelet on her wrist. After years of hardly ever wearing it, she decided to put it on this morning. She twists it slowly, admiring the charms and enjoying the sense of connection it gives her to her grandfather Markus.

Wendy returns with her cake. "So, fill me in, then. Is there a date for the trial? Have you seen any of the other guests? What's the latest?"

Sadie sighs. She's not supposed to talk about the case, but that doesn't stop everyone asking her for details. There's been plenty of information in the press, though, so she sticks to this and pretends it's all she knows.

"They're still collating evidence," she says. "There's no date yet."

"And Nina Averell's still locked up?"

"Yep."

Wendy's eyes are enormous. "I can't believe your mum was friends with a *murderer.*"

"It was only attempted murder," Sadie says weakly.

"I know, but — Nina was so devious, wasn't she? Hiring those people to refurbish the house, and they all believed her when she said she was the owner . . . And knocking back the poisoned gin herself, to try to make the rest of you drink it . . ."

"It was whiskey, actually. And the active compound had broken down, so it didn't have much effect anyway."

"Still." Wendy's eyes shine with admiration. "You're lucky to be alive. I was saying that to — actually, do you know what? You could step straight into that mermaid commercial now, if you still wanted it. I'd just need to make one call . . ."

Sadie laughs. "No, thanks — and listen. Don't go around talking about this too much, will you?"

"Gosh no, don't worry." Wendy nods seriously. "My lips are sealed."

They sip their coffees. Sadie closes her eyes for a moment, relishing the buzz of happy chatter all around them in the café. In fact, there have been two major developments in Nina's case — neither of which Sadie can share with Wendy.

Shortly after Nina learned the truth, in jail, about Beth being Markus's biological daughter, Beth was called back to the police station to be interviewed about a new accusation that Nina had leveled against Leonora. Nina is now claiming that Leonora sent Markus out onto the ice deliberately, knowing it was likely that he would fall through.

"My mother knew I wouldn't have carried on following Beth," Nina had stated to her solicitor. "She knew I'd have turned around and gone back to the house — I wasn't allowed to leave Raven Hall, or go into the village. So there was no need for her to send Dad out after me. But she sent him anyway, because she knew the ice was weakening, and she was desperate to silence him. She wanted to protect my fraudulent inheritance of Raven Hall."

Sadie and Beth can't agree on whether

they think this is even remotely possible.

"Leonora *loved* Markus," Beth said to Sadie afterward. "He meant everything to her. He was the love of her life."

"Was he?" Sadie replied. "Or did he always come second to Raven Hall?"

Beth had frowned. "Well, there's no way she could have known he'd fall through, anyway . . . No. Much as I'm happy to believe a lot of bad things about Leonora, I can't believe she'd stoop that low."

Sadie wants to believe her mum is right, but she still finds the very suggestion unsettling. While Nina awaits her trial in a cell, Leonora is out on bail for the historic poisoning of her daughter; she's still, as far as Sadie's aware, holed up in her little seaside cottage, brooding on the loss of her ancestral home. And in an ironic twist, Leonora is providing evidence for the other major development in the far-reaching investigation.

When the police collected the game cards that the dinner guests had been given, they noticed that the comments on them were uniquely personal. Sadie can still remember the gist of hers: *You must have been a great disappointment to your mother, unable to hold down a job . . .*

But in among the other sly, mean-spirited

380

jibes, one guest's card — its gravy-stained quarters carefully pieced back together — stood out for the specific and serious nature of its accusations. Nina's attempt to unsettle her guests and prick their consciences has resulted in a fierce spotlight being turned onto Roy Everett.

At the same time that the police began investigating the thinly veiled accusations on Roy Everett's card, several women who'd seen him on news footage of the incident at Raven Hall came forward to put on record that he'd behaved inappropriately toward them. Some of the allegations are worse, but Sadie and Beth aren't privy to the details. However, Roy Everett will be facing his own trial in due course, and Sadie trusts that justice will be served.

"Okay," Wendy says, dabbing crumbs from around her mouth. "I can see your mind's on other things. Have a brilliant time in America, won't you? Give me a ring when you get back."

Sadie gives her a quick hug good-bye. Hendrik has bought tickets for Sadie and Beth to fly out tomorrow, to visit him for a couple of weeks. Beth nearly declined the offer — not least, Sadie suspects, because she doesn't like the idea of being away from Joe for that long. But Sadie talked her into accepting it; the timing is perfect — they'll be back just before Sadie starts her new job. And she's looking forward to seeing her great-grandfather again in person. They Skype every few days, but it isn't the same.

But before they fly out, there's one more invitation that Sadie has talked Beth into accepting. The new owner of Raven Hall — a Mr. El Daly, former investment banker and inventor of an encryption process that made him a fortune — has offered to show them around the newly repaired and refurbished Raven Hall. Beth was hesitant at first, but she surprised Sadie by warming to the idea.

"I think it might help, actually," Beth had said, once she'd thought about it. "I'm done with trying to block out the past. This might make it easier to move on."

Sadie knows that Joe — or Jonas, as Beth still insists on calling him — has played a large role in Beth's newfound positivity. Beth has been staying with Sadie in Sadie's flat for the last few months, but the arrangement will come to an end soon, because Beth and Jonas are going traveling. They've planned a six-month round-the-world trip together, making up for the years they lost. It makes Sadie smile every time she thinks of it.

As Sadie climbs into her car, her mind drifts back to Wendy's other question: *"Have you seen any of the other guests?"*

She did, in fact, meet up with Nazleen and her wife for drinks a couple of months ago. They skirted around the subject of Raven Hall, and they made vague promises to meet again, but she's not convinced they'll follow through.

Genevieve, she saw in the distance at the police station a few weeks ago, when she and Beth went in to discuss their statements. Sadie pointed Genevieve out to Beth, but the young woman was too far away for them to attract her attention and say hello.

Zach, Sadie hasn't seen at all. Even Jonas commented that the doctor's son has been lying low since the accusations against his father began to rumble around the village.

Sadie finds it sad that, after those intense few hours they spent together at Raven Hall, Nina's seven intended victims have been scattered apart. Of course, Sadie and Jonas are connected now, by Beth, so they have each other to talk to when they need to off-load about the events of that night. But Sadie worries about the other innocent guests — Nazleen, Genevieve, and Zach. The police told her about Nina's daisy notebook, filled with observations Nina had made when she was spying on Beth's house and, it transpires, on the homes of Sadie, Everett, and Jonas too. Is it worse to be a targeted victim, like they were, or to be collateral damage, like the others?

Sadie puts all such questions out of her mind as she arrives at her flat to pick up Beth. It's time to return to Raven Hall.

LEONORA

She follows the same routine every morning. Takes a brisk walk to the beach and back. Makes a black coffee. Fires up the laptop she bought at great expense from the soft-spoken man in the computer shop. Checks the day's news headlines. Then she types in her usual search term: *"Raven Hall."*

After weeks of pulling up the same old news reports and photos, today she sees a new article at the top of the list. Her heart beats faster as she clicks on the link and waits for her feeble broadband to respond to her command. She's only sixty-four, but her joints are aching today, despite all the ginger tea she's been drinking and her frequent dips in the sea.

Finally, the article loads.

"Take an exclusive peek at the magnificent interior of newly refurbished Raven Hall," it says. *"Mr. El Daly, thirty-seven, shows us the grand new staircase and the luxuriously refitted reception rooms, all completed with care-*

fully sourced materials and ethically produced furniture to delight any guest."

She winces as she scrolls down.

"Following the devastating fire and near loss of life at Raven Hall a mere six months ago, many locals feared the house would once again fall into disrepair. But under the meticulous guidance of its proud new owner, the transformation is truly remarkable."

Leonora's smile is sour as she scrolls through the photos. How has it come to this? Nina, her only daughter, is languishing in a prison cell. And this stranger is now the legal owner of Raven Hall.

Leonora knows how hard Nina will be finding her loss of freedom. After Markus died, Nina never did settle at the seaside cottage. She moved out as soon as she turned sixteen, and she led an itinerant lifestyle for years: traveling with a loose group of friends, picking up temporary work, visiting Leonora only when it happened to suit her.

Sometimes, on those unannounced visits, Nina would bring gifts that hinted at where she might have been living — punnets of strawberries, baskets of apples, trugs of parsnips with the soil still clinging to them. Occasionally, she brought people with her, and Leonora would feed them all a hearty meal while sneaking glances at their matted hair and unwashed clothes. On one memorable occasion, Nina set down an apple basket in the hall as she came in, and it took Leonora twenty minutes to realize there was a baby inside it. Leonora dashed to the shop for formula milk, and the infant guzzled it as if it hadn't been fed for days.

Hoping to encourage Nina to settle down, Leonora transferred a hefty chunk of her inheritance into Nina's bank account. But if Nina ever spent more than a bare minimum of it on herself, Leonora saw no evidence of it, and Nina continued to disappear for months at a time.

Until last year.

Perhaps it was Leonora's relief at seeing Nina on her doorstep that made her drop her guard, last summer. She had no one else to share her secrets with, after all, but this time she went too far. She mentioned her ongoing desperate hope that Nina would one day inherit Raven Hall, and Nina's face had instantly hardened. Leonora kicked herself; Nina had accused her more than once of loving the house more than she loved Nina — Raven Hall was always a sensitive subject between them.

So Leonora had resigned herself to not seeing Nina for another few months after that. But to her surprise, Nina returned a few days later, and she carried on visiting weekly. She began to ask Leonora endless questions about her childhood, scrawling notes in her old daisy notebook, until Leonora felt decidedly uneasy.

"I've decided how I want to spend my Averell inheritance money," Nina announced one afternoon. "And you're going to help me, Mother — don't look at me like that. By the end of it, Raven Hall will belong to us again . . ."

Leonora should never have trusted her. But Nina was her daughter; what else could she do?

She still doesn't understand where she went wrong with Nina. Despite all the terrible things that happened to Leonora when she was younger, she never sought revenge — not on Roy Everett, not on Hendrik, not on anyone. All she wanted was to see Raven Hall returned to the Averell family. She's not even sure which caused her more pain — Nina's attempt to kill her, or Nina's attempt to destroy Raven Hall.

Raven Hall will always belong to the Averells, whatever the lawyers say. It seems unlikely, now, that Nina will ever set foot in it again, but Leonora hasn't lost all hope — quite the opposite. Her dreams about Raven Hall are stronger now than they've ever been.

She reaches out a trembling finger and touches the image of the house on the screen.

"Hold on a little longer," she whispers. "You will be ours again soon. I promise."

BETH

Raven Hall's gray facade gleams, untarnished, in the gentle Fenland sunlight. As Sadie brings her car to a halt on the gravel, I can't help thinking of Caroline: the way she drove me here on that first day, fully aware I was her daughter, unmoved by the fact that neither Markus nor I had the faintest idea we were related.

A stocky man with a broad smile bounds down the stone steps — Mr. El Daly, the new owner. And suddenly this visit feels absolutely right.

"You go and look around inside," I say to Sadie, "but I want to stay out here." I glance at the lake, thinking of Markus. "I'd like to be by myself, to say good-bye."

So Sadie and Mr. El Daly head into the house, and I stroll down the grassy decline, remembering all the times I ran down here with Nina and Jonas. I smile when I think of Jonas; after a lifetime of masking my feelings, I've discovered the power of talking, and Jonas is a patient listener. Only this morning, I rang him about an odd phrase of Nina's that was niggling at me: *I'm not obsessed with Raven Hall like them.*

"Why did she say *them*?" I asked Jonas. "Why not *her*? As in, Leonora."

Jonas had given it some thought. "She must have meant Markus, I guess — who else could have been as obsessed with Raven Hall as Leonora?"

I'm not convinced, but perhaps that's because I like to think better of Markus. As I approach the dock, sunlight dazzles on the water, and my eyes sting at the injustice of not knowing Markus was my father while he was alive. But I remind myself that the future is bright.

A noise up by the house makes me turn, and I see a dark-haired young woman slipping out through the front door. She trots down the steps, and when she notices me watching her, she presses a hand over her heart and gives a startled laugh. I hurry up the grass toward her.

"Sorry!" I call out. "I didn't mean to make you jump."

She frowns as I come closer. "Are you from the hot tub company? Only we weren't expecting you 'til three . . ."

"No, I was just . . ." A glint of jewelry catches my attention, and, without intending to, I reach out. "Do you mind — can I see — ?"

Her guarded expression gives way to delight, and she springs forward with her hand outstretched to show off a glittering diamond ring. "It's a beauty, isn't it? We're getting married next week. Just a small wedding — my grandmother on my side, and his parents on his . . . And then I'll be Mrs. El Daly of Raven Hall."

But it's not her ring I'm gazing at. "No, where did you get your bracelet from?"

"Oh, this?" She hooks up the delicate gold chain. "From my mum — it's the only thing she ever gave me. We're not close. I mean, she left me with my gran when I was a baby — in an apple basket, of all things. Gran brought me up. But my mum did show that she cares about me, in her own way, a few months ago. She dragged me into some crazy plan she'd dreamed up, but then she warned me to leave before it got too dangerous . . ."

She twists the bracelet around to show me the charms.

"Flag iris," I murmur, trying to hide my astonishment while my mind races to understand the implication of her words. "Greylag goose. Reed warbler." Jonas's question resounds in my ears — *Who else could have been as obsessed with Raven Hall as Leonora?* — and my heart pounds with the suspicion that the answer is standing right here in front of me.

"Do you know what I really like about it?" The young woman is still twisting the bracelet, gazing down at it, oblivious to my unease. Her faraway tone is so familiar, I feel I might have stepped thirty-one years into the past, to when I stood talking to Leonora in this very spot.

I shake my head, speechless.

"My gran loves the thought of me wearing this here. She always says this is where we both belong." She lifts her gaze to my face and blinks a few times, as if she's emerging from a trance. "Anyway, it's lovely to meet you . . ."

As her hand reaches for mine, I finally find my voice again. "Beth."

"I'm Genevieve." She smiles warmly at me. "Welcome to Raven Hall."

ACKNOWLEDGMENTS

This book wouldn't exist if it weren't for my two brilliant editors, Emma Beswetherick at Piatkus and Amanda Bergeron at Berkley. Thank you both for everything.

I'm also enormously grateful to Eleanor Russell, Kate Hibbert, Andy Hine, Helena Doree, Sareer Khader, Jin Yu, Diana Franco, and Danielle Keir. Thank you for helping my books reach so many readers.

Rebecca Ritchie of A.M. Heath is the best literary agent an author could wish for, and I'm ridiculously lucky to be represented by her. Thank you for believing in my writing, Becky.

I'm grateful to everyone who shared their knowledge with me for this book, even though the changes I made to the manuscript meant that some details were no longer needed. Particular thanks to Danielle Feasby, Colin Issitt, Claire Daniel, Anita Faul, and Sam Foord for being so generous with your expertise.

A special mention to the Mrs H. crew — Suzanne Harrison, Helen Richards, Susannah Jennings, Helen Harrison, Sylvie Martin, Val Watson, and Claire Thorne — who keep me sane on a near-daily basis.

And thank you to all my family, especially Brian, Will, Ed, and Arthur, for your unconditional support, as ever.

If you'd like to read about one family's mission to set up a small nature reserve in the East Anglian Fens, please take a look at the Facebook page for Madeleine's Patch: facebook.com/madeleinespatch.

■ ■ ■ ■

READERS GUIDE:
THE PERFECT
GUESTS

EMMA ROUS

■ ■ ■ ■

BEHIND THE BOOK

When I graduated from vet school back in 1997, I began working for a friendly veterinary practice in Huntingdon, in the east of England. It wasn't long before they sent me to cover a shift at their smallest branch surgery, which they described as being "out in the Fens," in a little town called Ramsey. The vet nurses had already discovered from accompanying me on home visits that I had no sense of direction, so they sketched me a map on the back of a lab-results fax and assured me the route was quite straightforward. I flung my stethoscope and drugs formulary onto the passenger seat of my battered old Volvo, and off I set.

I soon found myself in distinctively wide-open countryside. Long straight roads. Flat fields of crops stretching to a featureless horizon. A huge dome of washed-out blue above. And on all sides — in ditches, in reed-lined channels, in silvery sheets on the fields themselves — the glint of water.

I got lost, of course. In my defense, there aren't many obvious landmarks when you're a newcomer driving between endlessly similar fields. In any case, I'm perfectly used to being lost, so it didn't trouble me; instead it gave me a chance to appreciate the striking sense of space and solitude offered by the rural Fens. I paused at signposted junctions and studied village names that hinted at a preoccupation with the contours of the land: Ramsey Heights, Ramsey Hollow, Ramsey Mereside, Ramsey Forty Foot (which I later learned took its name from the Forty Foot Drain).

In the end, by approaching Ramsey from the "wrong" direction, I found myself driving in on the very road I was aiming for, which bore the rather intriguing name "Great Whyte." Even with my new-graduate brain distracted by the imminent prospect of meeting new colleagues and clients, I was surprised by just how *wide* the Great Whyte was — a remarkably broad street in this otherwise small and unassuming market town — twice as wide as the roads I was used to back in Huntingdon and Cambridge.

And I was startled when I discovered what lay *beneath* the Great Whyte. But to explain that, it helps to know a little of the history of the Fens.

The term *the Fens* is used to indicate a low-lying region of around fifteen hundred square miles in the east of England, encompassing parts of Lincolnshire, Cambridgeshire, Norfolk, and Suffolk, with its easternmost boundary along the coast. Once covered by ancient forest, it was reduced to peat bogs and marshland when the sea began to encroach upon it, and for a long time these wetlands were deemed uninhabitable by all but the hardiest of folk. Those tough few inhabitants built their homes on scattered "islands" of slightly raised ground and traveled in boats through shifting marsh channels and across lakes, which they called "meres." They lived primarily off the abundant fish and waterfowl — pike and eel, crane and heron, bittern and egret, and many more.

Then came a profound discovery: that the peat-rich earth lying just beneath the shallow waters was impressively fertile. And so began a series of attempts to drain the Fens.

The Romans made a start on it. Efforts continued through the Middle Ages. In 1620, King James I called in the expertise of Dutch engineers, including Cornelius Vermuyden. Water channels were dug and widened, coastal walls were built, and — despite bitter resistance from local residents — slowly but surely wind-powered pumps drained the marshes to expose a vast plain of rich agricultural land. In later centuries, the wind pumps were replaced by Victorian steam technology, then diesel-fueled engines, and finally modern electric pumps. Meanwhile, the crops that thrived on the black, peaty soil earned the Fens the nickname "the breadbasket of England."

As I drove my beloved Volvo down the surprisingly wide Great Whyte in Ramsey that day, I was only vaguely aware of this watery fenland history. And it was a fair while longer before I discovered that the word *whyte* here is believed to come from the Anglo-Saxon *waite* meaning *dock*.

Before the Fens were drained, Ramsey was one of the "islands" that could be reached only by boat, via either channels through the marshes or along a river called Bury Brook. In medieval times, the town of Ramsey flourished, not least due to the Benedictine Ramsey Abbey, which was founded there in AD 969. Goods were delivered to the townspeople along Bury Brook, and the section of the river where the boats docked was called the Great Whyte. But when the drainage of the Fens began in earnest in the seventeenth century, the very shape of the land and watercourses changed.

As the land area increased, the town of Ramsey was able to expand, and the Great Whyte now flowed not along the edge of an island but down the center of a broad street. Road links sprang up across the region. The "island towns" in the Fens were no longer wholly dependent on their waterways. And by the mid-nineteenth century, with the additional promise of the railway soon to come to Ramsey, the much-reduced Great Whyte had fallen into redundancy.

So in 1852, engineers built a set of brick tunnels to enclose the water that flowed down the middle of the street and conceal it underground. After that, the townspeople no longer needed a bridge to cross the Great Whyte; they could stroll back and forth between shops, banks, public houses (with names such as the Boat Inn, the White Swan, and the still-open Jolly Sailor), and eventually, of course, the veterinary surgery.

I continued to work at that surgery on Great Whyte, on and off, until 2016, when I left veterinary practice to start writing fiction. During that time, I learned about some of the other side effects of fenland drainage, both on the region's threatened wildlife and on the land itself. Year upon year, as the water continues to be drawn out, the peaty soil shrinks and the land sinks still farther.

In recent years, I've taken my children to Holme Fen to visit the lowest point in Great Britain, where a four-meter-high iron post marks the fall in land level between 1851 and now. I've explored some of the nature reserves in the region, and I've read about schemes to reflood parts of the Fens in winter months, not least to lock carbon into the peat to prevent its release from contributing to global warming. I've even tried a bit of wild swimming in the chilly fenland waters.

Little wonder that when I started mulling over ideas for the setting of *The Perfect Guests,* it was a patch of fenland that sprang to mind: an isolated house next to a remnant of what was once a great lake, surrounded by fields and water channels in every direction. Here, a child could grow up roaming freely but still be hidden away from the world. Here, no one could approach without fear of being spotted. Here, a fire could take hold without alerting the neighbors . . .

Raven Hall is a fictitious house set in a very real landscape. I hope, if you haven't already, you might one day get the chance to visit the Fens — to marvel at the rich-

ness of its wildlife and its wonderful conser-
vation projects, to catch a fascinating
glimpse of its history, and most of all to soak
up the glorious sense of open space under
that huge dome of a fenland sky.

QUESTIONS FOR DISCUSSION

1. In the early stages of Leonora's relationship with Markus, she worries that she's a bad person, and she hopes that Markus might help her "to change, to improve, to become more like him." Do you think Leonora's desire to be a good person counts for anything? Is it fair to say that in the end, it's Markus who becomes more like her?

2. Who was responsible for the cracks that formed in Beth and Nina's friendship? Do you think it was inevitable that things would go wrong?

3. Nina tells Beth, "My mother always loved this house more than she loved me." Do you think that's true? Does it fit with Leonora's behavior when she ignores Markus's instruction to phone the fire brigade and rushes upstairs into thick smoke to search for Nina?

4. Stephanie tried to be a good friend to Leonora, protecting Nina's identity and warning Leonora about Hendrik's visits. Do you think Stephanie did the right thing? If she'd decided not to keep Leonora's secrets, might the outcome have been better for Nina?

5. Do you feel Leonora and Markus bear equal responsibility for the initial "game"? Was it reasonable for them to assume it would be harmless for Beth?

6. If you could explore the life of one of the minor characters, which would you choose?

7. How do you feel about the choices Caroline made, both before Beth was born and afterward? Do you feel any sympathy for her?

8. In the aftermath of the 2019 events at Raven Hall, Beth says about her childhood there: "Most of the time — it was a pretty wonderful place to live." Does this statement surprise you?

9. Near the end, Sadie wonders whether it's worse to be a targeted victim of a crime or to be thought of as collateral damage. What do you think?

10. What would you like to see happen at Raven Hall in the days and weeks following the final chapter?

ABOUT THE AUTHOR

Emma Rous is a Cambridge University graduate who spent eighteen years working as a veterinary surgeon. She is now writing full-time and lives with her husband and three school-age sons.

The employees of Thorndike Press hope you have enjoyed this Large Print book. All our Thorndike, Wheeler, and Kennebec Large Print titles are designed for easy reading, and all our books are made to last. Other Thorndike Press Large Print books are available at your library, through selected bookstores, or directly from us.

For information about titles, please call:
(800) 223-1244

or visit our website at:
gale.com/thorndike

To share your comments, please write:
Publisher
Thorndike Press
10 Water St., Suite 310
Waterville, ME 04901